Intercultural Parenting

How do parenting styles differ globally? How do different, international, parenting practices impact on children's development? Can we bring together and hybridise different international parenting styles?

Intercultural Parenting explores the relationship between family, culture and parenting by reviewing established and evolving Western and Eastern parenting styles and their impact on children's development. Authoritarian, authoritative, permissive and neglecting approaches, as well as newer techniques such as helicopter parenting, are compared with filial, tiger and training approaches, and mixed parenting styles. Practical application sections show how cultural understanding can help demonstrate how professionals might use the information and ideas in their clinical work, whilst parental questionnaires encourage self-assessment and reflection. Dr. Foo Koong Hean brings together the traditional and evolving approaches to the art of parenting practices and also showcases relatively neglected research on Eastern parenting practices.

This book is important reading for childcare professionals such as health visitors, early years' teachers and those in mental health, as well as students in family studies and developmental psychology.

Dr. Foo Koong Hean is a psychotherapist and an adjunct senior lecturer at James Cook University, Singapore.

Intercultural Parenting

How Eastern and Western Parenting Styles Affect Child Development

Dr. Foo Koong Hean

LONDON AND NEW YORK

First published 2019
by Routledge
2 Park Square, Milton Park, Abingdon, Oxon OX14 4RN
and by Routledge
52 Vanderbilt Avenue, New York, NY 10017

Routledge is an imprint of the Taylor & Francis Group, an informa business

© 2019 Foo Koong Hean

The right of Foo Koong Hean to be identified as author of this work has been asserted by him in accordance with sections 77 and 78 of the Copyright, Designs and Patents Act 1988.

All rights reserved. The purchase of this copyright material confers the right on the purchasing institution to photocopy pages which bear the photocopy icon and copyright line at the bottom of the page. No other parts of this book may be reprinted or reproduced or utilised in any form or by any electronic, mechanical, or other means, now known or hereafter invented, including photocopying and recording, or in any information storage or retrieval system, without permission in writing from the publishers.

Trademark notice: Product or corporate names may be trademarks or registered trademarks, and are used only for identification and explanation without intent to infringe.

British Library Cataloguing-in-Publication Data
A catalogue record for this book is available from the British Library

Library of Congress Cataloging-in-Publication Data
Names: Foo, Koong Hean, author.
Title: Intercultural parenting : how Eastern and Western parenting styles affect child development / Foo Koong Hean.
Description: Abingdon, Oxon ; New York, NY : Routledge, 2019. | Includes bibliographical references and index.
Identifiers: LCCN 2018060675 (print) | LCCN 2019002443 (ebook) | ISBN 9780429507083 (Ebook) | ISBN 9781138580862 (hardback) | ISBN 9781138580879 (pbk.)
Subjects: LCSH: Parenting–Cross-cultural studies. | Child development–Cross-cultural studies.
Classification: LCC HQ755.8 (ebook) | LCC HQ755.8 .F66 2019 (print) | DDC 306.874–dc23
LC record available at https://lccn.loc.gov/2018060675

ISBN: 978-1-138-58086-2 (hbk)
ISBN: 978-1-138-58087-9 (pbk)
ISBN: 978-0-429-50708-3 (ebk)

Typeset in Dante and Avenir
by Swales & Willis, Exeter, Devon, UK

Contents

List of tables	vi
Preface	vii
Acknowledgements	x
Introduction	1
1 Family, parenting, and influencing factors	5
2 Fathering versus mothering	39
3 Western (individualistic) parenting styles	62
4 Eastern (collectivistic) parenting styles	88
5 Other relevant parenting styles	126
6 Comparing parenting styles	146
7 The role of significant others	179
8 Assessing your parenting style	198
9 Overview of parenting	223
Index	234

Tables

1.1	Pros and cons of small and large families	9
1.2	Summary of factors influencing parenting	30
2.1	Fathering versus mothering	57
3.1	Pros and cons of Western-style parenting	82
4.1	Pros and cons of Eastern-style parenting	115
5.1	Pros and cons of other parenting styles	139
6.1	Analysis of parenting styles	173
7.1	Pros and cons of parenting by significant others	194
8.1	Assessing your parenting style/practice	211
9.1	Common parenting behaviours	230

Preface

Parenting, I firmly believe, is a natural human behaviour. Given the nature of the mother (and now perhaps that of the father), with her given genes, hormones, and natural instincts, loving and caring for her baby is a natural process, though it may progress heuristically. Adding to the mother's learning in parenting is the experience from other mothers; for example, the grandmothers or mothers from other families. So, what is it with parenting (both parents) that it is now quite a major concern? I say "major" because fewer children are being born and raised in a family (I've called this "small family parenting", which is described in detail in the book *Negotiation Parenting*), and parenting thus becomes crucial to children's survival and success—a supposedly natural human behaviour has become an experimental process. An experimental process whereby the parents are experimenters and the children are the participants, going through a process of learning and unlearning for both sides.

The second reason for parenting to be a major concern is that parents believe they know much more than their children, so the latter have to be protected, fed, taught, and guided at all times in growing up. What parents have experienced, children must be taught. What parents fail at, children must not go through. What parents have done well, children must do, the same or better. What parents have not tried, children must not do until parents have discussed it. Children are seemingly a blank slate without knowledge, other than the basics.

Evolutionary nature, however, has informed us that somehow what parents know and do is passed down to their children through the genes. Neuroscience is unveiling this daily. You may know that, for example, as your father is a good chess player, you somehow love the game when you are young and play well as you progress learning it. Just like having a flair for it! Right?

A possible third reason for parenting to be a major concern is that children are not just offspring but pets and possessions. By "offspring", I mean they continue the family line. By "pets", I mean treasured things. By "possessions", I am referring to parents saying, "They are mine", "We cannot lose them or let them be hurt", "It is our duty to raise them well", and "It is our responsibility to care for them for life." Once parents hold these beliefs and thoughts, children are no longer beings free to develop.

Time passes generationally and sees parenting change for better or worse. I'd say better, because humans have gained and shared knowledge about parenting, thus improving the methods and processes of it. What is and is not to be done to a child by the mother or father is put in place for the betterment of the child's growth. Coupled with economic and intellectual growth, among other factors, parenting becomes of prime importance in a family, especially for the few children. What is missing or not done in the parents' lives or in the past is preferably not allowed to happen to the next generation, unless tradition dictates it, or some of it; hence, parenting becomes loving and caring for children to the best of one's abilities.

When I say parenting can change for the worse, I mean that, given the same advantages and shared knowledge about parenting, parents go to the extent of interfering with the child's natural growth, and possibly depriving the child of his or her freedom of personal choice to make themselves better human beings. What is more confusing is that given access to the internet, parents from developing and developed countries are "doing their best" to make their children better intellectuals; in the process, their children's natural growth and development are not realised, but rather the wishes and plans of the parents.

Simply said, parenting in the modern world is no longer a natural process. It has become a host of tactics for upbringing and survival—an experimental process, as said earlier. Hence the proliferation of varied sources on parenting to guide knowledge-hungry parents. Bearing in mind the numerous factors that mediate or moderate parenting, culture being a major force, parenting becomes ever more complex and puzzling.

Thus, this book attempts to put two and two together to inform interested parents and adults on the recognised literature and research on parenting to illuminate this critical act or process in life. The material on parenting, however, is broad and huge, including that in the public media and other languages besides English. So, the best I can do is to mention the fundamentals, provide the substance, summarise the necessary information, and list the references. Feedback from readers is most welcome on this provocative topic.

Acknowledgements

I would like to thank my loving, determined wife, Cindy Ang Lian Tee, for her endless support and tolerance while I was preparing this book. And the opportunities she gave me in observing at first hand, and occasionally hands-on, the day-care activities during the nine years when she ran a childcare centre in Singapore. I had many occasions to interact with the children and their grandparents and parents, and the teachers. The wealth of information gathered from these experiences is invaluable in understanding childcare from a non-parent perspective.

I would also like to thank students at James Cook University, Singapore, from 2007 to 2010 and 2013 to 2017 for their research work with me on parenting, and the research staff for their valuable comments on findings from the studies conducted in these years.

Fabulous responses on parenting also came from participants at international conferences and numerous school talks who attended my presentations on the topic.

Information on parenting also came from clients and patients whom I have worked with at our psychotherapy sessions at hospitals and private sessions for over 25 years. I am grateful for their sharing of real-life experiences on the topic.

I would also like to thank the School of Positive Psychology, Singapore, for the opportunities to present parenting topics there and accordingly obtain more feedback from the audience on them.

Last but not least, I would like thank all the families and actors that I have observed in over 30 countries where my wife and I have toured, and in the few countries where I have studied, worked, and done therapy sessions.

Introduction

For generations, people around the world have been bringing up or parenting their next cohort in their own cultural settings and ways. And people have evolved idiosyncratically with distinctive identities and behaviours in families of all sizes; for example, being American, British, Chinese, Danish, Japanese, or Maori,[1] and coming from a nuclear family of two, three, four, or more, or an extended family.

But as countries develop or modernise, with importations like business investments and tourism and exportations like working abroad and emigration, as well as sharing of information through multimedia resources, structural and procedural changes to families and their upbringing of children take place. A keen eye shows that small families, with three or fewer children, are trending in developed countries. This translates to a big change in parenting of children. No more leaving children to strive on their own. No more having many hands to help complete chores in family businesses. No more hustling and bustling at home. Instead, a calmer ambience prevails. But more attention is now paid to the few offspring, who justifiably become families' priceless treasures.

In literature, however, parenting has been defined to cover mainly beliefs, styles, and practices. Analogously, it is like talking about what is in the mind, what is the concept, and what we do in parenting.

Beliefs are internal convictions about what something means; they drive events in people's lives. Styles are distinctive manners in which things are done. And practices are the exact actions involved in doing those things. So, we have at least three viewpoints when discussing parenting. In this book, we focus on parenting styles.

Developmental psychology and neuroscience, among major disciplines, have added to the understanding and development of parenting styles emanating from parenting beliefs and practices in different cultures. Parenting styles have been classified variously by different schools and proponents. To cut the rigmarole on what classification is best to use, I would like to adopt *Eastern collectivistic* and *Western individualistic* as terms for types of parenting.[2] But as we know, with advances in science, humanities, and technology, particularly with globalisation and interconnection, even parenting has taken on mixed styles for many a modern family.

This book attempts to advise the reader on what to expect in intercultural parenting. It is divided into nine chapters.

Chapter 1 opens up with a quick look at select theories and models on parenting, the underpinning for further discussion. The terms "family" and "parenting" are then defined to give focus to these subject areas. The scope on family covers what constitutes a family, why we want children, the ideal size for a family, and the ideal setting for bringing up children. The pros and cons of small versus large families are summarised in Table 1.1. The focus on parenting covers select parenting systems and models, the attachment construct, and hand-picked significant factors that influence parenting (see Table 1.2).

Chapter 2 touches on the concept of what is necessary in being a man or woman before launching into the concepts of fathering and mothering. Examples of these by cultures are given. It is crucial here to scrutinise the professional views of the similarities and differences between the roles of father and mother. Snippets on stay-at-home dads and mums and a short section on new fathers and mothers add colour to the chapter. It wraps up with a final section comparing the effects of fathering and mothering on the children (see Table 2.1), giving some outcomes as food for thought for the reader.

Chapter 3 launches straight into the Western individualistic parenting styles that have been established in Western literature through decades of evidence-based research. An account of each generic style (for example, authoritative parenting) is given, supported by pertinent studies from its advocate(s) and from research in different parts of the Western world. The pros and cons of these parenting styles (see Table 3.1) wrap up the chapter for your reference and reading pleasure.

Chapter 4 launches into the other half of parenting styles: the Eastern collectivistic styles. Comparatively, these have been researched and studied increasingly in recent decades in Western literature with respect to the Western styles. Notably, these Eastern parenting styles are based on racial cultures; for example, Chinese parenting. The historical and cultural contexts behind them are mentioned first, backed up by studies in Eastern countries extracted from literature from the West. Some views on punishment and childrearing related to parenting styles from the Eastern viewpoint are added to the chapter. The pros and cons of these parenting styles (see Table 4.1) finish it.

Chapter 5 lists emerging parenting styles that are advocated in literature and the media and are gaining importance and relevance in parenting. These styles are sifted from both Western and Eastern countries. They add colour to parenting, and may be practised by many a parent instinctively. Once more, an account of each style is given, supported by relevant studies. The pros and cons of these parenting styles are summarised (see Table 5.1) at the end of the chapter.

Chapter 6 seeks to compare some or most of the Western and Eastern parenting styles that have been studied in research to give the reader an idea of which is better for his or her child. A little theory on attribution serves to organise the thoughts in this chapter. Then, due to the complexity of parenting and the diverse studies completed on it, I have selected studies that compared parenting in two or more countries regarding its outcomes. Each outcome has a heading (for example, "Parental love"), context with evidence from related studies, and a learning comment. To broaden the comparisons, parenting styles as perceived by parents and children are included. Snippets on immigrant parenting, consequences of punishment, and young versus older parents are included too. This chapter attempts to consider the compatibility of Western and Eastern parenting styles in a point-by-point analysis (see Table 6.1).

Chapter 7 looks at the roles of significant others in parenting, as many parents cannot be looking after their children full-time. The main significant others are nannies, grandparents, and domestic helpers.[3] The roles of significant others are examined, and whether they would a make a difference to parenting compared to that by the child's parents. The pros and cons of using the significant others to augment parenting in a family are summarised (see Table 7.1) as food for thought for the reader.

Chapter 8 covers what a parent may be looking for, that is, assessing *your* parenting style. First, select theories and models on how parenting is measured are highlighted. Then, some of the commonly used parenting measures for parents are described. Owing to space constraints, parenting measures for different outcomes (mainly for children) are merely cited for information. However, an important outcome involving academic achievement of children will be emphasised here. Finally, a composite parenting questionnaire consisting of various items borrowed from literature and media, but modified for use in this book, is laid out for your completion (see Table 8.1). Note that this is not a diagnostic or prescriptive tool in parenting, but rather a guide to the parenting style adopted by the adult caring for a child.

Chapter 9 wraps up the book with an overview of parenting, summarising what has been discussed so far, with some tips on what to do if parenting is not going as hoped for. Interestingly, the reader will find a list of practical parenting behaviours introduced here (see Table 9.1), and not earlier, to add flavour to your understanding of parenting.

At the end of each chapter is a list of reference sources for further reading.

Happy reading!

Notes

1 We now know that using single terms, such as "American", "British", or "Chinese", to address people in general from these countries is incorrect, as there are many races or ethnicities belonging to each of these nomenclatures.
2 I understand that *East* and *West* and their compounds are also arbitrary; the same applies for *collectivistic* and *individualistic*. Thus, I'd like to put them together for convenience in discussing the two main lines of parenting: Eastern collectivistic versus Western individualistic parenting styles.
3 "Nanny" is a generic term used for someone caring for a child. Thus, a grandparent or domestic helper is also a nanny. These three terms are used separately here as they are studied as such in the literature.

Family, parenting, and influencing factors

Bearing in mind the big picture painted in the introduction, let us move on to the topic proper.

To set the scene here, a quick look at select theories and models concerning parenting is presented. Theories and models make a good starting point for discussion, though they are wide-ranging and may not be preferred by some readers. Next, the terms "family" and "parenting" are defined sufficiently for dialogue. The focus on family covers why we want children, the ideal size for a family, the ideal setting for bringing up children, and what constitutes a family. Pros and cons of small versus large families are summarised in Table 1.1 for quick reference. The focus on parenting covers parenting systems and models, the attachment construct, and the significant factors that influence parenting. The list of the latter is long, but only relevant factors are covered here (see Table 1.2).

The chapter finishes with mentions of the styles of parenting, and an introduction to measuring their effects on parenting, which are elaborated on in later chapters. Do ponder the pointers in this chapter for later discussion on parenting. Do note that beside my opinion on parenting, many pointers come from research and studies by professionals and experts on family and parenting. Of course, the reader's standpoint is welcome too.

6 Family, parenting, and influencing factors

Theories and models

Undoubtedly, discourse on family and parenting cannot go on without making reference to natural human development that impinges on every aspect of life. Theories on human development across the life-span can be broadly classified into four or more groups: biological, socio-cultural, cognitive, and psychological theories (Browne, 2001); of late, cultural models have been developed, and in combination with ecology, like bioecocultural theories. Put simply, these theories concern the structures and processes of the body, the mind, and interaction between people and their environment.[1]

Specifically, some of these theories focus on the internal growth of the children, some on their externalising behaviours, and others on their interactions with parents or other adults. The developmental literature identifies mechanisms and processes of influence in parent–child relationships, including parental role modelling, differential treatment of girls and boys, differences in content and style of instruction towards sons and daughters, gendered expectations, opportunities provided, monitoring and management of children's activities, and emotional communication and regulation (Palkovitz, Trask, & Adamsons, 2014).

As for other major theories, in a nutshell the psychodynamic theory expounds human personality as an assimilation of human behaviour, feelings, and emotions. Each of these is guided by psychological forces resulting from a complex relationship between the unconscious and conscious mind. Childhood experiences are accountable for the development of this relationship. Cognitive-developmental theory expounds how humans gradually come to acquire, construct, and use knowledge. The social-psychological approach expounds the correlation between the socio-psychological needs of parents and characteristics of relationships in the family; the needs that emerge, form, and can be satisfied in the process of communication with another person. Social cognition theory expounds the interpersonal interaction or manner in which children analyse and interpret social behaviour.

Let us take a look at the evolutionary theory. Regarding parenting, it holds that human beings have an ability to parent, and a need to parent, particularly in mothers (Bardwick, 1974), and parents, for reproductive success, invest differently in each of their children (Keller, 2000). This is not to say fathers are not good parents, just that there is a requirement for different parenting skills. Investment (physical, psychological, and social) is dependent on the family climate of the parents. Low parental investment in a poor family climate commonly leads to many children and problems. High parental investment in a rich family climate normally leads to fewer children and better outcomes (Keller, 2000). Nonetheless, parent–child interactions lead to attachment, whether secure or insecure, and other outcomes for parents and children. These outcomes are richly discussed in later chapters, which is one of the main objectives of this book.

Hence, if we apply the above theoretical viewpoints to parenting, we could be looking at emotions, neuroscience or biology, beliefs and attitudes, sex differences, learning and behaviour, socialisation, and personality traits between parents and their children, and other caregivers. These aspects could be operationalised (defined in concrete statements), configured and measured individually (e.g., male), severally (e.g., female, mother, genes), as continuous dimensions (e.g., warmth, hostile), or holistic constructs (parenting style, parenting attitude); compared, related, linked, or cross-cased; and within one period or in the short or long term, to name the common methodology. These represent probably what most research and literature on parenting has been about until today. In other words, it is also about structure and process, role and function, or intercorrelation. Researchers' definitions, operationalisation of terms, measurements, and methodologies are varied, thought-provoking, and ever innovative. For this book, I'll just use *parenting style* to avoid too much wrangling over terms' usage and processes.

Jay Belsky's process of parenting model, published in 1984 and widely referenced within the scientific literature, premises that parenting is determined multiply and is influenced by characteristics of the parent, child, and social context. Accordingly, what creates different styles of parenting are:

> One, the personal characteristics of the parent; two, social-contextual influences such as the marital relationship, satisfaction with social support from network members, and the work–family interaction; and three, the personal characteristics of the child. These determinants of parenting are likely to influence unequally parental functioning. In fact, central to the model is the proposition that the characteristics of the parent are likely to be the most important because they exert a direct influence on the parent's parenting, and an indirect influence through their impact on marital relations, network relations, and occupational experiences.
>
> (Woodworth, Belsky, & Crnic, 1996, p. 681)

An interesting cultural model for parenting is the conceptualisation parenting model advocated by Heidi Keller and her colleagues (Keller et al., 2006). They contended that cultural models are expressed in the degree of familism, which informs socialisation goals that are embodied in parenting ethnotheories.

> Three cultural models (independent, interdependent, and autonomous-related) were adopted and tested with the following samples: German, Euro-American, and Greek middle-class women representing the independent cultural model; Cameroonian Nso and Gujarati farming women representing the interdependent cultural model; and urban Indian, urban Chinese, urban Mexican, and urban Costa Rican women representing the autonomous-related model. The results confirmed that socialisation goals mediate between broader socio-cultural orientations (familism) and parenting ethnotheories concerning beliefs about good parenting.
>
> (p. 155)

However, the model of autonomous relatedness needs further theoretical and empirical refinement.

Perhaps a more suitable model to explain parenting is Carol M. Worthman's composite bioecocultural model on child development (Worthman, 2010). Of particular importance in this model is the concept of a developmental microniche, which results from the interaction between the child and the developmental niche. The developmental niche is created by an interacting micro-system of settings, customs, and actors in the child's daily experience. This niche also includes elements to accommodate conditions or changes in the child and the societal and physical macro-environment. Additionally, the model includes moderators (parent characteristics, family status and relationships, and household conditions) to the developmental microniche and outcomes (habitus, emotion regulation, learning and adaptation, physical and mental health, and life history).

We now turn to the definition of *family*.

Family

Families are a cultural system that may serve to constrain parents' behaviours by the sex of members (Bussey & Bandura, 1999).

The first question that comes to mind is, why do we want children? Many couples have chosen not to have children—they were formerly called "childless", and are now "childfree"—so parenting takes on a different meaning and function for these people. For the majority who want children, two strategies have been adopted to bring them up (Csikszentmihalyi, 1993). One is to have as many children as possible, with general effort, so that some will survive to adulthood. This is not discriminating among children, but ensuring the adaptable ones survive better into adulthood. The other is to have few children but full effort is spent on them to adulthood.

Then comes the question of how many children to have in a family. With strong economies, many developed countries are observed to have small families—that is, three or fewer children—and adopt the second strategy above in childrearing. From my research, I have advocated at least four children in a family, and the more the better, within the parents' means, for reasons of strong sibling support, economies of scale, and the opportunity for more chances of children helping out the parents in their later age, among other reasons (see Table 1.1 on the pros and cons of small and large families). As to the roles of the members of a family, I am sticking to traditional and modern roles of the father and the mother (see the later chapter on fathering and mothering). Again, it is open to the choices of parents what and how parenting is to be done at home.

Table 1.1 Pros and cons of small and large families

	Pros	Cons
Small families (three children or fewer) Note: Many experts have advocated two children in a small family; I have advocated three, as one more in this family is still within the confines and terms of small-family parenting.	*Children get more attention from parents* Children get more quality attention from their parents as limited parental emotional and economic resources are not diluted. *Higher levels of education for children* With more focused resources and attention, children will likely achieve higher levels of education.	*Children may be more self-centred* For the only child, he or she is deprived of a sibling relationship, meaning he or she cannot learn to share. Even with a sibling or two, there may be less of a need to share. *Limited well-rounded development for children* Fewer children contribute less to the variety of talents in the family.

(Continued)

Table 1.1 (Cont.)

Pros	Cons
Smaller impact on family finances Fewer children means less impact (food, school, trips, gifts) on family finances or less pressure on family budgets, therefore relieving strain and emotional pressure. Thus, parents have more money for other uses for the family. *Economic success* All children will have an equal chance of achieving personal and economic success. *Better quality of life for the mother* Women are usually responsible for childrearing activities. Having fewer children would give the mother additional time to develop individually and professionally.	Children may be bored. *Children may not learn responsibility* Because of close parental attention, children may not learn self- and other-responsibility early; particularly for the only child, this is obvious. *Problems for the only child* The only child may feel lonely. If the child is sick, there will not be any family member to look after him or her when the parents are at work. If the only child is excessively pampered or loved, he or she may become wayward. They will not be with children of the other gender. *Parents may be overprotective and excessively attentive* Parents generally become over-caring and excessively attentive, not allowing their only child to play or explore. Co-dependency occurs both ways. The same may happen when parents have one or two siblings for the child. *Parents may face problems when they get old* When the parents are old and require help, they do not have enough children to take care of them. *Small support system* Support within the family is limited to the few members.

(Continued)

Table 1.1 (Cont.)

	Pros	Cons
Large families (four children or more)	*Lively family* There are always events going on for the large family, with no time to be bored and lots of opportunities for games and fun. Siblings can entertain one another. Less chance of lonely moments. *Strong support system* Many hands in the family lend support to everyone for whatever event that is to happen—e.g., going to school, visiting the doctor, shopping, going to the movies, outings. Peer support is present in siblings. Also, family members provide mutual support for one another in bad times. *Learning to socialise, share, and be responsible* Children learn to share and to be responsible (e.g., independence, assertiveness) for themselves and others physically, cognitively, and emotionally. Children learn about different sexes and personalities. The family can buy in bulk and save on spending, etc. *"Being parents" revisited* Parents revisit the pleasure of having a newborn each time a child is born, with the	Children get less attention from parents Children get less quality attention from their parents as limited parental emotional and economic resources are diluted. There may be a family pet envious of siblings. *Economic success* Not all children will make it in life personally and economically. Even with ample wealth, somehow at least one child can be left out. *Need to share* Everything has to be shared or split. *Costly family to run* It is definitely hard to run a large family financially, if parents are not well-to-do. Having to keep everyone satisfied and happy is not easy. There is a need for a bigger car and house, more childcare and babysitting services, more trips externally, and more presents. *Need better organisation* Parents have to get the family in the best shape for activities and events in the home or outside. *Less time for parents themselves* More children translates into less time for the parents for

(Continued)

Table 1.1 (Cont.)

	Pros	Cons
	expectations for each one and their future.	themselves—the before-having-children moments.
	Help within family Initially, parents spend time on their few children. As the family grows, the older siblings can help take care of the younger ones, fostering bonds and learning parenting early. Then, parents can move on to other matters for themselves and the family.	*Parents as referees* Children will at times be involved in conflicts or arguments where parents have to step in to intervene or settle the situation. There will be more drama in the family.
	Strong chances of children looking after parents When the parents are old and require help, they do have enough children to take care of them. If there are additional children in the family, they can all assist one another.	*Need for external support* There may be a need to get support from extended family or governmental agencies or support groups if resources within the family are insufficient or exhausted.
	Better well-rounded development for children More children in a family provide a variety of talents for each child to develop better all round.	
	Evolutionally, better odds There is a chance that at least one child will strike it rich. There are plenty of chances to make mistakes; in the worst case, if a child dies, there is always another.	

Next, a question in parents' minds: what sort of setting is best for bringing up children? An optimal growth environment or family for children is one where enjoyment in the activities of everyday life is found, especially one that allows the attainment of new skills and the growth of new potentialities (Csikszentmihalyi, 1993). Apparently, two opposing processes—namely, instrumental versus expressive, authoritative versus authoritarian,[2] or differentiation versus integration—are needed and synergised. Of course, optimal growth for children must go hand in hand with an optimal school and community (not discussed here, except regarding implications for teaching and teacher–parent interaction).

Noteworthy is the fact that human infants of today are more dependent on their mothers than ever before compared with other species through better environmental affordances (for example, nourishment and shelter) (Dodge, 2004). I would add that this occurs because of better understanding of growth and development through science and technology; particularly, discoveries on how the environment alters the expression of genes, how genes limit environmental effects, how biology and environment interact across time, and how maximising the gene–environment fit leads to optimal outcomes for children (Dodge, 2004), and the abundant learning opportunities made available to today's children.

So what, then, is family? *Family* is used to refer to everyone living in the same household, and likely consists of father, mother, and children. Other significant members may include grandparents, close relatives, and possibly pets. The dynamics of the family are multifaceted, though interesting to study and learn. The family is nonetheless dependent on social policies and culture (Oltedal & Nygren, 2015), and its definition varies within and between countries affected by many factors, such as proximity of living, matter of interpretation, and relationship (Sharma, 2013). Hence, with the passing of time and changes in societies, the definition of *family* has changed dramatically.

In this book, *family* refers to the living together of close members within a household for relationship and care. Generally, there is a father, a mother, and at least one child, all in typical conditions with regard to sexual orientation and health status. Noteworthy is the fact that the inclusion of a gay person or a person with autism would complicate the discussion on parenting. The contribution of a grandparent, an aunt or uncle, or a domestic helper may be included. The individual role of everyone in the family is crucial to its functioning, as well as collectively and developmentally (Parke, 2004). In other words, each member plays a special role in the family, and a group role if there are in-groups, and these relative functions are dependent on each member's stage of development.

The family-alliance model posits that there are four interactive functions in the family: group participation by all members; specific participation by each member; sharing of a common theme of activity; and sharing of affect among members (for details, see Favez, Frascarolo & Tissot, 2017). The model is useful in assessing the family functions and malfunctions. However, I would like to add that though members of the family have specific functions, by position (parent or child) and by sex (male or female), these should be limited to the individual. What this means is that without the presence of the father, the elder son could take over his function for the time being. Conversely, the daughter could take over the mother's functions if she is not available. This is more wholesome for the family. It is like role-play in therapy. The more we get into the shoes of others, and think and behave like them, the better we understand and empathise with them.

Delving a little deeper, three possible subsystems exist in a family: the parent–child, the marital, and the sibling (Parke, 2004). In the parent–child subsystem, parents serve as interactors, advisors, and managers of their children. In the marital subsystem, the marital relationship of the parents greatly influences their children's thoughts, emotions, and actions. In the sibling subsystem, the presence of siblings offers children a pathway and process to be with peers. Family socialisation strategies are reliant on the resources of the parent, the children's characteristics, and the sources of stress and support. Discussion on intercultural parenting focuses on the parent–child subsystem, reference to the marriage subsystem is minimal, and reference to the sibling subsystem is essential as families often involve more than one child.

Related to *family* is the term "familism". Familism is defined as a social structure in which the needs of the family come before those of family members. For example, the face of the Chinese family (face is akin to reputation but means much more; in Chinese families, the family's face comes before the individual's desires). Familism comprises loyalty, reciprocity, and solidarity within the members of the family; thus, the family is an extension of the self (Keller et al., 2006). Familism is alluded to each time the discussion turns to families from collectivistic societies or families that practise the collectivist system.

In summary, we have defined the family, that is, the presence of both parents and children, its subsystems, the growth environment for children, and familism. The family offers growth in the children towards their selves and socialisation abilities. The main players in bringing up children are definitely the parents and, if available, significant others, and, of course, the presence of siblings.

So, that's what we have in mind regarding family. What about parenting?

Parenting

The dual definition of *parenting* sees, first, mothers as reliable, structured, and discipline-consistent; and second, fathers as participative in family life and spending time with children. Mothering of children includes attention to detail and looking after fathers' participation. Fathering equals parenting (Pedersen, 2012). Parenting by mothers is natural, but by fathers is recent, similar to how women joining the workforce is recent and men working is routine (Pedersen, 2012). This is true in most families.

Four parenting systems have been examined in the literature: primary care, body contact, simulation context, and face-to-face context (Keller, 2000). Primary care is basically providing the child with food and shelter. The body contact system is carrying the child. The simulation context is the two-way interaction between mother and child. The face-to-face context is mutual exchanges between mother and child through the use of eye contact and language. These four parenting systems together constitute, in varying degrees, a parenting style. Preference for face-to-face contact, object play, and responsivity to positive infant signals is connected to the development of autonomy, whereas the preference for body contact, body stimulation, and responsivity to negative signals is linked to the development of relatedness (Keller et al., 2006).

Additionally, three cultural models of parenting are suggested: independent, interdependent, and autonomous-related (Keller et al., 2006). In the model of independence, concerning urban, educated families in industrialised societies, the individual is perceived as separate, autonomous, and self-contained. These individuals strive to support self-enhancement and self-maximisation. In the model of interdependence, concerning rural, farming families, the individual is interrelated with others, and heteronomous. These individuals accept norms and hierarchies for the smooth functioning of the family. In the autonomous-related model, concerning the urban, educated, middle-class families in societies with a cultural heritage, the individual is perceived as having the combined qualities of interpersonal relatedness and autonomous functioning. These individuals focus on harmonic integration into the family and autonomy. Aspects of the cultural models will be referred to in the book from time to time. Familism is expected to be higher in the interdependent and autonomous-related cultural models, and lower in an independent cultural model (Keller et al., 2006).

Thus far, parenting involves practices (parenting systems) and styles (cultural models). Researchers have attempted to differentiate the functions of parenting (e.g., Lee, Daniels, & Kissinger, 2006), like parenting influence, parenting style, parenting practice, parenting beliefs, and attitude and behaviour, for more precise measurement of the construct of parenting. For example, parenting style is considered general and indirect, but parenting practice is considered specific and direct. This book has chosen to use *parenting style* to mean a two-way process back and forth between parents and children, involving inputs (e.g., systems, models) and outputs (outcomes).

One of the well-studied outcomes of parenting is attachment (Jones, Cassidy, & Shaver, 2015). A famous revolutionary archetype on parenting is attachment theory, first propounded by John Bowlby in the 1950s (Kenny & Rice, 1995). With many research studies backing it—for example, by Mary Ainsworth, Marshall Klaus, and John Kennell—this stage-theory proposed that the quality of parental involvement, particularly that of the mother, in the growth of children affects their subsequent development and coping in life. It is often used to discuss the secure or insecure attachment of a child to his or her parents, which eventually safeguards or damages the child's future behaviour. No worthy theory or model is without comment or flaw. For instance, with working mothers and single-parent families, the said parent–child attachment may not occur appropriately. Besides, in any society, economic, political, and cultural influences impose on parenting practices (Hays, 1998). In her recent article, Heidi Keller (2013) proposes reconceptualising attachment theory as a culture-sensitive framework—see her article for details.

Notably, in some areas, parenting by both father and mother, whether in intact, separated, or divorced families, is also referred to as *co-parenting* (Sim, 2017). This is implied in this book by *fathering and mothering*, though this is not exactly sharing the role of looking after children. Further, parenting may include parenting children other than one's own, which is called *social parenting* (Stevens, 2016). Social parenting is interesting, but complex, and thus is not covered here.

With the definitions of *family* and *parenting* made clear, let us turn to the factors influencing parenting.

Influencing factors

Many factors play a part in influencing the state or process of parenting; some are helpful, some are unhelpful, and some adjust it. The list is lengthy, thus only a host of more relevant ones are mentioned herein as food for thought (see Table 1.2 for a summary): birth order of children; children's behaviour; communication; culture and religion; education/literacy of parents; family breakup/changes; feeding practice, physical activity, and health; fertility rates and new reproductive technologies; intercultural marriage; internet use; parental attitude, affection, and control; perception of parenting; personality traits of parents and children; preference for male children; significant others; social economic status; and work–family balance.

Birth order of children

Knowingly or not, many parents nurture their children differently as they are born. The first child is often very precious and much-awaited. Much time and effort will be spent on parenting him or her, to the extent of seeking help from experts (like doctors and midwives) and the experienced (grandparents and nannies). The child's reactions and behaviours will also provoke much anxiety and angst in the parents. The second child is a different story; unless it is of a different sex from the first, when there will be new trials and learning. Otherwise, much will be done similar to the first, and it is only necessary to observe the reactions of the second. As more children pile in, parenting becomes automatic, and it is likely the older children will assist in the caring of the younger siblings; the parents will be extremely busy and exhausted.

In summary, a child's birth order affects parenting. It is normal for parents to dote on their first-born and the few children (perhaps three at most, which I consider a small family) in the family. It is also normal for parents to relegate parenting responsibilities to their older children when there are more than four children in the family (which I consider a large family). Generally, first-borns perceive their parents as stricter (more authoritarian) with them than their younger siblings, who perceive their parents as more authoritative and even permissive (Stansbury & Coll, 1998).

From the children's standpoint, many would envy being the firstborn, many would choose to be at least second-born (second-borns often behave differently from the first, such as being themselves more than being under parental control and guidance), and many regret coming from a large family. Whatever opinion we have, we shall take into consideration the views from parents and children, and from literature, studies, and parenting experts.

Children's behaviour

It is obvious that for every action there is a reaction, and for every reaction there is another action. The chain of actions and reactions goes on until one party stops reacting. This translates as meaning that, from time immemorial, whatever parents do to their children, they will react again to their children's reaction. In other words, children's behaviour also shapes parents' behaviour (Osofsky, 1970). Understandably, stricter parents may produce obedient children but with negativity, and lenient parents may produce wilder children but with some positivity. Unsuitable parenting may bring about aggression in children, all else remaining constant (Kawabata, Alink, Tseng, van IJzendoorn, & Crick, 2011). In summary, parental control, if not properly activated, will lead to problem behaviour in children (Aunola & Nurmi, 2005). A crucial point to bear in mind.

Communication

Perhaps the most significant factor in a family is communication among members of it. Sounds incredible, but in reality, other than parents giving instructions and children responding accordingly, many parent–child interactions lack adequate constructive conversations to iron issues out. Especially in today's world of internet usage, where electronic devices like mobile phones, notebooks, and electronic tablets are frequently used by almost everyone everywhere; people are not having face-to-face chats and proper conversations on daily living.

More so with growing children who are bogged down by school work, studies, peers, and multimedia; parents are losing control over them, even in talking to them in the ordinary way. One of the most difficult challenges families face today is finding time to spend together (Varghese & Nivedhitha, 2014).
This is linked to the later section on internet use.

Culture and religion

Culture, as defined by sociologists, is the beliefs, way of life, art, and customs shared and accepted by people in a particular society. Therefore, as long as people exist, culture will never stop existing (Kerfoot, 2015).

> It is any kind of ritualised behaviour that becomes meaningful for a group and that remains more or less constant and is transmitted down through the generations. Culture is an essential part of understanding us as humans, making it necessary to describe what we understand by culture correctly.
>
> (Astobiza, 2017, p. 1)

Variability in activities is an inherent property in culture and parenting (McNaughton, 1996). Ways of knowing and ways of doing, constituting a culture, are constructed at two levels: personal and collective. Parents act as socialising agents to their children to promote their cultural identity. Parents construct a personal culture from the collective culture. Cultural diversity leads to different styles in parenting. Parenting style is most influenced by cultural value orientation (Otto, 2016).

Religion is part of culture, and it pays to talk a little about religion as it plays a major role in culture, which in turn affects parenting. Religion is a powerful tool in culture for believers; it helps move people, families, and individuals. Further, it helps people to bond early in life, similar to the parent–child relationship. Youth-centred religious conversations in a strong parent–child relationship may bring about better positive behaviours in the child (Dollahite & Thatcher, 2008). Heterosexual couples who observe religious beliefs and carry out religious practices have greater marital satisfaction and do better in child supervision (Ahmadi & Hossein-Abadi, 2009). Fundamentalist religious parents tend to shape their children's faith towards theirs (Danso, Hunsberger, & Pratt,

1997). Parental religiousness is associated with more controlling parenting, which will increase child problem behaviours. Children relate religiousness to parental rejection, whereas parents relate it to parental efficacy and warmth (Bornstein et al., 2017).

Education/literacy of parents

Parents with low levels of education are generally less involved and have lower levels of motivation for involvement with their children (Newland et al., 2013). Conversely, parents who are more educated will often be more involved, supportive, and more controlling of their children (Hsieh, Dopkins Stright, & Yen, 2017). Notably, the education level of parents is predictive of the success of children many years later (Dubow, Boxer, & Huesmann, 2009). Certainly, education has become a must-have in parenting children. It is generally believed that education is the first answer to many human problems; for example, some types of addiction, and the need for a better life. Most parents will spare no effort in getting the best education for their children from the best institution.

Associated with this topic are instructional styles of teachers; though not a focus of this book, they have a strong bearing on parenting. For one, many parenting benefits can be undone in school, and vice versa. For another, parent–teacher coordination in teaching children may bring about stronger benefits for the children, say, in reading and spelling (Kiuru et al., 2012). Parental influence on teachers is significant in making the latter more prosocial, that is, more involved in educational policies and in being an advisor to parents, including updating parents on their children and doing more to assist weaker students or be more caring towards them (Shaheen, Gupta, & Kumar, 2016).

Family breakup/changes

Family research has found delays in the commencement of parenthood, increases in the breaking up of families through divorces, and climbing rates of single-parent families among other changes in the family. Such breakups and changes have tremendous impact on parenting children. Hopefully, these are transient and reversible. Sometimes, they occur for the good of each party. Whatever happens, the upbringing of children is affected. Although parents promise to continue nurturing their children in spite of the circumstances they are in, parenting will take on a twisted path.

For example, research has found that overt parental conflict is related strongly to children's emotional and behavioural problems. That is, if parents are in disagreement over childrearing they will not be consistent in handling children, and this may be linked to the development of behavioural disorders (Jenkins & Smith, 1991). A study (Spruijt, Eikelenboom, Harmeling, Stokkers, & Kormos, 2005) found that parental alienation syndrome occurred significantly more often when decisions relating to children were not taken together by the parents but were determined in court.

Feeding practice, physical activity, and health

A key process in parenting is the feeding practice of parents that is imposed on their children. Given the foods of today, many of which feature artificial chemicals in their manufacturing and transporting processes, parents play a crucial role in selecting the right types of food for their children from day one. Early correct learning about food, nutrition, and health will lead to a longer life for many people with less major illness. However, many a parent does not have food knowledge, and is swayed instead by advertisements and business gimmicks. In any case, parenting styles affect their feeding styles (Hubbs-Tait, 2008) and may be responsible for obesity in children (Ventura & Birch, 2008), to cite a well-known phenomenon. Authoritative parents are easier on their children's choices of food, whereas authoritarian parents will ensure children eat what they are told to have, and permissive parents model food eating for their children. However, a study (Johnson, Welk, Saint-Maurice, & Ihmels, 2012) has found that the permissive parenting style is associated with more obesogenic environments.

Note that children may be picky eaters from as young as one year of age. Picky eating and feeding difficulty behaviours occurring frequently are associated with caregiver stress when feeding, and a negative impact on family relationships. Such common feeding behaviours are eating slowly or holding food in the mouth, refusing food (particularly fruits and vegetables), eating sweets and fatty foods instead of healthy foods, food neophobia, eating snacks instead of meals, and accepting only preferred types of food (Goh & Jacob, 2012).

There is a possibility that feeding difficulty behaviours will cause the children to be less energetic, and may lead to lower weight and stature. They are also related to certain attitudes and perceptions of parents or grandparents. Of these, pressure to eat (such as raising the voice and threatening the child until the food is finished, and making the child eat when not hungry) is positively associated with persistent behaviour. Common coping strategies are consulting a doctor about the child's eating habits, allowing a maid/caregiver to feed the child, and giving the child milk from a bottle (Goh & Jacob, 2012). A study (Crookston, Forste, McClellan, Georgiadis, & Heaton, 2014) has found that if parents have more schooling, and household wealth increases, with the ability to provide more nutrition, child growth will improve, with better cognitive achievement.

Linked closely with feeding practice is the health of children, obviously. And clearly we are looking at many obese children today, with affluence in families; nonstop supplies of foods of all sorts, boosted by mouth-watering commercial advertising in the media; and children being couch potatoes, watching shows and playing games on electronic screens. A study (Jago et al., 2011) found that maternal permissive parenting was associated with higher levels of physical activity than authoritative parenting. Maternal logistic support was associated with female children's physical activity, whereas paternal logistic support was associated with male children's physical activity. Logistic support concerns enrolling children in activities, and providing transportation to parks and playgrounds.

Fertility rates and new reproductive technologies

Advances in laws and medicine have helped the decreasing fertility rates in humans through new reproductive technologies and processes. Such advances include adopting children; artificial insemination; cloning; cryopreservation of embryos, oocytes, and sperm; embryo transfer; hormone treatment; in-vitro fertilisation; sperm/egg donation; and surrogate motherhood (Van Zyl, 2002). Parenting takes on additional meanings where children are born out of these technologies.

At the same time, contraceptive devices have disjoined sex from procreation and provided control over the instances and timing of childbearing—not reproductive success. Thus, through contraceptive ingenuity, humans have outwitted and taken control over their evolved reproductive system (Bussey & Bandura, 1999).

Intercultural marriage

Being an intercultural couple is both interesting and challenging, particularly if they live in a world not quite ready for such a mixed marriage. Difficulties facing them include having to decide on a place of residence, going through cultural transitions, realignment following the birth of a child in the family, and selecting the better intercultural parenting style and identity for that family (Crippen & Brew, 2007).

Children of intercultural marriages take on additional roles, like searching for one's true identity and religious affiliation, to name two. My personal experience with these couples, particularly their children, indicates how complex their lives can be if they are not acknowledged by their relatives and friends, and the public. It is easy for a couple to fall in love, but to gain acceptance on top of being the usual couple is quite a challenge, if not a major obstacle to surmount.

Internet use

The internet dominates the lives of many people around the world today, particularly in developed countries, so much so that many problems come with the benefits of having the internet at our fingertips. The main benefit is its speed for communication (Tur-Porcar, 2017). In fact, the internet has changed most human behaviours from home to school to workplace to public areas—almost every aspect of human living. Parents have a hard time controlling the use of the internet by their children, more so if they are internet savvy and addicted themselves.

A recent study (Li, Lei, & Tian, 2018) meta-analysed 79 studies exploring the relationship between positive and negative indicators of parenting style and internet addiction among 44,650 Mainland Chinese teenagers. Positive indicators of parenting style include emotional warmth and understanding, and negative indicators include excessive interference, overprotection, refusal or denial, punishment, strictness, and over-indulgence. The results show that higher numbers of positive parenting behaviours correlate with a lower degree of teenagers' internet addiction. Positive parenting increases the level of children's mental health, self-esteem, life satisfaction, and self-control, and the children develop more positively. Negative parenting leads to a stronger tendency for children to be addicted to the internet.

Parental attitude, affection, and control

This is perhaps one of the most important groups of factors in parenting. No doubt, most parents are positive about having children, but in some cases parents do not want their children, for reasons best known to themselves. With positive parental attitude comes positive parental involvement and acceptance; thus, children develop better thinking styles in terms of higher levels of creativity and autonomy, and are ready to explore the world without much fear (Fan & Zhang, 2014). Alternatively, children from parents who exercise a lot of authority will show conservative thinking styles. This is a huge topic for discussion later.

Parental behavioural control would include rules, supervision and monitoring, and disciplining. Parental psychological and emotional control would range from shaming and love-withdrawal to providing warmth, psychological autonomy, and demandingness (Stolz, Barber, & Olsen, 2005). More parental psychological control would lead to increases in internalising and externalising problems in female adolescents, but only internalising problems in male adolescents. More parental knowledge would lead to decreases in male adolescents' internalising and externalising problems. Generally, adolescents often perceive their mothers as using more psychological control and having more knowledge on adolescents' whereabouts, friends, and activities than their fathers (Lansford, Laird, Pettit, Bates, & Dodge, 2014).

A recent study (Kimmes & Heckman, 2017) using data from the National Longitudinal Survey of Youth 1997 in the US examined how parents influence the higher education decision-making process of young adults. The results show that parenting is indirectly associated with college enrolment through prior associations with young adults' subjective probability of completing college, time preferences, academic achievement, cognitive ability, and parental expectations. Thus, parenting style impacts the child's beliefs, expectations, and attitudes, all of which ultimately play a role in the decision over whether or not to enrol in college.

Inconsistency in parenting is a situation children fear just as a trainee fears inconsistency in training of any sort. Not only is the child confused as what to do next, but parents are equally unaware of it. A study (Dwairy, 2008) has found that parental inconsistency, whether from one or both parents, is an important factor in psychological disorder symptoms among adolescents who are more connected to their parents.

This influencing group of factors does include the life story of the parents. How one went through one's childhood and upbringing would, no doubt, affect the way one would manage his or her own children. Hopefully, what is learned best and is worthwhile is passed on, and not the ugly matters. Details on the topic of the neurobiological perspective of parenting are available (see, for example, Lomanowska, Boivin, Hertzman, & Fleming, 2017).

Perception of parenting

This is a major issue in parenting. Everything starts with a perception (where seeing is mostly mentioned because sight is 80% of our senses), then thoughts and emotions, followed by action. If it stops after perception, then nothing else follows. Unfortunately, when we perceive something, it does not stop there. We tend to think about it, put some feelings into it, add more thoughts and feelings, and take some action. Most importantly, as a psychotherapist I would say (to my clients), "If you perceive and don't interpret, nothing will happen; but if you do, then you are to take note of it, take charge if need be, or else manage it." The same happens in parenting and other mental events.

Therefore, parents will always perceive themselves as playing their parental roles correctly, or even perfectly, for their children. Parents will go to great lengths to play their roles at their best, consulting books, social media, friends and relatives, and even experts on parenting. They will have the "Anything that is good for my children, I'll go for it" attitude, and the "Anything that is unsafe for my children, I'll avoid it" attitude. *I'll punish my children for wrongdoings so that they will grow up morally righteous. I'll reward my children for doing right and the best for themselves (and perhaps their family). Don't tell me my parenting style is wrong. It is for their own good. Just tell me how to do better.* These self-talks by parents or among parents in a family are prevalent.

Unfortunately, children might not perceive things as their parents do. First, they are of a different age, a different generation. Second, they are growing up in a different environment than that of their parents and being influenced differently. Most important of all, children perceive their way of life if they could finance and manage it. Hence, there could be conflicts of interest in parenting. It is best if parents and children agree; worse if they are completely opposite.

Literature abounds with definitions of perception (for example, self-perception), its function, and its outcomes. These are not covered here.

Personality traits of parents and children

Individual differences in personality traits are inborn or heritable. Research has shown that genes are 40% to 50% responsible for these differences (Bratko, Butkovic, & Hlupic, 2017). So almost half of children's behaviour comes from their parents, like it or not and no matter how hard they try to change them. The more manageable part is the other half, which is moulded by the environment. Present-day research in neuroscience has shown that changing one's behaviour may alter one's genes, delaying or preventing them for expressing themselves in the life of the person. This is good news for parenting!

Consequently, good parental traits or characteristics may lead to secure attachment of children to them and vice versa (Carranza & Kilmann, 2000). Indian parents, for example, may attribute the positive behaviours of children to parenting and the personality of the child (Montemayor & Ranganathan, 2012). It is a challenge for good parents to look after badly behaved children—another topic of major discussion, but not discussed in detail here.

Research has also shown that as children share about half of their genes with each biological parent, the same genetic factors that influence hostile parenting might also affect the expression of child aggression; thus, an association between hostile parenting and child aggression is the product of shared genes rather than a direct effect of caregiving (Stover et al., 2012). A study (Laukkanen, Ojansuu,

Tolvanen, Alatupa, & Aunola, 2014) found that children's low positivity is associated with low maternal affection, whereas children's negative emotionality is associated with mothers' many attempts at psychological and behavioural control. Notably, the more active and the less positive a mother perceives her child to be, the lower will be her well-being and, consequently, the more psychological control she will apply.

Further, many studies have found strong associations between parents' antisocial traits, marital conflict, and negative parenting. Note that antisocial and other personality traits are defined as a set of enduring characteristics that affect behaviour and perceptions (Stover et al., 2012). For example, mothers in individualistic cultures show personality traits that are more affectionate and compassionate, and stronger interest in learning about a diversity of things than mothers of collectivistic cultures. Mothers in collectivistic cultures tend to be more susceptible to social influence and group pressure, more eagerly seek formal and informal association with others, and are more easily upset and worried over inconsequential matters than mothers in individualistic cultures (Bornstein et al., 2007). A mother's psychotic manner and introversion may increase a child's depression disorder (Babaee & Jain, 2009). Low levels of neuroticism and psychopathology and high levels of agreeableness, extraversion, and conscientiousness are associated with adaptive parenting (McCabe, 2014). Neuroticism and an authoritarian parenting style are positively related to socially prescribed perfectionism (Miller & Speirs Neumeister, 2017).

Preference for male children

In many societies, families still hold a preference for procreating male children who can succeed their lineage, and who are believed to be able to earn more income to look after aged parents. For these families, it is extremely sad or even disastrous to have no sons. Some countries have been known to have high incidences of infanticide of female babies. Many grandparents have urged their sons to take in an additional wife to bear them sons or grandsons. Chinese families pray for the first-born of their eldest sons to be male, and worship their grandsons. Psychoanalysts have called this "penis envy". I would rather term it "penis worship".

Research has shown that fathers often estimate males as having higher scores in logico-mathematical and spatial intelligence (Furnham, Reeves, & Budhani, 2002). Differences between males and females in physical, mental, and emotional performances are present and undeniable. These again pose challenges to parenting if not carefully understood and managed.

In India, for example (Lin & Adserà, 2013), sons are needed for the cremation of the deceased parents, because only they can light the funeral pyre. Also, when sons are preferred over daughters, the latter get to do much more housework. There is the belief that girls should be good at housework skills in order to be socially fit once they are mature and are married. Notably, the increase in hours of housework is associated with wealth and urban–rural differences in the demand for housework. Families in rural areas tend to live in conditions that involve more labour-intensive work (for example, farmland that must be tended) and require more housework in their daily activities than those in urban areas; both areas are linked with the hours of housework performed by children. Furthermore, when mothers have more sons than daughters, childbearing is likely to be discontinued (Chaudhuri, 2012). And sons receive more childcare time than daughters, they are breastfed longer, and they get more vitamin supplementation (Barcellos, Carvalho, & Lleras-Muney, 2014).

Significant others

Significant others in a family refers to grandparents, aunts and uncles, domestic helpers, baby sitters, and any child-carer that contributes some time to looking after the children.

Significant others who are not in the common group, like those with chronic illnesses, transgender people, stepparents, etc., pose different parenting issues, and are not discussed here. For example, children with parents with chronic illnesses have more internalising problem behaviours and some externalising behaviours (Sieh, Meijer, Oort, Visser-Meily, & Van der Leij, 2010). Parenting of children with disabilities is filled with issues concerning barriers (Parchomiuk, 2014). And being brought up by same-sex parents is not always easy for children to accept and deal with when the truth is out (Lytle, Foley, & Aster, 2013). Children can also find a stepparent or stepsiblings difficult to accept (Cassoni & Caldana, 2012).

On the whole, significant others often augment parenting of children; or the consequences can be worse for the children. For example, domestic helpers often carry out parental orders to such an extreme that the children are over-pampered—another major factor to contend with in parenting.

Social economic status

Definitely, wealth is a major influence on the provision of food, shelter, and education for children, to name the most important issues. This factor (some researchers call it "class") greatly affects many other influencing factors regarding parenting. For example, over-provision or incorrect provision of food may lead to child obesity or poor health. Too good a life means "hardship" is not the in-word for children from wealthy families. On education, what is meant here is the choice of going to the school preferred by the child or parent. Often the latter prevails, because parents know best. True or false? It is true that children from families with low incomes often do not do so well in education. With helpful educational programmes (Benzies, Tough, Edwards, Mychasiuk, & Donnelly, 2011) and government subsidies or scholarships, these children would stand a better chance of success in schooling. Children from families of low social economic status can have a string of problems, ranging from physical to behavioural to emotional ones; for instance, poor health, violent behaviour, and being mentally unfit or unstable.

A study (Olivari, Hertfelt Wahn, Maridaki-Kassotaki, Antonopoulou, & Confalonieri, 2015) contended that in middle-class families parent–child relationships are more accepting and equalitarian, whereas in working-class families they are oriented towards discipline and obedience. Perhaps, as basic needs are satisfied in the case of middle-class families, there is more time for scrutinising parent–child relationships; whereas when basic needs are not easily met, time at home is spent more on getting the children on the right path to success, that is, behaviour.

Economic distress has constantly revealed direct associations with marital hostility and indirect associations with marital conflict on parenting (Stover et al., 2012). On the other hand, affluent parents will use their financial, educational, and cultural resources to transfer their class privilege to their children through active involvement in their children's lives (Park, 2018).

Work–family balance

With more women encouraged to join the workforce comes the issue of work–family balance. This is in addition to the discussion on work–life balance for men. But work–family balance seems to affect mothering more than fathering as women still have to grapple with housework and looking after children when home after work. The new roles of career women, organisational policies to effect them (Hunt & Hunt, 1982), and generational conflicts are hotly discussed (Bennett, Beehr, & Ivanitskaya, 2017).

Today, it is acceptable for fathers to stay home as house husbands to look after the children while the mothers work as breadwinners. Parenting takes on a different route once again.

Table 1.2 Summary of factors influencing parenting

	Description	*Food for thought*
Birth order of children	Many parents nurture their children differently as they are born. First-born is often doted on, second-born less but is freer to follow his or her preferences. Third child onwards is dependent more on parents' and child's personality.	Personality, characteristics, and behaviours peculiar to children.
Children's behaviour	Children's behaviour also shapes parents' behaviour as they are parented.	Be mindful of reactions from children too. Only let the child be in charge when it is deemed safe and necessary to do so.
Culture and religion	Culture and religion strongly influence parenting style, particularly if they are strictly adhered to.	Children from such families may have little leeway for their own preferences in life.
Communication	Although members of families live together, constructive communication is lacking due to interference; e.g., the internet.	Need for parents and children to have more meaningful conversations.

(*Continued*)

Table 1.2 (Cont.)

	Description	Food for thought
Education/ literacy of parents	Parents who are more educated will often be involved, be supporting, and be more controlling of their children.	Need for parents to be better informed.
Family breakup/ changes	Family breakups and changes have tremendous impact on parenting children.	Mostly affected are children, who may in turn follow the footsteps of their parents in bad marriages.
Feeding practice, physical activity, and health	Early correct learning about food, nutrition, physical activity, and health leads to a longer life for many people. However, many a parent does not have food knowledge, and is swayed instead by advertisements and business gimmicks.	Need to be better informed on food, nutrition, physical activity, and health matters.
Fertility rates and new reproductive technologies	Advances in laws and medicine have helped the decreasing fertility rates in humans through new reproductive technologies and processes.	Would children born of such technologies be different in the long run?
Intercultural marriage	These marriages bring the best of both worlds to the children.	Children of intercultural marriages take on additional roles, like searching for one's true identity and religious affiliation, to name two.
Internet use	The internet dominates the lives of many people around the world today, particularly in developed countries, so much so that most people cannot live without it.	The benefits of internet use may overshadow the accompanying problems.
Parental attitude, affection, and control	A major factor in parenting.	Note the positive and negative effects of this factor.
Personality traits of parents and children	About 50% of children's personality traits come from their parents; the rest are theirs.	What to change and what cannot be changed as a result of heredity of genes.

(Continued)

Table 1.2 (Cont.)

	Description	Food for thought
Perception of parenting	Hopefully, parents and children see eye-to-eye on the parenting style(s) applied in the family. Parents may adopt different parenting styles for their children.	Which style is best for each child? It depends on many factors, among them traits, situation, condition, and outcome.
Preference for male children	In many societies, families still hold a preference for procreating male children to succeed their lineage and earn more income to look after aged parents.	Need to progress with equality for female children.
Significant others	*Significant others* in a family refers to grandparents, aunts and uncles, domestic helpers, baby sitters, and any child-carer that contributes some time to looking after the child or children.	These significant others can contribute to problems in parenting, particularly for parents who want their own ways.
Social economic status	No doubt, wealth is major factor in the provision of food, shelter, and education for children.	Is wealth everything for living?
Work–family balance	This is about the working mother managing her career and motherhood, and about the modern stay-at-home-dad.	What is the right formula for work–family balance? For that matter, work–family–life balance too?

Conclusion

We have discussed family, parenting, and important influencing factors. The reader may like to retain these descriptions and discussion at the back of their mind while reading on. On the whole, parenting is complex and challenging, but possible and worthy.

Before discussing the types of parenting styles, the difference between fathering and mothering has to be ironed out, and this is the gist of the next chapter.

Notes

1 The environment is everything outside of the individual, from the air around him or her to the people and land, and to the faraway space. It includes the tangible (for example, food, house, people) and the intangible (talks, policies, etc.). It helps to explain what and how we develop along the lifeway, whether as a child, a parent, or any adult. And onward to models on parenting that have been advocated by many experts; such are found abundantly in literature on the shelves of book shops, libraries and schools.
2 In the psychology literature, *authoritarian parenting* refers generally to strict, unquestioning parenting, whereas *authoritative parenting* refers to firm but flexible parenting. Details of parenting styles are given in the chapters on Western and Eastern parenting.

References

Ahmadi, K., & Hossein-Abadi, F. H. (2009). Religiosity, marital satisfaction and child rearing. *Pastoral Psychology*, 57(5), 211–221. doi:10.1007/s11089-008-0176-4.

Astobiza, A. M. (2017). What is culture in "cultural economy"? Defining culture to create measurable models in cultural economy. *Arbor: Ciencia*, 193(783). doi:10.3989/arbor.2017.783n1007.

Aunola, K., & Nurmi, J. (2005). The role of parenting styles in children's problem behavior. *Child Development*, 76(6), 1144–1159. doi:10.1111/j.1467-8624.2005.00841.x.

Babaee, E., & Jain, S. (2009). *Relation between aspects of mother's personality and children's behavior disorders*. Mobile: Project Innovation.

Barcellos, S. H., Carvalho, L. S., & Lleras-Muney, A. (2014). Child gender and parental investments in India: Are boys and girls treated differently? *American Economic Journal: Applied Economics*, 6(1), 157–189. doi:10.1257/app.6.1.157.

Bardwick, J. M. (1974). Evolution and parenting. *Journal of Social Issues*, 30(4), 39–62. doi:10.1111/j.1540-4560.1974.tb01754.x.

Bennett, M. M., Beehr, T. A., & Ivanitskaya, L. V. (2017). Work–family conflict: Differences across generations and life cycles. *Journal of Managerial Psychology*, 32(4), 314–332. doi:10.1108/JMP-06-2016-0192.

Benzies, K., Tough, S., Edwards, N., Mychasiuk, R., & Donnelly, C. (2011). Aboriginal children and their caregivers living with low income: Outcomes from a two-generation preschool program. *Journal of Child and Family Studies*, 20(3), 311–318. doi:10.1007/s10826-010-9394-3.

Bornstein, M. H., Hahn, C., Haynes, O. M., Belsky, J., Azuma, H., Kwak, K., ... de Galperín, C. Z. (2007). Maternal personality and parenting cognitions in cross-cultural perspective. *International Journal of Behavioral Development*, 31(3), 193–209. doi:10.1177/0165025407074632.

Bornstein, M. H., Putnick, D. L., Lansford, J. E., Al-Hassan, S. M., Bacchini, D., Bombi, A. S., ... Alampay, L. P. (2017). "Mixed blessings": Parental religiousness, parenting, and child adjustment in global perspective. *Journal of Child Psychology and Psychiatry, 58*(8), 880–892.

Bratko, D., Butkovic, A., & Hlupic, T. V. (2017). Heritability of personality. *Psychological Topics, 26*(1), 1–24.

Browne, T. (2001). Human development theories. *Futurics, 25*(1/2), 50–71.

Bussey, K., & Bandura, A. (1999). Social cognitive theory of gender development and differentiation. *Psychological Review, 106*, 676–713. doi:10.1037/0033-295X.106.4.676.

Carranza, L. V., & Kilmann, P. R. (2000). Links between perceived parent characteristics and attachment variables for young women from intact families. *Adolescence, 35*(138), 295–312.

Cassoni, C., & Caldana, R. H. (2012). Parenting style and practices in stepfamilies. *Psychology Research and Behavior Management, 5*, 105–111. doi:10.2147/PRBM.S34966.

Chaudhuri, S. (2012). The desire for sons and excess fertility: A household-level analysis of parity progression in India. *International Perspectives on Sexual and Reproductive Health, 38*(4), 178–186.

Crippen, C., & Brew, L. (2007). Intercultural parenting and the transcultural family: A literature review. *Family Journal, 15*(2), 107–115. doi:10.1177/1066480706297783.

Crookston, B. T., Forste, R., McClellan, C., Georgiadis, A., & Heaton, T. B. (2014). Factors associated with cognitive achievement in late childhood and adolescence: The young lives cohort study of children in Ethiopia, India, Peru, and Vietnam. *BMC Pediatrics, 14*(1), 253. doi:10.1186/1471-2431-14-253.

Csikszentmihalyi, M. (1993). Contexts of optimal growth in childhood. *Daedalus, 122*(1), 31–56.

Danso, H., Hunsberger, B., & Pratt, M. (1997). The role of parental religious fundamentalism and right-wing authoritarianism in child-rearing goals and practices. *Journal for the Scientific Study of Religion, 36*(4), 496–511.

Dodge, K. A. (2004). The nature–nurture debate and public policy. *Merrill-Palmer Quarterly, 50*(4), 418–427. doi:10.1353/mpq.2004.0028.

Dollahite, D. C., & Thatcher, J. Y. (2008). Talking about religion: How highly religious youth and parents discuss their faith. *Journal of Adolescent Research, 23*(5), 611–641. doi:10.1177/0743558408322141.

Dubow, E. F., Boxer, P., & Huesmann, L. R. (2009). Long-term effects of parents' education on children's educational and occupational success: Mediation by family interactions, child aggression, and teenage aspirations. *Merrill-Palmer Quarterly, 55*(3), 224–249. doi:10.1353/mpq.0.0030.

Dwairy, M. A. (2008). Parental inconsistency versus parental authoritarianism: Associations with symptoms of psychological disorders. *Journal of Youth and Adolescence, 37*(5), 616–626. doi:10.1007/s10964-007-9169-3.

Fan, J., & Zhang, L. (2014). The role of perceived parenting styles in thinking styles. *Learning and Individual Differences, 32*, 204–211. doi:10.1016/j.lindif.2014.03.004.

Favez, N., Frascarolo, F., & Tissot, H. (2017). The family alliance model: A way to study and characterize early family interactions. *Frontiers in Psychology, 8*, 1–11. doi:10.3389/fpsyg.2017.01441.

Furnham, A., Reeves, E., & Budhani, S. (2002). Parents think their sons are brighter than their daughters: Sex differences in parental self-estimations and estimations of their children's multiple intelligences. *Journal of Genetic Psychology*, 163(1), 24–39. doi:10.1080/00221320209597966.

Goh, D. Y., & Jacob, A. (2012). Perception of picky eating among children in Singapore and its impact on caregivers: A questionnaire survey. *Asia Pacific Family Medicine*, 11(1), 5. doi:10.1186/1447-056X-11-5.

Hays, S. (1998). The fallacious assumptions and unrealistic prescriptions of attachment theory: A comment on "parents' socioemotional investment in children". *Journal of Marriage and Family*, 60(3), 782–790.

Hsieh, Y., Dopkins Stright, A., & Yen, L. (2017). Child characteristics, parent education and depressive symptoms, and marital conflict predicting trajectories of parenting behavior from childhood through early adolescence in Taiwan. *Family Process*, 56(3), 734–751. doi:10.1111/famp.12253.

Hubbs-Tait, L. (2008). Parental feeding practices predict authoritative, authoritarian, and permissive parenting styles. *Journal of the American Dietetic Association*, 108(7), 1154–1161. doi:10.1016/j.jada.2008.04.008.

Hunt, J. G., & Hunt, L. L. (1982). The dualities of careers and families: New integrations or new polarizations? *Social Problems*, 29(5), 499–510. doi:10.1525/sp.1982.29.5.03a00060.

Jago, R., Davison, K. K., Brockman, R., Page, A. S., Thompson, J. L., & Fox, K. R. (2011). Parenting styles, parenting practices, and physical activity in 10- to 11-year olds. *Preventive Medicine*, 52(1), 44–47. doi:10.1016/j.ypmed.2010.11.001.

Jenkins, J. M., & Smith, M. A. (1991). Marital disharmony and children's behaviour problems: Aspects of a poor marriage that affect children adversely. *Journal of Child Psychology and Psychiatry, and Allied Disciplines*, 32(5), 793–810. doi:10.1111/j.1469-7610.1991.tb01903.x.

Johnson, R., Welk, G., Saint-Maurice, P. F., & Ihmels, M. (2012). Parenting styles and home obesogenic environments. *International Journal of Environmental Research and Public Health*, 9(4), 1411–1426. doi:10.3390/ijerph9041411.

Jones, J. D., Cassidy, J., & Shaver, P. R. (2015). Parents' self-reported attachment styles: A review of links with parenting behaviors, emotions, and cognitions. *Personality and Social Psychology Review*, 19(1), 44–76. doi:10.1177/1088868314541858.

Kawabata, Y., Alink, L. R. A., Tseng, W., van IJzendoorn, M. H., & Crick, N. R. (2011). Maternal and paternal parenting styles associated with relational aggression in children and adolescents: A conceptual analysis and meta-analytic review. *Developmental Review*, 31(4), 240–278. doi:10.1016/j.dr.2011.08.001.

Keller, H. (2000). Human parent–child relationships from an evolutionary perspective. *American Behavioral Scientist*, 43(6), 957–969. doi:10.1177/00027640021955694.

Keller, H. (2013). Attachment and culture. *Journal of Cross-Cultural Psychology*, 44(2), 175–194. doi:10.1177/0022022112472253.

Keller, H., Lamm, B., Abels, M., Yovsi, R., Borke, J., Jensen, H., ... Chaudhary, N. (2006). Cultural models, socialization goals, and parenting ethnotheories: A multicultural analysis. *Journal of Cross-Cultural Psychology*, 37(2), 155–172. doi:10.1177/0022022105284494.

Kenny, M. E., & Rice, K. G. (1995). Attachment to parents and adjustment in late adolescent college students: Current status, applications, and future considerations. *Counseling Psychologist, 23*(3), 433–456. doi:10.1177/0011000095233003.

Kerfoot, K. (2015, July 2). Defining culture. *University Wire*.

Kimmes, J. G., & Heckman, S. J. (2017). Parenting styles and college enrollment: A path analysis of risky human capital decisions. *Journal of Family and Economic Issues, 38*(4), 614–627. doi:10.1007/s10834-017-9529-4.

Kiuru, N., Aunola, K., Torppa, M., Lerkkanen, M., Poikkeus, A., Niemi, P., ... Nurmi, J. (2012). The role of parenting styles and teacher interactional styles in children's reading and spelling development. *Journal of School Psychology, 50*(6), 799–823. doi:10.1016/j.jsp.2012.07.001.

Lansford, J. E., Laird, R. D., Pettit, G. S., Bates, J. E., & Dodge, K. A. (2014). Mothers' and fathers' autonomy-relevant parenting: Longitudinal links with adolescents' externalizing and internalizing behavior. *Journal of Youth and Adolescence, 43*(11), 1877–1889. doi:10.1007/s10964-013-0079-2.

Laukkanen, J., Ojansuu, U., Tolvanen, A., Alatupa, S., & Aunola, K. (2014). Child's difficult temperament and mothers' parenting styles. *Journal of Child and Family Studies, 23*(2), 312. doi:10.1007/s10826-013-9747-9.

Lee, S. M., Daniels, M. H., & Kissinger, D. B. (2006). Parental influences on adolescent adjustment: Parenting styles versus parenting practices. *Family Journal, 14*(3), 253–259. doi:10.1177/1066480706287654.

Li, S., Lei, H., & Tian, L. (2018). A meta-analysis of the relationship between parenting style and internet addiction among mainland Chinese teenagers. *Social Behavior and Personality, 46*(9), 1475–1487. doi:10.2224/sbp.7631.

Lin, T., & Adserà, A. (2013). Son preference and children's housework: The case of India. *Population Research and Policy Review, 32*(4), 553–584. doi:10.1007/s11113-013-9269-6.

Lomanowska, A. M., Boivin, M., Hertzman, C., & Fleming, A. S. (2017). Parenting begets parenting: A neurobiological perspective on early adversity and the transmission of parenting styles across generations. *Neuroscience, 342*, 120–139. doi:10.1016/j.neuroscience.2015.09.029.

Lytle, M. C., Foley, P. F., & Aster, A. M. (2013). Adult children of gay and lesbian parents: Religion and the parent–child relationship. *Counseling Psychologist, 41*(4), 530–567. doi:10.1177/0011000012449658.

McCabe, J. E. (2014). Maternal personality and psychopathology as determinants of parenting behavior: A quantitative integration of two parenting literatures. *Psychological Bulletin, 140*(3), 722–750. doi:10.1037/a0034835.

McNaughton, S. (1996). Ways of parenting and cultural identity. *Culture & Psychology, 2*(2), 173–201. doi:10.1177/1354067X9600200203.

Miller, A. L., & Speirs Neumeister, K. L. (2017). The influence of personality, parenting styles, and perfectionism on performance goal orientation in high ability students. *Journal of Advanced Academics, 28*(4), 313–344. doi:10.1177/1932202X17730567.

Montemayor, R., & Ranganathan, C. (2012). Asian-Indian parents' attributions about the causes of child behavior: A replication and extension with parents from

Chennai, India. *Journal of Genetic Psychology, 173*(4), 374–392. doi:10.1080/00221325.2011.614649.

Moor, J. A., & de Graaf, P. M. (2016). Temporary and long-term consequences of bereavement on happiness. *Journal of Happiness Studies, 17*(3), 913–936. doi:10.1007/s10902-015-9624-x.

Newland, L. A., Chen, H., Coyl-Shepherd, D. D., Liang, Y., Carr, E. R., Dykstra, E., & Gapp, S. C. (2013). Parent and child perspectives on mothering and fathering: The influence of ecocultural niches. *Early Child Development and Care, 183*(3–4), 534–552. doi:10.1080/03004430.2012.711598.

Olivari, M. G., Hertfelt Wahn, E., Maridaki-Kassotaki, K., Antonopoulou, K., & Confalonieri, E. (2015). Adolescent perceptions of parenting styles in Sweden, Italy and Greece: An exploratory study. *Europe's Journal of Psychology, 11*(2), 244–258. doi:10.5964/ejop.v11i2.887.

Oltedal, S., & Nygren, L. (2015). Local family definitions matter. *Journal of Comparative Social Work, 10*(1), 1–5.

Osofsky, J. D. (1970). The shaping of mother's behavior by children. *Journal of Marriage and Family, 32*(3), 400–405.

Otto, W. J. (2016). What teachers should know about why these students perform so well: An examination of Korean-American achievement through student perspectives of East Asian parenting beliefs, styles and practices. *International Electronic Journal of Elementary Education, 9*(1), 167–181.

Palkovitz, R., Trask, B. S., & Adamsons, K. (2014). Essential differences in the meaning and processes of mothering and fathering: Family systems, feminist and qualitative perspectives. *Journal of Family Theory & Review, 6*(4), 406–420. doi:10.1111/jftr.12048.

Parchomiuk, M. (2014). Social context of disabled parenting. *Sexuality and Disability, 32*(2), 231–242. doi:10.1007/s11195-014-9349-5.

Park, J. (2018). Public fathering, private mothering: Gendered transnational parenting and class reproduction among elite Korean students. *Gender & Society, 32*(4), 563–586. doi:10.1177/0891243218771551.

Parke, R. D. (2004). Development in the family. *Annual Review of Psychology, 55*(1), 365–399. doi:10.1146/annurev.psych.55.090902.141528.

Pedersen, D. E. (2012). The good mother, the good father, and the good parent: Gendered definitions of parenting. *Journal of Feminist Family Therapy, 24*(3), 230–246. doi:10.1080/08952833.2012.648141.

Shaheen, M., Gupta, R., & Kumar, Y. L. N. (2016). Exploring dimensions of teachers' OCB from stakeholder's perspective: A study in India. *Qualitative Report, 21*(6), 1095–1117.

Sharma, R. (2013). The family and family structure classification redefined for the current times. *Journal of Family Medicine and Primary Care, 2*(4), 306–310. Retrieved from: www.jfmpc.com/text.asp?2013/2/4/306/123774.

Sieh, D. S., Meijer, A. M., Oort, F. J., Visser-Meily, J. M. A., & Van der Leij, D. A. V. (2010). Problem behavior in children of chronically ill parents: A meta-analysis. *Clinical Child and Family Psychology Review, 13*(4), 384–397. doi:10.1007/s10567-010-0074-z.

Sim, C. T. K. (2017). Co-parenting conversation process: A qualitative study of Chinese Singaporean parents: Co-parenting conversation process. *Journal of Family Therapy, 39*(2), 217–237. doi:10.1111/1467-6427.12140.

Spruijt, E., Eikelenboom, B., Harmeling, J., Stokkers, R., & Kormos, H. (2005). Parental alienation syndrome (PAS) in the Netherlands. *American Journal of Family Therapy, 33*(4), 303–317. doi:10.1080/01926180590962110.

Stansbury, V. K., & Coll, K. M. (1998). Myers–Briggs attitude typology: The influence of birth order with other family variables. *Family Journal, 6*(2), 116–122. doi:10.1177/1066480798062006.

Stevens, H. (2016, February 25). "No impact man" expands definition of parenting; Colin Beavan says it should include mentoring kids in the community. *Times Colonist*.

Stolz, H. E., Barber, B. K., & Olsen, J. A. (2005). Toward disentangling fathering and mothering: An assessment of relative importance. *Journal of Marriage and Family, 67*(4), 1076–1092. doi:10.1111/j.1741-3737.2005.00195.x.

Stover, C. S., Connell, C. M., Leve, L. D., Neiderhiser, J. M., Shaw, D. S., Scaramella, L. V., ... Reiss, D. (2012). Fathering and mothering in the family system: Linking marital hostility and aggression in adopted toddlers. *Journal of Child Psychology and Psychiatry, 53*(4), 401–409. doi:10.1111/j.1469-7610.2011.02510.x.

Tur-Porcar, A. (2017). Parenting styles and internet use. *Psychology & Marketing, 34*(11), 1016–1022. doi:10.1002/mar.21040.

Van Zyl, L. (2002). Intentional parenthood and the nuclear family. *Journal of Medical Humanities, 23*(2), 107–118. doi:10.1023/A:1014842031013.

Varghese, T., & Nivedhitha, D. (2014). Indian teenagers and their family relations in the social networking era. *Rajagiri Journal of Social Development, 6*(1), 21.

Ventura, A. K., & Birch, L. L. (2008). Does parenting affect children's eating and weight status? *International Journal of Behavioral Nutrition and Physical Activity, 5*(1), 15. doi:10.1186/1479-5868-5-15.

Woodworth, S., Belsky, J., & Crnic, K. (1996). The determinants of fathering during the child's second and third years of life: A developmental analysis. *Journal of Marriage and Family, 58*(3), 679–692. doi:10.2307/353728.

Worthman, C. M. (2010). The ecology of human development: Evolving models for cultural psychology. *Journal of Cross-Cultural Psychology, 41*(4), 546–562. doi:10.1177/0022022110362627.

Fathering versus mothering

2

Parenting is mainly about the roles played by both the father and mother for their children. Naturally, the father is a male and the mother is female. Because of the inherent sex[1] differences between them, the role they play for their children would undoubtedly depend on their being male or female.

This chapter kicks off with a little talk on what being a man or woman entails. After a quick mention of the roles of members of a family, the definitions and scope of fathering and mothering are provided. Examples of these by culture are given. The pros and cons of fathering versus mothering are summarised in Table 2.1. Snippets on stay-at-home dads and mums and a short section on new fathers and mothers add flavour to the chapter. It wraps up with a final section comparing the effect of fathering and mothering on children, giving some outcomes as food for thought for the reader.

Noteworthy is the fact that, at present, same-sex marriages have unseated or upset fathering or mothering in parenting. In my opinion, no matter how able same-sex parents are in parenting, there are bound to be some matters relating to sexual preference that cannot be emulated. Same-sex parenting is not taken up here.

The strength of a marriage between a heterosexual couple is important for fathering and mothering, or simply parenting, to work. Studies have shown that divorce affects fathering more than mothering and weakens the father–child relationships (see, for example, Coiro & Emery, 1998). For most of this chapter, it is assumed that the parents are working together on parenting their children successfully. In spite of this assumption, hiccups in parenting due to differences or conflicts between the father and mother do occur. These are given some attention from time to time, but not delved into in detail.

What makes us man and woman?

According to biological theories, familial genes act as the transmission agent of sex differentiation across generations (Bussey & Bandura, 1999). Sex differences arising from the distinctive reproductive roles played by men and women form the basis of sex role development and differentiation. Thus, biologically or physically, we are man or woman. In general, a man is stronger, with more muscles and less fat, and taller, with more hairs on the body, a lower voice, and so forth. Generally, a woman is less strong with fewer muscles and more fat, and is shorter and less hairy, with a higher voice, and so forth. There are subtle brain differences in men and women. For example, men's brains are slightly larger, perhaps 8–10% (Hall, 2013), and have areas in them that are configured slightly differently—read books on neuroscience featuring these interesting facts if you would like to know more.

Psychological theories tend to emphasise within-the-mind or intrapsychic processes concerning sex development. These theories emphasise the cognitive construction of sex conceptions and styles of behaviour within the familial transmission model (Bussey & Bandura, 1999). Two psychological differences between men and women are highlighted here. One, the communication centre inside a woman's brain is larger than that in the man's brain. Thus, women are better at processing language. This means women pay more attention to spoken words, read between the lines, and notice the body language of people at the same time as their facial expressions. Two, men prefer to solve problems themselves rather than sharing them with others, as preferred by women. Thus, if a woman shares her problems with a man and he answers curtly, she will be disappointed.

Emotionally, women are believed to be more empathetic (Hall, 2013). Men in general can make decisions without being emotionally affected, whereas women in general take into consideration emotional factors before making decisions. This is possibly why male belligerent leaders tend to go to war. A common stereotype is that men should not show their emotions, and that real men do not cry. In reality, men certainly show the world much less of their emotional side; they would rather show their emotions to close or trusted people, or when alone.

Sociological theories focus on socio-structural determinants of sex role development and functioning, emphasising the social construction of sex roles mainly at the institutional level (Bussey & Bandura, 1999). Sociologically, on average, husbands are older than wives, men are more aggressive and violent, males and females have spatial and behavioural differences, females do more direct childcare, and sex imbalances are present in careers—there are fewer women in maths, science and engineering (Hall, 2013).

Behaviouristic theories have given prominence to parents in shaping and regulating sex-linked conduct (Bussey & Bandura, 1999). Generally, women are wired to avoid conflict. Men are more aggressive in general. Thus, a woman would try to avoid conflict and maintain peace, whereas a man would not back off if someone threatened or challenged him.

Personality-wise, let us refer to the Jungian archetypes to explain the behaviours of man and woman. According to Carl Jung's archetypal psychology (Enns, 1994), we have four archetypes: one, the persona, a mask one wears for the self and others; two, the shadow, the animalistic and antisocial side of one that must be tamed; three, the anima, which represents the unconscious feminine part of a man's psyche; and four, the animus, which represents the unconscious masculine part of a woman's psyche. These archetypes drive what is in each of us and make us different, depending on situation and context.

Some sex differences are biologically originated, but most of the stereotypic characteristics and roles related to sex come from cultural designs (Bussey & Bandura, 1999). Culture is a significant factor in our lives, without which we have less of a feeling of belonging.

In sum, this section delineates what is it to be a man or woman, the main sexes on earth for human beings. Biology aside, we are dominated by our thoughts, feelings, actions, and interactions with one another. Bearing in mind too that no matter how theories and hypotheses inform us about ourselves, each and every one of us is different no matter how much we try to group ourselves by race, ethnicity, religion, and whatever other category is used.

Let us now turn to our roles in a family.

Roles of members of a family

Family roles, that is, what is expected of each family member, represent a central construct of the family systems theory. The most basic types of roles are father, mother, daughter, son, and so forth. Each member of the family has a number of implicit or explicit culturally shaped ideas about what is to be expected by people and society in each of these roles. Different cultures, subcultures, and families have their own nuanced interpretations about what fathers, mothers, and children are supposed to do and what they should not do in families. All families, and all family subsystems, are dynamic; the individual components and the nature of their interactions change. Because of the developmental and circumstantial changes that different family members experience daily, unavoidable changes are brought into the ways that families interact, what children come to expect of fathers and mothers, and how they understand and respond to fathering and mothering roles (Palkovitz, Trask, & Adamsons, 2014).

As to the roles of parenting in a family, I am sticking with traditional and modern roles of the father and the mother. This means a father is a father and a mother is a mother. As primary caregivers for children, mothers are expected to get their children ready in life regarding language, behaviour, appearance, physical and intellectual skills, health, and hygiene. Such an intensive mothering role requires a significant amount of time, money, and devotion. Today's dads are now more nurturing and involved; fathers' supportive involvement in childrearing will enhance children's self-esteem, life satisfaction, and social competence (Park, 2018). But if either chooses to switch roles or do something different from that dictated by tradition, it is acceptable too. Here, I am not covering same-sex marriages and single-parenthood in parenting children. Note that fathering and mothering can both be different and complementary.

Noteworthy is the fact that parents are also linked interdependently through their children's activities and communication with peers outside the home. Parents, in return, offer social support and guidance on how to manage difficulties that arise in peer relations (Bussey & Bandura, 1999).

In addition to family roles, family rules also influence the events that parents engage in or abstain from. Family rules are the (often unspoken and unwritten) norms about how the family operates (Palkovitz et al., 2014). This aspect of family is alluded to from time to time. So, we will concentrate on the father and mother.

Fathering

In the past, literature on fathering emphasised four areas: cultural representations of and discourses about fatherhood; conceptual and empirical analyses of the diverse forms of fatherhood and paternal involvement; linkages between dimensions of the father–child relationship and children's well-being and development; and the interpretive practices surrounding paternal identity and fathering (Marsiglio, Amato, Day, & Lamb, 2000).

Fathering is in the limelight currently for the following reasons. One, fathers spend significant amounts of time with their children, especially sons, though not always. Two, fathers often occupy a dominant position in the family, being deferred to in important decisions, bringing crucial resources to the family, and perhaps playing the role of protector against outside forces. Three, children develop strong attachments to fathers as well as mothers, and respond differently towards fathers and mothers. Four, although fathers' relationships with their children in many ways parallel those of mothers, in other respects they are distinct. And five, fathers also have a unique role to play in the identity formation of their sons and as models of gender-appropriate behaviour (DeKlyen, Speltz, & Greenberg, 1998).

Therefore, good fathering emphasises meeting the needs of the next generation more than reacting to societal expectations or changing social roles. A father figure is important for emotional security within a family as well. The paternal involvement construct consists of the direct interaction of the father with the child in caregiving or leisure, and the accessibility and availability of the father to the child, rather than merely the performance of the child (Pickard, 1998).

Some evidence from early childhood indicates that those fathers who perform 40% or more of the within-family childcare show more cognitive competence, a greater internal locus of control, more empathy, and less gender-role stereotyping. Among school-aged children, positive paternal engagement is linked with a cluster of outcomes, including self-control, self-esteem, life skills, and social competence, which remain through adolescence. These adolescents hold less traditional views about dual-earner couples and about parents sharing childcare. The positive outcomes of paternal involvement continue to build, as high positive paternal engagement is significantly associated with lower frequency of internalising and externalising symptoms and higher sociability, as well as carrying out responsibilities and doing what parents ask of both male and female adolescents (Pickard, 1998).

Children who experience positive father involvement are more likely to develop their personal resources and social competencies, while paternally deprived children are at risk of suffering from psychological problems, depending on their biological predisposition and social circumstances. Interestingly, when men and women are present, men decrease their level of parenting activity compared to women, and women increase their level of interaction with children compared to men (Pickard, 1998).

As to mothers' view of fathering, mothers report being more satisfied with their spouse or partner when fathers share the parental role more equitably. Paternal competence and satisfaction are associated with positive effects on fathers' development and community participation. In the transition into the parental role, longitudinal research indicates that fathers of boys generally decline in self-esteem over the transition, while fathers of girls increase in self-esteem. The explanation is that achieving the status of fatherhood has an overall positive effect, while the difficulties fathers experience in caring for boys lower self-esteem to a great degree. Providing childcare associated traditionally with the female role may decrease masculinity and increase femininity, causing these fathers to feel as if they are projecting an inadequate role model of masculinity to their sons (Pickard, 1998).

Fathering self-efficacy and marital satisfaction are positive predictors of father involvement. That is, older fathers are more involved in childrearing than younger fathers because of the former's maturity and sense of responsibility; and fathers with greater marital satisfaction participate more in childrearing. Thus, it is important to promote father involvement to improve marital satisfaction and enhance fathering self-efficacy.

Marital satisfaction acts as a buffer that reduces the negative impact of low fathering efficacy for the following reasons. One, a positive marital relationship may cushion parenting stress caused by low fathering efficacy. Two, marital satisfaction creates a good family atmosphere, encouraging fathers to be more involved in fathering, even those with low fathering efficacy. And three, high marital satisfaction moderates the impact of low fathering efficacy through the mother's encouragement and through the father's motivation to show his love and affection to his wife. Fathering efficacy can be enhanced by enabling fathers to learn about the childrearing process, for instance through workshops (Kwok, Ling, Leung, & Li, 2013).

When fathering, men hold multiple images within their fathering identities that reflect meanings aligned with more traditional expectations of the breadwinning father as well as more recent expectations of involved fathering. The four common fathering images or identities are: provider, role model, partner, and nurturer. *Provider* means providing financially for their family. *Role modelling* means modelling appropriate behaviour for their children and guiding them on how to grow into good people. *Partner* means being a good spouse, which entails helping out with responsibilities such as the diaper changing and feeding, being involved in doctor's appointments, and being there during important developmental markers. *Nurturer*, the most involved notion of fathering, means being available, involved, and "being there as much as possible" for their children; the ideals and aspirations associated with this image mean going above and beyond the call of duty as a father (Humberd, Ladge, & Harrington, 2015).

As fathers take on more caregiving and other family tasks, workplace canons may inhibit the development of a father's identity. Fathers seek to reconcile the multiplicity by defending a particular image within their fathering identities, maintaining the multiplicity within their fathering identities, by either embracing the positive synergy among images or accepting the inconsistency among multiple notions of fathering. Men hold multiple images of themselves as fathers that are sustained through norms and expectations in their day-to-day work and personal contexts (Humberd et al., 2015).

On the whole, however, fathering is less defined than mothering by social convention, and men are less socialised as caregivers compared with women (Coiro & Emery, 1998). Thus, fathers may require the support of mothers to describe their parenting role.

Examples of fathering by culture

African American fathering

A study (White, 2006) offers practical insights and recommendations for understanding the best practices of some African American fathers who connect with their children despite societal barriers. Apparently, African American fathers are most negative in the fathering model due to their steadfast belief in the patriarchal model. However, there are fathers who challenge the patriarchal model and adopt the feminist fathering model in today's world. These working fathers are financially supporting their children. These fathers have pointed out five areas of concern: nurturance and emotional intimacy with children, politically conscious parenting, nonviolent discipline, supportive social arrangements, and open attitudes concerning parenting of a child.

These fathers emphasised fathering as a personal and relational experience. When nurture is placed at the centre of fatherhood, multiple levels of care (physical, emotional, intellectual, and spiritual) are emphasised. These fathers actively raise their children to oppose racist, sexist, and heterosexist beliefs and practices. They shun the use of corporal punishment (e.g., spanking, slapping, and hitting) in the home. Violence permits and encourages behaviours inconsistent with nurturance. These fathers have working partners, flexible jobs, and people willing to help them parent (e.g., grandparents, friends, and other relatives). They expand the idea of what represents a legitimate family and how responsibility for childcare must be dissociated from both gender and heterosexuality in radical ways. For instance, gay and bisexual men can be effective fathers too.

Each father's personal commitment to feminist principles reflected how he went beyond wanting the best for his child and included what was best for women, African American communities, broad societal change, and the psychosocial development of African American men.

Stay-at-home dads

In the last 10 years, there has been much media focus on the stay-at-home dads in Canada and the US. *Stay-at-home dad* is defined as a father who leaves full-time paid work for intermittent or extended periods of time. This means having the spouse or partner as the breadwinner in the household. This could mean equal parental leave for fathers and mothers. Stay-at-home dads may be divided into fathers who are home by choice and fathers who are home through forced choice or termination of employment—that is, fathers in transition; fathers working flexibly, at home, as self-employed, as freelancers, or in part-time jobs; and fathers taking a break from paid work. Two concerns of stay-at-home dads are: men's disadvantages and potential loss of male power as a result of being at home for several years with little or minimal connection to paid work and its socio-economic benefits; and the relation to wider feminist debates about gender equality in caregiving and breadwinning (Doucet, 2016).

Overall, in recent years, new literature has emerged describing contributions fathers make to the development of very young children. Experts suggest that active play may be a specific area of parenting in which fathers are primary and, further, that this type of play helps children experience intense emotions and learn to regulate them. Regular active physical play between fathers and young children is associated with improved developmental outcomes. However, moderate amounts of active play are associated with better outcomes for children, but too little or too much active play is associated with worse outcomes, especially for children with more reactive temperaments. Importantly, these data are not seen in relation to other types of parenting activities in which fathers engage, such as reading to children or engaging at mealtime, suggesting that there is a special relationship between this type of play and children's development. Furthermore, studies demonstrate that children with high emotional reactivity may benefit the most from active playtime with their fathers (Bocknek et al., 2017).

The notion of fathers is notably absent in most children's literature. However, some research has indicated that scenes featuring fathers with children, some forms of physical contact (e.g., various forms of touching), or fathers caring for children are not significantly less likely to feature in UK picture books than equivalent scenes featuring mothers, perhaps reflecting a more progressive portrayal of "involved" fatherhood (Adams, Walker, & O'Connell, 2011). The same may be said of books in other cultures.

Let us turn to mothering.

Mothering

Women have faced two critical issues since time immemorial: being a natural woman allowing herself to be biologically determined as such, and facing societal expectations for being of the female sex. If women challenge the second issue, regarding cultural tradition, they are considered less feminine; if they conform, they are considered passive and dependent. Worse still, if they join the workforce, they are in multiple roles that might conflict with one another if not well managed.

Ideologies are patterns of beliefs, ideas, opinions, and values that are used to create meanings. The traditional "good mother" ideology defines her as full-time, at home, middle-class, and entirely fulfilled through domestic aspirations. Thus, the traditional mothering ideology, based on expectations of full-time stay-home mothering, perpetuates cultural hegemony. The traditional ideology is also influenced by social status characteristics, including race, class, sexual orientation, and sex, among others. Three themes emerge in the constructions of the ideal mother: accessibility (being there for the child sacrificially), mother–child happiness, and separation of spheres (work versus home). Women could alter the construction of these themes, depending on their own maternal work status (Johnston & Swanson, 2006).

As to intensive mothering, it is a child-centred, expert-guided, emotionally absorbing, labour-intensive, financially expensive ideology in which mothers are primarily responsible for the nurture and development of the treasured child. Negative and positive effects are promoted by intensive mothering expectations. Intensive mothering expectations create relationships that confuse dependency with intimacy, place sole maintenance of relationships on the mother, and model the self-sacrifice of women. Intensively mothered children may suffer from a sense of entitlement, lack of initiative, inability to establish relationships based on mutuality, and an inability to assume responsibility. On the positive side, intensive mothering expectations value involvement with children, development of children's self-esteem, and emotional care. To surmount expectations of intensive mothering, a mother may select to stay home and abandon her work, or select a career that rejects intensive mothering expectations. Alternatively, a mother may separate her work and mother identities, or shift between work and mother identities at different times, such as staying home when the child is young and returning to a career when the child reaches school age. Neutralisation may necessitate cutting corners on employment and child commitments to do both simultaneously. The most sophisticated response is reframing. A mother may reframe her construction of intensive mothering expectations and career opportunities in such a way that tension no longer exists. For example, a mother may reframe intensive mothering as highly involved interactive parenting without continual accessibility (Johnston & Swanson, 2006).

The feminist movement has been a strong advocate for shared parenting (Olarte, 2000), or *co-parenting* as it is popularly called. So, fathers, please stay home more and do more for the children.

Stay-at-home mums

Many mothers are 100% stay-at-home mums if they are not working. At-home mothers construct a mother identity consistent with cultural at-home versus employed mothers' rhetoric, and most mothers perceive a lack of cultural support for their mother role (Johnston & Swanson, 2004). Literature abounds on what women go through as stay-at-home mums or as working mums with part-time mothering—please refer to it as desired.

Examples of mothering by culture

Christian mothers

Among Christian mothers, the image of the mother is favourable. Often the image of the child is missing, or has a neutral emotional nature (in some cases, a negative emotional nature). The same goes for interaction with the child. These mothers have states of anxiety and self-doubt. These mothers are not likely to accept the societal level of mothering. Termination of pregnancy is acceptable for reasons of financial situation (housing problem, low income), marital status (unmarried, husband does not want to have children), and personal interests (*I have not lived myself yet, I don't want to settle down*). The number of children desired averaged less than two. They desire one to two children, and a later age for marriage (Razina, 2014).

Buddhist mothers

Buddhist women expand motherhood to include other people (husband, parents, other relatives, etc.). They hold a low level of anxiety. For them, group social norms are acceptable. Pregnancy may be terminated for a variety of reasons: marital situation (poor relationship with the husband, unmarried, divorced, illegitimate child, etc.), due to the child having a disability, and issues related to the woman's health. The average number of children these women would like to have is two. These women prefer a later age for marriage and having children (Razina, 2014).

Muslim mothers

Among Muslim mothers, the image of the child is very favourable, and the value of the life of the future child is very high. These mothers are likely to accept the societal level of mothering. For them, abortion is not acceptable under any circumstances, because it poses a threat to the mother's life. These women do not think that children will stop them from living life. Children will not be a burden and to have children means not minding the extra work or problems. *It is far better to live for our pleasure.* They desire at least three children and an earlier age for marriage (Razina, 2014).

On the whole, though women's participation in the labour market has increased substantially in recent decades, men have not taken up tasks traditionally performed by women, such as housework and childcare, to the same extent (Buchler, Perales, & Baxter, 2017). Conflicts may arise over employment and housework, leading to marital dissatisfaction because baby care is heavy-duty (Walzer, 1996).

New fathers and mothers

Parenting seems to imply that parents are naturally good at looking after their children. However, parenting is critical for new parents, that is, first-time fathers and mothers.

Undoubtedly, new fathers and mothers are very anxious about their first child. Literature abounds on what these new parents could do for their child.

New mothers, nevertheless, do three things regarding their baby compared to new fathers. One, they think about their babies, even at work, whereas fathers do not necessarily do that, because they work to support the family. Mothers do that because they care for the baby and are socially expected to do so. Two, mothers frequently process information about baby care (e.g., food) as part of the work of taking care. And three, mothers often make decisions on the division of labour on baby care with fathers, so as not to relinquish control of motherhood (Walzer, 1996). Thus, it seems that new fathers are less caring or at a disadvantage. This is not the case; it is just that new mothers, by nature being female, are more caring about a new life.

The novelty of the first wears off a little upon the birth of the second child. This, however, is not necessarily the situation if the second child is of a different sex to the first. It is like having a new child, except that it is experience with a child of the other sex. Suddenly, the father or mother comes to life, because they wonder, "Is this child is going to be more like me?" As more children come into the family, parenting may eventually be shared by the older sibling. This may be a good thing because when is a better time to learn and practise parenting with support from adults?

Comparing fathering and mothering

Globally, across a vast array of cultural diversity, fathers and mothers share similar parenting goals of survival, protection, teaching, and fostering self-fulfilment in their offspring. Although fathers and mothers often share ideals, values, roles, and involvement in parenting, household work, and well-being, they seldom do so equally (Palkovitz et al., 2014).

The most common family parenting styles are those in which both parents display the same style of parenting. Having two authoritative parents is associated with the most positive outcomes for adolescents. In the absence of this optimal family parenting style,[2] there is evidence that having one authoritative parent can, in most cases, buffer a child from the deleterious consequences associated with less-optimal styles of parenting (Simons & Conger, 2007).

Research investigating mother–child interactions has focused on aspects of parenting such as sensitivity, intrusiveness, and detachment, as well as the overall quality of the mother–child relationship, whereas work done on fathering has largely been concerned with the quantity of time spent on parenting tasks relative to mothers, or has focused on contrasts between parenting styles and attitudes of father and mothers. Studies show that fathers spend a larger portion of their parent–child interactions in physical play, whereas mothers devote a larger proportion of their time with the child to basic care (Woodworth, Belsky, & Crnic, 1996).

Ample research literature linking negative and positive aspects of the father–child relationship with early-onset conduct problems is available. For example, studies show that negative (e.g., harsh, angry, and physically punitive) and positive (involvement, warmth, and secure attachment) dimensions of fathering, as well as aspects of the marital relationship, appear to be linked with the emergence of early-onset conduct problems among pre-schoolers (DeKlyen et al., 1998).

In different societal contexts, fathers and mothers are also held to different standards and are judged by how well they perform their parental roles. It is common for fathers and mothers to hold unique individual appraisals of and aspirations for their children's development and well-being. Hopes and dreams, concerns, and fears of parents may also be qualitatively different for their sons and daughters. Therefore, fathers and mothers tend to treat sons and daughters differently. Simply stated, it is likely that sons and daughters learn different roles in different ways from their observations of and interactions with their parents. That is, within families, fathers and mothers interact with their children in convergent yet distinct ways, characterised by different meanings and processes that yield different expectations and developmental outcomes (Palkovitz et al., 2014).

Let us have a word on parenting and marriage here.

Family systems theory has an explanation for the links between marriage and parenting. Within this framework, families are hierarchically organised systems with multiple subsystems including the interparental, parent–child, and sibling relationships. The interdependence of these subsystems allows for the influence of emotional and behavioural dynamics within the interparental subsystem to impact the parent–child subsystem. Another theory to explain this interdependence is the spill-over hypothesis, which suggests: "(a) highly conflicted marriages place emotional distress on parents, leading to deterioration in parenting quality; and/or (b) emotions aroused in one family relationship spill over into another" (Stover et al., 2012, p. 402). Studies have supported this theory that marital hostility is associated with increases in parent–child hostility and parental rejection. Antisocial personality traits are related to a more hostile/conflicted marital relationship and to hostile parenting. In addition, subjective financial strain is uniquely associated with marital hostility and child aggression. Some studies have even suggested that fathers' parenting may be more sensitive to marital problems than mothers' (Stover et al., 2012).

Some outcomes

An overview of qualitative research on fathers paints a rich view of meanings and processes of fathering that diverges in substantive ways from those with mothers. Children have different experiences with their fathers and mothers by virtue of their parents' physical and psychological differences. These differences lead to different cognitive and affective experiences in their children. On one level, parents raise children with similar hopes and goals, striving hard to achieve them regardless of their sex. On another level, the political, social, and institutional contexts that men experience over their life course cause the experience of parenting to become one that is highly gendered. Consequently, men enact parenthood from a different starting point compared to that of women, and their experiences and trajectories diverge in many ways over time (Palkovitz et al., 2014).

The characteristics of fathers are most predictive of average levels of fathering and changes in fathering. The most powerful predictors of fathers' personality constructs are extraversion and neuroticism. Extroversion is the enjoyment of being in the company of others; hence the extrovert is outgoing and social. Neuroticism is the more-than-averagely-experienced feeling of anxiety, worry, anger, fear, guilt, frustration, and jealousy, among other emotions. The next powerful predictors are social support satisfaction and family socio-economic status. Fathers possessing greater psychological, social, and economic resources control their sons in ways considered to reflect a more harmonious father–child relationship (Woodworth et al., 1996). Their psychological control could be directly linked to adolescents' emotional symptoms, that is, adolescents' difficulties in emotion regulation. Proximal (last year's) adverse life events experienced (e.g., a death in the family) are also strongly linked with difficulties in emotion regulation (McEwen & Flouri, 2009). Father's absence is associated with frequent giving and depriving of support to sons by the mother; and mother's offering and depriving her son of support are associated with a more feminine semantic style by her son (Longabaugh, 1973).

Where mental health is concerned, aspects of early father functioning play an important role in the cognitive, psychosocial, and academic development of pre-school-aged children with behaviour problems. Early paternal depressive symptoms portend some aspects of children's outcomes three years later, including internalising and externalising problems, social skills deficits, and lower cognitive and academic functioning, and foretell changes in children's internalising, externalising, and social problems across the pre-school years. Paternal socio-economic status also consistently predicts children's later functioning across these domains. Furthermore, self-reported paternal attention deficit hyperactivity disorder symptoms and laxness, as well as observed frequent commands, are linked with later externalising problems in children. Paternal depressive symptoms and laxness mediate the relation between paternal attention deficit hyperactivity disorder symptoms and child functioning (Herbert, Harvey, Lugo-Candelas, & Breaux, 2013).

Children's low positivity is associated with low maternal affection, whereas children's negative emotionality is associated with mothers' frequent attempts at psychological and behavioural control. The more active and the less positive a mother perceived her child to be, the lower her well-being and, consequently, the more psychological control she applied (Laukkanen, Ojansuu, Tolvanen, Alatupa, & Aunola, 2014).

High levels of parental affection and behavioural control, as well as their combination in terms of an authoritative parenting style, are shown to have adaptive impacts on child development. They have been associated with, for example, well-adjusted children, school achievement, and well-being, as well as with low levels of problem behaviours among both children and adolescents. A high level of psychological control, in turn, has been shown to lead to more maladaptive outcomes among both children and adolescents, including problem behaviour, low self-esteem, and low academic achievement. Children with difficult temperamental characteristics seem to be at heightened risk of eliciting parenting, especially mothering, that is negative, angry, or coercive, and highly controlling (Laukkanen et al., 2014).

An authoritative parenting style is also associated with a reduction in sedentary screen time, and a neglectful parenting style with an increase in sedentary screen time, especially in boys and in children whose mother has a medium education level (Van Der Geest, Mérelle, Rodenburg, Van De Mheen, & Renders, 2017). Authoritative mothering is found to relate to higher self-esteem and life satisfaction and to lower depression. Paternal parenting styles are likewise related to psychological adjustment. Although the advantage of authoritative mothering over permissive mothering is evident for self-esteem, depression, and life satisfaction, the advantage regarding paternal styles is only evident for depression (Milevsky, Schlechter, Netter, & Keehn, 2007).

A girl's sense of continuity with her mother leads her to be socially connected; that is, to perceive herself in relation to others. Daughters whose mothers have been absent since early childhood are less connected than daughters whose mothers have been absent later in the daughters' lives, or daughters who have never been separated from their mothers (Tolman, Diekmann, & McCartney, 1989).

When mothers travel for work, families embody cultural contradictions between work and parenting as they navigate their stances regarding breadwinning and family work. One way the families demonstrate this, from the perspectives of each member within families, is by emphasising the value of independence. Family members become interdependent—when one is gone, things change in the families and these changes tend to be perceived both as challenging but also in large measure as worthwhile because they foster independence and growth. Travel is seen as a respite for women, which is consistent with the problematic nature of mothers' leisure. Women's jobs and thereby their contribution to family breadwinning are not problematic in these families. For men, wives' travel is problematic, because it increases men's burden of work and because many men do not take on household management, scheduling, orchestration, or emotion work through communication to the extent that the family is used to having these elements of family work accomplished by the women. Some work demands may challenge traditional notions of work and family, requiring families to reconstruct their lived experience and the meaning they ascribe to parenting (Swenson & Zvonkovic, 2016).

Wives have greater influence upon the behaviour of fathers than do husbands on the behaviour of mothers, especially when considering families and cultural training of men and women in their roles as parents. In some families, the roles of spouse and parent may not be compatible. Study data have indicated that husbands and wives who engage in conversations regarding topics not related to the baby are relatively unlikely to be actively engaged in parenting. That is, in some families, certain types of husband-and-wife conversation (e.g., non-baby-related) may preclude parents from being actively involved with their young children. Furthermore, in some families, attention directed towards the child provides the basis for pleasurable interaction between husband and wife. In summary: (1) wives may have a greater influence on fathering than do husbands on mothering, (2) in some families spousal interaction may preclude active involvement in parenting, and (3) in other families active parental involvement may provide the basis for pleasurable spousal interaction (Belsky, 1979).

Overall, fathers and mothers do overlap their roles in parenting (see Table 2.1 for a summary of fathering versus mothering). Where it concerns mental health of children, it has been found that: (a) mothers' behavioural control is relatively more important than fathers' in explaining sons' subsequent antisocial behaviour, (b) fathers' support is relatively more important than mothers' support in explaining subsequent youth social initiative, and (c) mothering and fathering tend to have a cross-gendered effect on early adolescents' depression (Stolz, Barber, & Olsen, 2005).

Lately, a study (Buchler et al., 2017) has found that while both Australian and British men become more enthusiastic towards being involved in the care and upbringing of their children after experiencing parenthood, Australian women become less likely to agree that fathers should do so. This is why couples engage in more traditional gender divisions of labour after parenthood. This suggests that men's involvement in childcare is not only constrained at the institutional and employment levels, but also by their female partners becoming more reluctant to support an active fathering role. More broadly, such research shows that first births are an important life-course marker, and parenthood has the capacity to shift how men and women perceive their familial roles and their broader roles in society.

Table 2.1 Fathering versus mothering

Fathering	Mothering	Remarks
Tradition: Traditional role of male—father, husband, provider, role model, authority, protector of family, disciplinarian, less self-efficacious as parent. Cultural role—leader, religious, may be bigamous, prefer to have son as heir to family inheritance, pleasing grandparents and continuing family lineage. General male characteristics: muscular strength, rough and tough, external-oriented, more action, uses aggression in conflict, heroic, head of family, and protector.	Traditional role of female—full-time mother, intensive mothering, wife, nurturer, carer, self-efficacious as parent. Cultural role—subordinate, religious teacher at home, prefer to have son as heir to family inheritance, pleasing grandparents and continuing family lineage. General female characteristics: gentler, home-focused, more emotion, uses reasoning in conflict, supportive, co-head of family, and defender of children.	Same-sex marriages, being employed, and gender equality have changed these roles. With the death of a parent, the eldest son/daughter may assume that parent's role.
Characteristics: Want authority and control; may be authoritarian. Nurturer; spends less time with children. Paternal influence, e.g., like father like son. Ensures children follow family's religious affiliation.	More authoritative and approachable. Intensive caregiver; spends most time with children. Maternal influence; like mother like daughter. Supports family's religious faith and teaches it at home.	Parents may use different parenting styles. Enlisting a nanny or caregiver for children changes this. But the opposite gender attracts, to ensure parents take care of other-gender offspring. Staunch religious parents demand their children follow suit. Easy-going parents allow freedom of worship.
Modern-day: Continuation of traditional role of male—father,	Continuation of traditional role of female—full-time mother, wife, nurturer,	All kinds of equality have surfaced to allow more

(Continued)

Table 2.1 (Cont.)

Fathering	Mothering	Remarks
husband, provider, role model, protector of family.	carer, self-efficacious as parent.	women into the workplace and men to stay home.
Continuation of cultural role—leader, religious, prefer to have son as heir to family inheritance, pleasing grandparents and continuing family lineage. Modern role could be stay-at-home dad or part-time worker and dad, or remain working but partake in more fathering.	Continuation of cultural role—subordinate, religious teacher at home, prefer to have son as heir to family inheritance, pleasing grandparents and continuing family lineage. Modern role could be provider, or multiple-role-player, or stay-at-home mum.	The work–life–family balance is a present-day focus for both men and women. Marital satisfaction is important. Staying unmarried or child-free is an option.
Questions: Could the father do just as well as a parent or worker? Will he lose masculinity, so to speak? Will the society undermine his male role?	Questions: Could the mother do just as well as an employer or worker? Will she become more masculine, so to speak? Will the society undermine her mother role?	

Conclusion

The social cognitive theory of gender-role development and functioning integrates psychological and socio-structural determinants under a conceptual framework. In this viewpoint, sex or gender conceptions and role behaviour are the products of a broad network of social influences operating both in the family and in the many societal systems that happen in everyday life (Bussey & Bandura, 1999). The social cognitive theory posits that when men and women in emerging adulthood remember their parents sharing childcare and paid labour more equitably, they will be planning for a future where men are involved in childcare. Men who remembered their fathers caring for them would feel more competence in childcare tasks themselves. For example, college men and women were able to construct family roles that do not adhere to the breadwinner–caregiver model when their parents modelled a less traditional division of labour in their childhoods (Fulcher, Dinella, & Weisgram, 2015).

So, fathering and mothering can be as simple as being a father and a mother, or being caring parents, both of whom are nurturing the child or sharing parenting roles that can be separate or fused. But if one parent tries to dominate the situation, and the other attempts to do just as well, we have an issue. Sounds like a simple problem? No way. With outspoken and eager parents of today, not to mention the opinions of significant others, like parents-in-laws, this can be a complex situation that may lead to headaches, frustration, anger, and a parting of the ways.

Notes

1 Sociologists are particular about using the word "sex" or "gender" to identify the sexual orientation of an individual. *Sex* is meant to refer to biological anatomy, and has a sexual connotation to it, whereas *gender* is meant to refer to sexual orientation or affiliation. To me, *sex* is good enough to mean "male" or "female", passing over all other thoughts about it and definitions about it, to save wrangling.
2 To me, the authoritative parenting style is optimal only if the children are easy to manage.

References

Adams, M., Walker, C., & O'Connell, P. (2011). Invisible or involved fathers? A content analysis of representations of parenting in young children's picture books in the UK. *Sex Roles*, *65*(3), 259–270. doi: 10.1007/s11199-011-0011-8.

Belsky, J. (1979). The interrelation of parental and spousal behavior during infancy in traditional nuclear families: An exploratory analysis. *Journal of Marriage and Family*, *41*(4), 749–755.

Bocknek, E. L., Dayton, C., Raveau, H. A., Richardson, P., Brophy-Herb, H. E., & Fitzgerald, H. E. (2017). Routine active playtime with fathers is associated with self-regulation in early childhood. *Merrill-Palmer Quarterly*, *63*(1), 105–134. doi: 10.13110/merrpalmquar1982.63.1.0105.

Buchler, S., Perales, F., & Baxter, J. (2017). Does parenthood change attitudes to fathering? Evidence from Australia and Britain. *Sex Roles*, *77*(9), 663–675. doi: 10.1007/s11199-017-0757-8.

Bussey, K., & Bandura, A. (1999). Social cognitive theory of gender development and differentiation. *Psychological Review*, *106*, 676–713. doi: 10.1037/0033-295X.106.4.676.

Coiro, M. J., & Emery, R. E. (1998). Do marriage problems affect fathering more than mothering? A quantitative and qualitative review. *Clinical Child and Family Psychology Review*, *1*(1), 23–40. doi: 10.1023/A:1021896231471.

DeKlyen, M., Speltz, M. L., & Greenberg, M. T. (1998). Fathering and early onset conduct problems: Positive and negative parenting, father–son attachment, and the marital context. *Clinical Child and Family Psychology Review, 1*(1), 3–21. doi: 10.1023/A:1021844214633.

Doucet, A. (2016). Is the stay-at-home dad (SAHD) a feminist concept? A genealogical, relational, and feminist critique. *Sex Roles, 75*(1), 4–14. doi: 10.1007/s11199-016-0582-5.

Enns, C. Z. (1994). Archtypes and gender: Goddesses, warriors, and psychological health. *Journal of Counseling and Development, 73*(2), 127–133.

Fulcher, M., Dinella, L. M., & Weisgram, E. S. (2015). Constructing a feminist reorganization of the heterosexual Breadwinner/Caregiver family model: College students' plans for their own future families. *Sex Roles, 73*(3), 174–186. doi: 10.1007/s11199-015-0487-8.

Hall, H. M. D. (2013). Gender differences: What science says and why it's mostly wrong. *Skeptic, 18*(19–25), 64.

Herbert, S. D., Harvey, E. A., Lugo-Candelas, C. I., & Breaux, R. P. (2013). Early fathering as a predictor of later psychosocial functioning among preschool children with behavior problems. *Journal of Abnormal Child Psychology, 41*(5), 691–703. doi: 10.1007/s10802-012-9706-8.

Humberd, B., Ladge, J. J., & Harrington, B. (2015). The "new" dad: Navigating fathering identity within organizational contexts. *Journal of Business and Psychology, 30*(2), 249–266. doi: 10.1007/s10869-014-9361-x.

Johnston, D. D., & Swanson, D. H. (2004). Moms hating moms: The internalization of mother war rhetoric. *Sex Roles, 51*(9), 497–509. doi: 10.1007/s11199-004-5460-x.

Johnston, D. D., & Swanson, D. H. (2006). Constructing the "good mother": The experience of mothering ideologies by work status. *Sex Roles, 54*(7), 509–519. doi: 10.1007/s11199-006-9021-3.

Kwok, S. Y. C. L., Ling, C. C. Y., Leung, C. L. K., & Li, J. C. M. (2013). Fathering self-efficacy, marital satisfaction and father involvement in Hong Kong. *Journal of Child and Family Studies, 22*(8), 1051–1060. doi: 10.1007/s10826-012-9666-1.

Laukkanen, J., Ojansuu, U., Tolvanen, A., Alatupa, S., & Aunola, K. (2014). Child's difficult temperament and mothers' parenting styles. *Journal of Child and Family Studies, 23*(2), 312–323. doi: 10.1007/s10826-013-9747-9.

Longabaugh, R. (1973). Mother behavior as a variable moderating the effects of father absence. *Ethos, 1*(4), 456–465. doi: 10.1525/eth.1973.1.4.02a00070.

Marsiglio, W., Amato, P., Day, R. D., & Lamb, M. E. (2000). Scholarship on fatherhood in the 1990s and beyond. *Journal of Marriage and Family, 62*(4), 1173–1191. doi: 10.1111/j.1741-3737.2000.01173.x.

McEwen, C., & Flouri, E. (2009). Fathers' parenting, adverse life events, and adolescents' emotional and eating disorder symptoms: The role of emotion regulation. *European Child & Adolescent Psychiatry, 18*(4), 206–216. doi: 10.1007/s00787-008-0719-3.

Milevsky, A., Schlechter, M., Netter, S., & Keehn, D. (2007). Maternal and paternal parenting styles in adolescents: Associations with self-esteem, depression and life-satisfaction. *Journal of Child and Family Studies, 16*(1), 39–47. doi: 10.1007/s10826-006-9066-5.

Olarte, S. W. (2000). The female professional: Parenting, career, choices and compromises. *American Journal of Psychoanalysis, 60*(3), 293–306. doi: 10.1023/A:1001929922264.
Palkovitz, R., Trask, B. S., & Adamsons, K. (2014). Essential differences in the meaning and processes of mothering and fathering: Family systems, feminist and qualitative perspectives. *Journal of Family Theory & Review, 6*(4), 406–420. doi: 10.1111/jftr.12048.
Park, J. (2018). Public fathering, private mothering: Gendered transnational parenting and class reproduction among elite Korean students. *Gender & Society, 32*(4), 563–586. doi: 10.1177/0891243218771551.
Pickard, M. J. (1998). *Fatherhood in contemporary society*. Minneapolis, MN: National Council on Family Relations. doi: 10.2307/585625.
Razina, N. V. (2014). Attitudes to motherhood in different cultures. *Psychology in Russia, 7*(2), 93–104. doi: 10.11621/pir.2014.0209.
Simons, L. G., & Conger, R. D. (2007). Linking mother–father differences in parenting to a typology of family parenting styles and adolescent outcomes. *Journal of Family Issues, 28*(2), 212–241. doi: 10.1177/0192513X06294593.
Stolz, H. E., Barber, B. K., & Olsen, J. A. (2005). Toward disentangling fathering and mothering: An assessment of relative importance. *Journal of Marriage and Family, 67*(4), 1076–1092. doi: 10.1111/j.1741-3737.2005.00195.x.
Stover, C. S., Connell, C. M., Leve, L. D., Neiderhiser, J. M., Shaw, D. S., Scaramella, L. V., ... Reiss, D. (2012). Fathering and mothering in the family system: Linking marital hostility and aggression in adopted toddlers. *Journal of Child Psychology and Psychiatry, 53*(4), 401–409. doi: 10.1111/j.1469-7610.2011.02510.x.
Swenson, A. R., & Zvonkovic, A. M. (2016). Navigating mothering: A feminist analysis of frequent work travel and independence in families. *Sex Roles, 74*(11), 543–557. doi: 10.1007/s11199-015-0545-2.
Tolman, A. E., Diekmann, K. A., & McCartney, K. (1989). Social connectedness and mothering: Effects of maternal employment and maternal absence. *Journal of Personality and Social Psychology, 56*(6), 942–949. doi: 10.1037/0022-3514.56.6.942.
Van Der Geest, K. E., Mérelle, S. Y. M., Rodenburg, G., Van De Mheen, D., & Renders, C. M. (2017). Cross-sectional associations between maternal parenting styles, physical activity and screen sedentary time in children. *BMC Public Health, 17*(1), 1–10. doi: 10.1186/s12889-017-4784-8.
Walzer, S. (1996). Thinking about the baby: Gender and divisions of infant care. *Social Problems, 43*(2), 219–234. doi: 10.1525/sp.1996.43.2.03x0206x.
White, A. M. (2006). African American feminist fathers' narratives of parenting. *Journal of Black Psychology, 32*(1), 43–71. doi: 10.1177/0095798405283528.
Woodworth, S., Belsky, J., & Crnic, K. (1996). The determinants of fathering during the child's second and third years of life: A developmental analysis. *Journal of Marriage and Family, 58*(3), 679–692. doi: 10.2307/353728.

Western (individualistic) parenting styles

3

In the previous two chapters, we have defined and described parenting (fathering and mothering) within the human family, and some important factors that influence parenting.

Now you are ready to look at the big picture on parenting around the world, based on peer-reviewed published literature, my presentations at conferences and talks, my personal therapy sessions with clients, and years of keen observations of family behaviour in public. I have grouped parenting styles generally into two schools, following the way human behaviours are classified in literature for discussion: parenting in individualistic societies (generally in Western countries) versus parenting in collectivistic societies (generally in Eastern countries). Although such classification is confronted by criticism that it is too simplistic and polarising compared with the real world, which is complex and ever-changing (the same challenge arises in talking about the world as East and West), for ease of discussion I am sticking to just that. This is because many people are still individualistic and many are still collectivistic, though many are now between these two extremes, depending on their situation. Of course, many are not in these groups, and prefer other metaphorical descriptions.

Because of length restrictions, this chapter covers only the Western individualistic parenting styles. The next chapter covers the Eastern collectivistic parenting styles. The contexts behind them are first mentioned, backed up by studies extracted from the literature. More evidence for these styles is discussed in terms of their applicability in the West or East respectively. Some views on punishment and childrearing related to parenting styles proposed by their respective advocates are added to each chapter.

Some quick revision here. *Individualistic* means that a person is all for himself or herself first. For example, they act to achieve personal goals, take failure upon themselves, think and make decisions without the need to consult others, feel internally and express emotions as appropriate to the situation without need to consult others, and also feel hurt without attempting to seek advice from others. The list goes on and on. This does not mean that the individual is not right, or uncaring, or uncooperative; it is just that he or she thinks, feels, and acts within his or her individual resources.

Compare this with the collectivistic person, for whom it is all-for-the-group-first. For example, he or she will consider (either tacitly or openly) the group's thoughts, feelings, or actions before attempting something. Thus, the group's aims and goals come before those of the individual. The belief here is that whatever is done is good for the group. Real-life examples come from cultural and institutional groups.

There are, of course, those who are individualistic as well as collectivistic. This means the person may do something for himself or herself if it does not hurt the family, but will consider the family together if deciding on an outing in a group.

So, parenting is generally divided into Western-style individualistic parenting and Eastern-style collectivistic parenting. Then there is the middle group that takes on mixed parenting styles from both the Western and Eastern ones; I will call this the *mixed parenting group*. Note, however, of late many "new" parenting styles have come to the fore from experts or parents advocating that these styles work better for their families under their existing conditions. Examples of such styles are tiger parenting and helicopter parenting. And, of course, my filial parenting (Foo, 2013). These are covered in Chapter 5.

This chapter focuses on the Western parenting styles and some related issues like punishment and childrearing, with a brief look at parenting measurement.

Western individualistic parenting

A popular topic when considering Western parenting styles is Baumrind's parenting typology (Baumrind, 1966, 1967, 1971, 1994, 1997). This has been augmented by one from Maccoby and Martin (1983); see also Maccoby (1992) and Lamborn, Mounts, Steinberg, and Dornbusch (1991). The latter contended that permissive parenting consists of indulgent and neglectful behaviours when examining the combined effects of warmth and demandingness among parenting styles. From here, these two typologies are combined and referred to as the four Western parenting styles.

Then came the Integrative Parenting Model by Nancy Darling and Laurence Steinberg (1993). Darling and Steinberg contended that the four Western parenting styles meant more for the white middle class in the US, did not answer specific cultural differences in parenting, and were not operationalised well for testing and measurement. Therefore, their model was developed to integrate the studies of specific parenting practices and global parent characteristics. Parenting style is seen as a setting that moderates the influence of specific parenting practices on the child. Thus, the Integrative Parenting Model encompasses parenting goals, practices, and style—more of a model for measuring parenting than a particular Western parenting style. Hence, it will not be discussed here but in Chapter 8.

Thus, we have the four Western parenting styles for research and study: authoritarian, authoritative, permissive or indulgent, and neglectful or uninvolved. Baumrind's parenting typology is discussed first, followed by Maccoby and Martin's addition.

Baumrind's parenting typology

More than half a decade ago, Diana Baumrind (1966), a clinical psychologist, developed three prototypes of parenting styles—namely permissive, authoritarian, and authoritative—then specifically focused on the authoritative parenting model, the ideal one.

Permissive or indulgent parenting style

This is best described in Baumrind's own words (1966, p. 889):

> The permissive parent attempts to behave in a non-punitive, acceptant, and affirmative manner toward the child's impulses, desires, and actions. She consults with him about policy decisions and gives explanations for family rules. She makes few demands for household responsibility and orderly behavior. She presents herself to the child as a resource for him to use as he wishes, not as an ideal for him to emulate, nor as an active agent responsible for shaping or altering his ongoing or future behavior. She allows the child to regulate his own activities as much as possible, avoids the exercise of control, and does not encourage him to obey externally defined standards. She attempts to use reason and manipulation, but not overt power, to accomplish her ends.

To put it in a contemporary way, permissive parenting is characterised by few parental demands and the belief that the child can regulate his or her own activities. These parents are non-controlling and may be warm and loving or neglectful, depending on their nature (Akhtar, Malik, & Begeer, 2017).

Authoritarian parenting style

Again, this is best described in Baumrind's own words (1966, p. 890):

> The authoritarian parent attempts to shape, control, and evaluate the behavior and attitudes of the child in accordance with a set standard of conduct, usually an absolute standard, theologically motivated and formulated by a higher authority. She values obedience as a virtue and favors punitive, forceful measures to curb self-will at points where the child's actions or beliefs conflict with what she thinks is right conduct. She believes in keeping the child in his place, in restricting his autonomy, and in assigning household responsibilities in order to inculcate respect for work. She regards the preservation of order and traditional structure as a highly valued end in itself. She does not encourage verbal give and take, believing that the child should accept her word for what is right.

To put it in a contemporary way, authoritarian parenting is defined as a parenting style in which parents are highly directive and children are not allowed to question values or decisions. Parents demand obedience from the child. This style is characterised by parental detachment, a lack of parental warmth, and use of punitive measures (Akhtar et al., 2017).

Authoritative parenting style

Again, this is best described in Baumrind's own words (1966, p. 891):

> The authoritative parent attempts to direct the child's activities in a rational, issue-oriented manner. She encourages verbal give and take, shares with the child the reasoning behind her policy, and solicits his objections when he refuses to conform. Both autonomous self-will and disciplined conformity are valued by the authoritative parent. Therefore, she exerts firm control at points of parent–child divergence, but does not hem the child in with restrictions. She enforces her own perspective as an adult, but recognizes the child's individual interests and special ways. The authoritative parent affirms the child's present qualities, but also sets standards for future conduct. She uses reason, power, and shaping by regime and reinforcement to achieve her objectives and does not base her decisions on group consensus or the individual child's desires.

To put it in a contemporary way, authoritative parents provide clear and firm directions for their child, and are characterised by warmth, reason, flexibility, and verbal give and take (Akhtar et al., 2017).

Comparatively (with the so-called contemporary way), nothing beats using Baumrind's own words to depict her parenting typology, which is self-explanatory and alluring. What many authors have done while citing her work is choose to discuss or refine aspects of it or interpret or measure it. Thus, the reader is not able to get a real favour of the typology. I believe the reader will enjoy reading her words (or work) directly, which makes most sense. Better still, read her original papers, if desired. However, details of some of Baumrind's studies are elaborated on in the next section.

Evidence for Baumrind's parenting typology

Let us see some evidence from Baumrind's own studies.

In an earlier study published in 1966 (Baumrind, 1971), the findings regarding children differing in social and emotional behaviour were: parents of the children who were the most self-reliant, self-controlled, explorative, and content were themselves controlling and demanding; but they were also warm, rational, and receptive to the child's communication. This combination of strong control and positive encouragement of the child's autonomous and independent strivings was called "authoritative parental behaviour". Parents of children who were discontented, withdrawn, and distrustful were themselves detached and controlling, and somewhat less warm than other parents. These were called "authoritarian" parents. Parents of the least self-reliant, explorative, and self-controlled children were themselves non-controlling, non-demanding, and relatively warm. These were called "permissive" parents (Baumrind, 1971).

A second previous study (Baumrind, 1967) of nursery school children and their parents also supported the position that authoritative control can achieve responsible conformity with group standards without loss of individual autonomy or self-assertiveness.

In another of her early studies, published in 1971, the findings regarding preschool children and their families were: authoritative parental behaviour was associated with independent, purposive behaviour for girls but only associated with such behaviour for boys when the parents were nonconforming. Authoritative parental control was associated with all indexes of social responsibility in boys compared to authoritarian and permissive parental control, and with high achievement in girls, but not with friendly, cooperative behaviour. Parental nonconformity was not associated with a lack of social responsibility in either boys or girls (Baumrind, 1971).

In yet another of her early studies, published in 1978, the findings regarding middle-class preadolescent children were: parents who were both demanding and responsive (the engaged pattern and the authoritative prototype) were likely to produce children who were socially responsible and socially agentic (Darling & Steinberg, 1993). Parents who were weak in both dimensions (the unengaged pattern and the rejecting/neglecting prototype) were likely to have children who either scored poorly on both social responsibility and social assertiveness, or on non-sex-normed competencies (social responsibility for boys and social assertiveness for girls).

Parents who were highly demanding but not responsive (the restrictive pattern and the authoritarian prototype) were likely to have daughters who were socially assertive and not highly socially responsible. Parents who were highly responsive but not demanding (the lenient pattern and the permissive prototype) were likely to have daughters who were not socially assertive but who were moderately socially responsible, and sons who were similar to sons from authoritarian families.

By the early 1980s, Baumrind's three-way model was firmly established, and served as the heuristic for discussions about parental influence on children's development (Darling & Steinberg, 1993).

Maccoby and Martin's additional parenting style

In a persuasive review published in the *Handbook of Child Psychology*, Eleanor Maccoby and John Martin (1983) updated Baumrind's typology by defining parenting styles using two dimensions: parental demandingness (control, supervision, demands for a child to show maturity) and parental responsiveness (warmth, acceptance, involvement). The interaction between the two dimensions produced four distinct parenting styles. Maccoby and Martin differentiated between two types of permissive parenting.

Baumrind's comments (1991, p. 748, as cited in Darling & Steinberg, 1993) regarding this addition were:

> Demandingness refers to the claims parents make on the child to become integrated into the family whole by their maturity, demands, supervision, disciplinary efforts and willingness to confront the child who disobeys. Responsiveness refers to actions which intentionally foster individuality, self-regulation and self-assertion by being attuned, supportive and acquiescent to the child's special needs and demands.

So, we have the fourth parenting style.

Uninvolved or neglectful parenting style

Uninvolved parenting, sometimes referred to as *neglectful* parenting, is a style characterised by a lack of responsiveness to a child's needs.

Uninvolved parents make few to no demands of their children and they are often indifferent, dismissive, or even completely neglectful. Uninvolved or neglectful parents have little emotional involvement with their children. While they provide for basic needs like food and shelter, they are uninvolved in their children's lives; that is, they have little vigour for their children. The degree of involvement may vary considerably. Some uninvolved parents may be relatively hands-off with their children, but may still set some basic limits, such as curfews. Others may be flatly neglectful or even reject their children entirely. They place few expectations on their children and offer little or no supervision about education. They may be focused on their career or earning an income, not recognising that they are uninvolved with their children, perhaps, or find it easier to take a hands-off approach to raising their children (Kuppens & Ceulemans, 2019).

Evidence for Maccoby and Martin's parenting style

A previously mentioned study (Lamborn et al., 1991) attested to the existence of Maccoby and Martin's addition to Baumrind's parenting typology. Over 4,000 families of adolescents were classified into the four parenting styles based on adolescents' ratings of their parents on two dimensions: acceptance/involvement and strictness/supervision. The adolescents were then contrasted using four sets of outcomes: psychosocial development, school achievement, internalised distress, and problem behaviour. The results show that adolescents with authoritative parents score highest on psychosocial competence and lowest on psychological and behavioural dysfunction; and vice versa for adolescents with neglectful parents. Adolescents with authoritarian parents are obedient and conform to the standards of adults but have relatively poorer self-conception. Adolescents with indulgent parents display a strong sense of self-confidence but have a higher frequency of substance abuse and school misconduct, and are less engaged in school.

The reader may be interested to know that in the research literature there is a vast amount of studies related to the four Western parenting styles of Baumrind and Maccoby and Martin.

A few decades on, as alluded to above, many experts and authorities on parenting have applied much thought to the three parenting models regarding different cultures. What has resulted is that the definitions, standards, and measurements of the original models have gone wider or narrower, which may be puzzling to the reader and confusing in terms of the implementation of parenting.

So Baumrind (1997) wrote another article with the following comments. She contended that each model contains its own truth. For example, with the liberal permissive model, autonomy and self-will are to be cultivated, not punished. With the conservative authoritarian model, discipline, from time to time confrontational or punitive, is required to socialise the child's self-indulgent wilfulness. Each polarised model, however, demonises the other and both fail to distinguish between mitigated and unmitigated agency, equating self-assertive individuality with unbridled aggression and egoism. The development of optimal competence in children requires the cultivation of the ability to disobey and accept unpleasant consequences, and to comply with legitimate authoritative directives.

Baumrind (1997) contended that the authoritative model she developed represents an integration of the authoritarian–permissive (or conservative versus liberal) polarity. It is not about enforcement of restrictive directives (as in authoritarian relationships) or avoidance of extrinsic motivators and externally imposed rules and structure (as in permissive relationships). It is about interdependent objectives of behavioural compliance and psychological autonomy. With the authoritative parenting model, children are encouraged to respond habitually in prosocial ways and to reason autonomously about moral problems, to respect adult authorities, and to learn to think independently.

In a nutshell, a parenting style is about a child's associated behavioural patterns:

- Authoritative style (high levels of both responsiveness and demandingness): Assertive, self-reliant.
- Authoritarian style (low responsiveness and high demandingness): Discontented, withdrawn.
- Permissive style (high responsiveness and low demandingness): Low self-control and low self-reliance.
- Uninvolved style (low levels of both responsiveness and demandingness): Poor self-control, low self-esteem, and aggression.

Western (individualistic) parenting styles 71

Punishment

In addition to developing the parenting typology, Baumrind (1966) also put in a word on punishment, emphasising the effects of severe versus mild punishments. Punitive and unjust disciplinary practices (including rejection) are related to cognitive and emotional disturbance in the child, including hostile withdrawal, acting out, dependency, personality problems, nervousness, and reduced classroom efficiency. The benefits of mild punishment, physical or otherwise, may include more rapid re-establishment of affectional involvement following emotional release, and imitation of the aggressive parent, resulting in prosocial assertive behaviour. Other siblings will gain and learn from it, and there will be a reduction in feelings of guilt following a transgression, and the child will have an increased ability to endure punishment for a desired end. Baumrind (1966) concluded that:

1. Punishment has inevitable harmful side effects and is an ineffective means of controlling a child's behaviour.
2. Close supervision, strong demands, and other forms of parental authority provoke rebelliousness in children, particularly with adolescents.
3. Firm parental control generates passivity and dependence.
4. Parental restrictiveness decreases normal self-assertiveness and buoyancy.
5. Permissiveness frees the child from the authority of the parent, and the child becomes aggressive.
6. Controlling parents are compelled by fear of loss of control to restrict the child's self-directed, autonomous efforts.
7. Firm control inhibits the child's creative thrust.
8. Similar patterns of childrearing affect boys and girls differently.

She concluded that parental control and allowance of freedom for children may represent an antinomy or a synthesis—interesting food for thought.

The prudent use of punishment within the context of a cultural, childrearing-responsive, supportive parent–child relationship is a necessary tool in the disciplinary encounter. It is how discipline is administered that counts. Within the context of an authoritative childrearing relationship, behavioural compliance is necessary but not sufficient.

The disciplinary encounter is intended to control children's immediate behaviour and to influence behaviour in the long run. Dispositional tendencies (for example, competitiveness, divergent intelligence, individuation, and willingness to dissent) are encouraged by confrontational parental training. Disputations are adaptive even though they may conflict with societal norms and dispositional compliance. The effectiveness of a disciplinary practice is about the desired outcome, whereas efficacy is the demonstrated power to produce the desired effect when properly used. Efficacious discipline is contingent upon the child's behaviour—prompt and rational, with knowledge and consideration of the child's developmental level and temperament (Baumrind, 1997).

Parents who adopt authoritative or permissive parenting styles will object to the use of corporal punishment as a means of childrearing to a far greater extent than authoritarian parents (Shechory-Bitton, Ben David, & Sommerfeld, 2015). Compared to parents from non-abusive families, parents from both abusive and neglectful families can be expected to be less responsive, and neglectful parents to also be less demanding (Baumrind, 1994).

Where attribution of punishment is concerned, Westerners are more influenced by attributes of the actors and the deed, whereas Easterners are more influenced by information about the actors' role relationship to others in the scenario. Thus, Westerners would choose sanctions that isolate the individual, and Easterners are likely to choose sanctions that emphasise restitution and maintaining relationship roles (Poasa, Mallinckrodt, & Suzuki, 2000).

Childrearing

Baumrind studied childrearing practices in preschool children (Baumrind, 1967). She found that parents of mature children (self-reliant, self-controlled, and explorative) were communicative and nurturant, though controlling and demanding, whereas parents of immature and dependent children were non-controlling, and parents of discontented and distrustful children were non-nurturant.

To Baumrind, the childrearing goals are to foster moral character and optimal competence. She added that authoritative parents are both highly demanding and highly responsive, in contrast with authoritarian parents, who are highly demanding but not responsive; permissive parents, who are responsive but not demanding; and unengaged parents, who are neither demanding nor responsive (Baumrind, 1997).

To reiterate, *parenting responsiveness* refers to warmth, reciprocity, and attachment, and *parenting demandingness* refers to coerciveness, confrontation, monitoring, supervision, consistent discipline, and corporal punishment. For the child, he or she has to use a range of responses to induce the parent to adjust his or her schedule to consider the child's needs. The child, however, can only have as much influence as the parent permits, and the parent's willingness to respond is a function of affective warmth. Affective warmth is the parent's emotional expression of love, which is associated with the development in children of conscience and an internalised moral orientation, and its absence with aggressive tendencies. Warmth frees the child to explore, whereas overprotection inhibits the child from exploring. Mothers of secure children achieve the difficult balance of being warm but not intrusive. Reciprocity is based on the expectation of contingent reinforcement or exchange between parent and child. Attachment is the strength of the bond between parent and child—secure or insecure.

Application of the four Western parenting styles typology

Now that we have understood Baumrind's typology and Maccoby and Martin's additional parenting style, let's see how they fare in individualistic Western countries (this chapter) and collectivistic Eastern countries (Chapter 4).

For simplicity's sake, *the Western world* refers to North and South America, Europe, Australia and New Zealand, and parts of Latin America, whereas *the Eastern world* refers to nations in Asia, Africa, the Indian subcontinent, and the Middle East.

Western countries

A study in the Netherlands (Wel, 1994) investigated 2,918 youths regarding bonding with parents and friends. Adolescence is a period considered to be of heightened tension between young persons and their parents, and friends play a significant role in expanding the social network of adolescents. As parental influence wanes when children grow up, friendship between peers builds. The study's results show that youths in early adolescence and early adulthood are experiencing more favourable parental relations than those in late adolescence. These results give the impression of fairly harmonious relations between the generations in the Netherlands, in which communication is conducted on a more or less equal footing, as among friends. Noteworthy is the fact that family relations are currently established less on authority than on negotiation, and that young people are raised more freely now than they were in the past. In particular, 15- to 17-year-olds perceive social support from friends as being of vital importance in the area of free time, whereas the mother is most important in the relational area, and the father is the key figure in educational matters.

A study in Russia (Hart, Nelson, Robinson, Olsen, & McNeilly-Choque, 1998) investigated 207 families of nursery-school-age children regarding parenting styles and marital interactions associated with childhood aggressive behaviour. The results show that parental coercion, lack of responsiveness, and psychological control (mothers only) are correlated with children's overt aggression with peers. Marital conflict is also linked to more overt and relational aggression for males.

A study in the US (Simons & Conger, 2007) investigated 451 intact families regarding parenting styles and their effects on delinquency, depression, and school commitment for adolescents. The results show that having two authoritative parents is linked with the most positive outcomes for adolescents. Having at least one authoritative parent can, in most cases, buffer a child from the deleterious consequences associated with less optimal styles of parenting.

Another study in the US (Milevsky, Schlechter, Netter, & Keehn, 2007) examined 272 students in grades 9 and 11 regarding adolescent adjustment to maternal and paternal parenting styles. The results show that authoritative mothering is related to higher self-esteem and life satisfaction, and to lower depression. Paternal parenting styles are also related to psychological adjustment. However, though the advantage of authoritative mothering over permissive mothering is obvious, for paternal styles the advantage is only evident for depression.

A study in Australia (Heaven & Ciarrochi, 2008) assessed over 784 high school students on the association between perceived parental style, conscientiousness, and academic grades at three different times. The results showed that students with more authoritative parents experienced less of a decrease in conscientiousness at time two. Parental authoritativeness at time one was related to outcomes in English, religious studies, and history at time three, but not for science and math achievement. This is probably because performance in science and math relies more on innate academic ability and acumen, and less on conscientiousness and, by extension, less on authoritativeness. Thus, authoritativeness differs in its ability to predict results across different academic areas.

A study in Greece (Georgiou, 2008) investigated 377 young Greek Cypriot children and their mothers regarding parental style and bullying in school. The results show a line of influence exists between maternal responsiveness, overprotection, and child victimisation experiences at school. Maternal responsiveness precedes low scores in child bullying behaviour. That is, children who are accepted and respected by their parents learn to respect their peers. Permissive mothers, who score highly in responsiveness, have children with the highest score in victimisation experience. That is, overprotected children lack the ability to defend themselves against bullying attacks, while presenting behaviour that invites such attacks. Monitoring and supervision of children's behaviour, which are included in the demandingness dimension of parental style, are negative correlates of bullying and victimisation experiences at school. Authoritative parents have children with higher school achievement and lower bullying and victimisation experiences than children of parents who use other parental styles.

Another study in the US (Hoeve et al., 2008) used data from the Pittsburgh Youth Study (ages 10–19) to investigate the trajectories of adolescent delinquent development and childhood parenting styles. Five distinct delinquency trajectories differing in both level and change of seriousness over time are identified: non-delinquent, minor persisting, moderate desisting, serious persisting, and serious desisting trajectories. More serious delinquents tended to frequently engage in delinquency, and a higher proportion of theft. Proportionally, seriously persistent delinquents are the most violent of all trajectory groups. Neglectful parenting is more frequent in moderate desisters, serious persisters, and serious desisters. Thus, poor parenting would lead to high levels of delinquency in young people.

A study in Spain (García & Gracia, 2009) examined 1,416 teenagers on the parenting styles of their parents and related outcomes concerning self-esteem (academic, social, emotional, familial, and physical), personal competence (social and grades), psychosocial maladjustment (hostility/aggression, negative self-adequacy and worldview, and emotional instability), and problem behaviour (school misconduct, delinquency, and drug use). The results show that authoritative and indulgent parenting styles are linked to better outcomes. The conclusion is that the indulgent parenting style, characterised by lots of warmth and little strictness, is optimal for Spain.

A study in Canada (Rinaldi & Howe, 2012) investigated 59 parents regarding parental reports of their parenting styles in relation to toddlers' externalising, internalising, and adaptive behaviours. The results show that parents are congruent in their parenting styles, whether authoritative, authoritarian, or permissive. An authoritarian parenting style adopted by fathers, which includes physical coercion, verbal hostility, and lack of reasoning with children, is linked with internalising and externalising child behaviours. Authoritative parenting adopted by fathers, which includes more warmth, reasoning, and autonomy support, is correlated with more adaptive child behaviours, and fewer externalising behaviours.

In particular, permissive parenting by mothers and authoritarian parenting by fathers significantly forecast toddlers' externalising behaviours.

A European study (Calafat, García, Juan, Becoña, & Fernández-Hermida, 2014) examined 7,718 adolescents, from Sweden, the UK, Spain, Portugal, Slovenia, and the Czech Republic, on parenting styles and adolescent substance use. The results show that the warm and strict authoritative parenting style and the warm, but not strict, indulgent parenting style are linked with lower levels of substance use in the countries analysed. On the other hand, the neither-warm-nor-strict neglectful parenting style and the strict-but-not-warm authoritarian parenting style are associated with the highest level of tobacco and illegal drug use, alcohol use being higher for the neglectful than the authoritarian parenting style.

A study in Sweden (Trifan, Stattin, & Tilton-Weaver, 2014) examined changes in family roles and authoritarian parenting practices over the last 50 years. Data came from 1,049 young to middle-age adults living in a suburb of Stockholm. The results show a dramatic decrease in parents' directive control. Also, parents are increasingly allowing children to express anger towards them. Parents' roles have changed from stereotyped versions of fathers as decision makers and mothers as caregivers to both parents sharing decisions and garnering respect from children. Overall, authoritarian parenting practices in Sweden have declined dramatically and moved towards more egalitarian family environment.

A study in Germany (Donath, Graessel, Baier, Bleich, & Hillemacher, 2014) investigated 44,610 ninth-grade students regarding adolescent suicide and parenting. Authoritative parenting is found to be protective, and rejecting-neglecting parenting is found to be risky, when it comes to predictors of suicide attempts. Other relevant significant variables are attention deficit hyperactive disorder, being female, smoking, binge drinking, absenteeism/truancy, the student's migration background, and parental separation events.

A study in North America (Hibbard & Walton, 2014) explored 231 mixed undergraduates regarding the associations between parenting characteristics of demands and warmth, and perfectionism. The results show that the authoritarian parenting style is linked to maladaptive aspects of perfectionism (e.g., concerns about mistakes, doubting one's abilities), whereas authoritative parenting buffered individuals from these maladaptive aspects. In general, indulgent parenting is linked to fewer feelings of criticism from parents, whereas neglectful parenting is related to more feelings of criticism. None of the parenting styles is related to adaptive perfectionism (e.g., personal standards, organisation). Generally, patterns of association are similar for males and females.

A study in Iran (Esmali Kooraneh & Amirsardari, 2015) assessed 357 undergraduate students on the use of Baumrind's parenting typology to predict maladaptive schemas. The results show that the authoritative parenting style adopted by parents displays high levels of warmth or encourages children to express their divergent opinions. On the other hand, the authoritarian parenting style reveals parental traits of heartlessness, impassiveness, strictness, and lack of attention to the children's developmental needs.

Two studies in South Africa (a diverse country that has evolved from separatism and segregation) examined parenting styles and outcomes. The first (Roman et al., 2015) investigated the role of parenting styles, basic psychological needs, and well-being in the adoption of goals and aspirations by 853 South African adolescents. The results show that authoritative and authoritarian parenting styles influence the adoption of life goals and psychological well-being of adolescents; fathers' negative parenting reduces adolescent well-being. Extrinsic life goals are a predictor of positive affect, while need frustration is a predictor of negative affect. The second study (Roman, Makwakwa, & Lacante, 2016) investigated 746 university students on the parenting styles across ethnic groups—classed as Black, White, and Coloured. The results show that the maternal authoritative parenting style is the most prevalent across the groups, perhaps because mothers are more involved with their children. Black African fathers score lower on the authoritative and authoritarian parenting styles than Whites, perhaps because they are less involved with their children. More males indicated that they received or benefited from their mothers' authoritarian style, whereas more females received an authoritative parenting style from their mothers.

Another study in the US (Majumder, 2016) examined the causal link between parenting style and children's educational outcomes using data from the National Longitudinal Survey of Youth 1997. The results show that the authoritative parenting style is the best among all types of parenting styles. Children reared by authoritative parents have more years of schooling and more chances to obtain higher qualifications, whereas children reared by uninvolved parents are more likely to be high school dropouts.

Another study in Valencia, Spain (Tur-Porcar, 2017), examined 433 adolescents (aged 15–18) regarding the links between internet use and the parenting styles that shape parent–child interactions. Internet use accounts for the majority of adolescents' leisure time. Results show that the neglecting parenting style encourages indiscriminate internet use. For males, authoritarian parenting has the strongest relationship with compulsive internet use. Intensive, addictive internet use among males also occurs when there is a mix of the four parenting styles. Seemingly, a lack of consistency and disciplinary contradictions between parents steer adolescents toward the internet.

From a different viewpoint, positive parenting styles (i.e., authoritativeness) are positively linked to social skills and negatively associated with impulsiveness, withdrawal, assertiveness, and overconfidence. Negative parenting styles (i.e., authoritarian and permissive) are negatively linked to social skills and positively associated with impulsiveness, withdrawal, assertiveness, and overconfidence (Akhtar et al., 2017).

Eastern countries

This section is not about parenting in the Eastern collectivistic cultures. It is rather about how the four Western parenting styles of Baumrind and Maccoby and Martin fare in Eastern countries.

First of all, critiques have it that the four parenting styles are not universal across countries and cultures. For one, Baumrind's parenting typology is defined and meant for the white middle-class culture. Therefore, when comes to its application, say to the Islamic culture, much difficulty is met. And it is also not suitable for families of Asian descent in the US.

For another, Baumrind's typology is defined as constructs encompassing a few dimensions (for example, authoritative parenting lumps warmth, involvement, and inductive discipline into one) rather than specific dimensions, such as acceptance or the orthogonal dimension of warmth–hostility and detachment–involvement (Darling & Steinberg, 1993; Stewart & Bond, 2002).

To cut the story short, the problems facing the four Western parenting styles are the use of typology versus dimensions, measures of parenting styles versus actual practices, the limited items in current measuring scales versus the variety in practice domains, the absence of meaning of culture-specific behaviour, and gender differentiation in other cultures. Styles are general behaviours across different situations (universal), whereas practices are situation-specific behaviours. In summary, this means there is a lack of standardisation of parenting measures across cultures (Stewart & Bond, 2002).

Furthermore, where adolescents are concerned, their perceptions of their parents' style of parenting as authoritarian are not necessarily homogeneous. Examinations of their personal adjustment and social variables have found maladjusted as well as well-adjusted behaviours. Undoubtedly, adolescents in the maladjusted group have low self-esteem, poor self-reliance, poor interpersonal relations, and a heightened sense of inadequacy; that is, they have poorer attitudes towards school and teachers compared to adolescents in the well-adjusted group, who are just the opposite. This means that the authoritarian parenting style could have a different cultural meaning for Asians (Ang & Goh, 2006).

On the other hand, some researchers have argued for the applicability of Baumrind's models across countries.

Several cross-cultural studies (Sorkhabi, 2005) examined in this article show that Baumrind's parenting styles and parenting dimensions (e.g., warmth, control) are similarly differentiated in cultures that are said to emphasise interdependence and independence. Moreover, commonalities between US and Chinese participants in the structure of authoritarian and authoritative parenting also show that parenting constructs emphasised in Chinese culture—such as encouragement of modesty, sharing, maternal involvement, and protection—are also applicable to parenting in the US. The cultural differences in the links between Baumrind's parenting styles and child outcomes have been explained in three different ways. One, the authoritarian parenting style is associated with positive parental characteristics in collectivist cultures and negative parental characteristics in individualist cultures. Two, training is a culture-specific form of parenting that is distinct from Baumrind's parenting styles and parenting dimensions of warmth and control. Three, the positive versus the negative perceptions of adolescents in collectivist and individualist cultures respectively mediate and ameliorate the negative effects of authoritarian parenting (Sorkhabi, 2005).

A longitudinal study (Zhang, Wei, Ji, Chen, & Deater-Deckard, 2017) investigated 2,173 urban Chinese adolescents regarding the subtypes of Chinese maternal parenting styles and their stability over the transition to early adolescence. The results identified four subtypes of parenting styles: authoritative, authoritarian, average-level undifferentiated, and strict-affectionate. Adolescents of authoritative mothers display the best overall adjustment, whereas adolescents of authoritarian mothers show the worst adjustment. Adolescents of strict-affectionate mothers generally adjust as well as those of authoritative mothers, except they present with lower academic achievement. Further analysis reveals high stability of parenting styles during early adolescence.

How are Western parenting styles measured?

This section offers a glimpse of the measurement of the established parenting styles, Western and Eastern and others. Details on this topic are found in Chapter 8.

One measurement is the single dimension (e.g., acceptance) or the orthogonal dimension (e.g., warmth–hostility and detachment–involvement). Another measurement is demandingness and responsiveness. A third is autonomy-granting (Stewart & Bond, 2002). Many more measurements of parenting are devised by researchers: acceptance/rejection, dominance/submission, emotionally involved/uninvolved, democratic/autocratic, responsiveness/unresponsiveness, control/non-control, and restrictiveness/permissiveness.

Generally, parenting is measured by forced-choice questions (for example, true/false and multiple choice), gathered into a list called a questionnaire or scale. The Parent Authority Questionnaire (Reitman, Rhode, Hupp, & Altobello, 2002) is a good example. In other instances, researchers have designed a behaviour checklist for parents to observe and tick accordingly. An example is the Child Behaviour Checklist (Achenbach, 2001). Occasionally, the researcher will add open-ended options for the participants to insert in writing what may be omitted by a lack of design information due to cultural differences. But this is rare, as open-ended questions will lead to complicated and additional analyses.

Conclusion

In summary (see Table 3.1), Western parenting is about giving the child individualistic abilities and skills to go on with his or her future life. However, this may be done by parents strictly, loosely, reasonably, or indulgingly. There is no one type of Western parenting style. Arguably, authoritative parenting is the desired style for bringing up children. But, with a better understanding of children's traits and behaviour and those of the parents, and the environment (everything else outside of the parent and child and their interactions), authoritative parenting may not be the desired parenting style.

Imagine you have a very mischievous child, who breaks things, throws tantrums with the slightest provocation, and is always angry and wild, and this is not due to a personality disorder or organic problem. What do you do as his or her parent? This is food for thought. Read on.

Table 3.1 Pros and cons of Western-style parenting

	Pros	Cons
Authoritarian parenting	Parent: - Little responsiveness and lots of demandingness. - Controlling, directive, strict with standard of conduct. - Values obedience without explanation. - Status-oriented. - Favour punishments. - Assigns household responsibilities. - Inculcates respect for work. - More one-way communication or instruction. - Provides well-ordered and structured environments with clearly stated rules. Child: - Fulfils parent's demand and wishes.	Parent: - Detached and lacks warmth. - Having to maintain style may be stressful. - Cannot really express love and care openly. - May surprise others from different families/cultures who are not expecting this. Child: - Discontented. - Withdrawn. - Not much choice in life. - Little social responsibility and competencies. - Lots of social assertiveness.
Authoritative parenting	Parent: - Lots of responsiveness and demandingness. - Provides clear and firm directions. - Warm, reasonable, and flexible. - Enjoys give and take. - Solicits objections from child. - Values autonomy, self-will, and disciplined conformity. - Exerts firm control at parent–child divergence, but does not hem child in with restrictions. - Enforces perspective as adult, but recognises child's individual interests and special ways. - Affirmative with future standards.	Parent: - Difficult to manage wilful, adamant children. - More roles and responsibility for parents (e.g., making and reviewing rules). Child: - May still feel parents are controlling, leading to low self-esteem.

(Continued)

Western (individualistic) parenting styles 83

Table 3.1 (Cont.)

	Pros	Cons
	- Provides reasons and shape by regime and reinforcement. - Bases decisions on group consensus or the individual child's desires. Child: - Becomes responsible, self-reliant, self-controlled, explorative, content, and responsible. - Conforms with group standards, self-assertive, independent, high achieving, friendly, and cooperative. - Performs academically well and obtains more skills.	
Neglectful or uninvolved parenting	Parent: - Little responsiveness and demandingness. - Provides for basic needs like food and shelter. - Places few expectations. - Offers little or no supervision about education. Child: - In the world more or less on his/her own.	Parent: - Often indifferent, dismissive, or even completely neglectful. - Has little energy or is uninvolved in children's lives—relatively hands-off or may have some basic limits, or be downright neglectful or even reject child outright. - Has little emotional involvement. - Unaware of their uninvolvement. Child: - Displays a strong sense of self-confidence but has a higher frequency of substance abuse and school misconduct, and is less engaged in school. - Low self-esteem. - Aggressive. - Poor self-control.

(Continued)

Table 3.1 (Cont.)

	Pros	Cons
Permissive or indulgent or non-directive parenting	Parent: - Lots of responsiveness and little demandingness. - Non-punitive, acceptant, affirmative. - Consults child on policy decisions. - Gives explanations for family rules. - Few demands for household responsibility and orderly behaviour. - Is a resource. - Lenient. - May be warm and loving. Child: - Free to regulate own behaviour or activities.	Parent: - Not a role model and a non-active agent for behaviour shaping or modification. Child: - May have higher self-esteem, better social skills, and lower levels of depression. - Little self-control and little self-reliance. - May be wayward without proper guidance. - Not socially assertive.
Overview of Western parenting style	Concepts: individualistic; independent; autonomy; self-determination; internalising. Tradition, customs, and practices are maintained, but there is freedom of expression and choice. Parental socialisation goals: emphasise self-development and independent interpersonal relationships; self-esteem; self-efficacy; self-reliance; self-expression; self-regulation. Child goal: fulfil own wishes and goals. Childrearing (four types of parenting): - Parents' choice—respond, demand, neglect, loving, hands-off, give and take, warm, accepting, controlling. Punishment: - Parents prefer grounding, time-outs, reasoning, carrot and stick. - Teach responsibility to child; enforce age-appropriate consequences. - Build on the positive; ignore the negative; set regular times to talk with children. Perception of others: - Less caring and controlling of children. - May turn out misbehaving, spoilt, unsuccessful children.	

(Continued)

Table 3.1 (Cont.)

Pros	Cons
	Ongoing issues: - Is there shared parenting between father and mother? - Should parents adopt one or two different parenting styles? - Do parents really ignore the group goals?

References

Achenbach, T. M. (2001). *The child behavior checklist for ages 6–18*. ASEBA. University of Vermont.

Akhtar, P., Malik, J. A., & Begeer, S. (2017). The grandparents' influence: Parenting styles and social competence among children of joint families. *Journal of Child and Family Studies, 26*(2), 603–611. doi: 10.1007/s10826-016-0576-5.

Ang, R. P., & Goh, D. H. (2006). Authoritarian parenting style in Asian societies: A cluster-analytic investigation. *Contemporary Family Therapy, 28*(1), 131–151. doi: 10.1007/s10591-006-9699-y.

Baumrind, D. (1966). Effects of authoritative parental control on child behavior. *Child Development, 37*(4), 887–907.

Baumrind, D. (1967). Child care practices anteceding three patterns of preschool behavior. *Genetic Psychology Monographs, 76*, 43–88.

Baumrind, D. (1971). Current patterns of parental authority. *Developmental Psychology Monographs, Part 2, 4*, 1–103.

Baumrind, D. (1994). The social context of child maltreatment. *Family Relations, 43*(4), 360–368.

Baumrind, D. (1997). The discipline encounter: Contemporary issues. *Aggression and Violent Behavior, 2*(4), 321–335. doi: 10.1016/S1359-1789(97)00018-9.

Calafat, A., García, F., Juan, M., Becoña, E., & Fernández-Hermida, J. R. (2014). Which parenting style is more protective against adolescent substance use? Evidence within the European context. *Drug and Alcohol Dependence, 138*, 185–192. doi: 10.1016/j.drugalcdep.2014.02.705.

Darling, N., & Steinberg, L. (1993). Parenting style as context: An integrative model. *Psychological Bulletin, 113*(3), 487.

Donath, C., Graessel, E., Baier, D., Bleich, S., & Hillemacher, T. (2014). Is parenting style a predictor of suicide attempts in a representative sample of adolescents? *BMC Pediatrics, 14*(1), 113. doi: 10.1186/1471-2431-14-113.

Esmali Kooraneh, A., & Amirsardari, L. (2015). Predicting early maladaptive schemas using Baumrind's parenting styles. *Iranian Journal of Psychiatry and Behavioral Sciences, 9*(2), e952. doi: 10.17795/ijpbs952.

Foo, K. H. (2013). Filial parenting is not working! In P. Mandal (Ed.), *Proceedings of the International Conference on Managing the Asian Century* (pp. 343–351). Singapore: Springer. doi: 10.1007/978-981-4560-61-0_39.

García, F., & Gracia, E. (2009). Is always authoritative the optimum parenting style? Evidence from Spanish families. *Adolescence, 44*(173), 101.

Georgiou, S. N. (2008). Parental style and child bullying and victimization experiences at school. *Social Psychology of Education, 11*(3), 213–227. doi: 10.1007/s11218-007-9048-5.

Hart, C. H., Nelson, D. A., Robinson, C. C., Olsen, S. F., & McNeilly-Choque, M. K. (1998). Overt and relational aggression in Russian nursery-school-age children: Parenting style and marital linkages. *Developmental Psychology, 34*(4), 687–697. doi: 10.1037/0012-1649.34.4.687.

Heaven, P. C. L., & Ciarrochi, J. (2008). Parental styles, conscientiousness, and academic performance in high school: A three-wave longitudinal study. *Personality and Social Psychology Bulletin, 34*(4), 451–461. doi: 10.1177/0146167207311909.

Hibbard, D. R., & Walton, G. E. (2014). Exploring the development of perfectionism: The influence of parenting style and gender. *Social Behavior and Personality: An International Journal, 42*(2), 269–278. doi: 10.2224/sbp.2014.42.2.269.

Hoeve, M., Blokland, A., Dubas, J. S., Loeber, R., Gerris, J. R. M., & Laan, P. H. V. D. (2008). Trajectories of delinquency and parenting styles. *Journal of Abnormal Child Psychology, 36*(2), 223–235. doi: 10.1007/s10802-007-9172-x.

Kuppens, S., & Ceulemans, E. (2019). Parenting styles: A closer look at a well-known concept. *Journal of Child and Family Studies, 28*(1), 168–181. doi: 10.1007/s10826-018-1242-x.

Lamborn, S. D., Mounts, N. S., Steinberg, L., & Dornbusch, S. M. (1991). Patterns of competence and adjustment among adolescents from authoritative, authoritarian, indulgent, and neglectful families. *Child Development, 62*(5), 1049–1065. doi: 10.1111/j.1467-8624.1991.tb01588.x.

Maccoby, E., & Martin, J. (1983). Socialization in the context of the family: Parent-child interaction. In P. H. Mussen (Ed.), *Handbook of child psychology* (pp. 1–101). New York: Wiley.

Maccoby, E. E. (1992). The role of parents in the socialization of children: An historical overview. *Developmental Psychology, 28*(6), 1006–1017.

Majumder, M. A. (2016). The impact of parenting style on children's educational outcomes in the United States. *Journal of Family and Economic Issues, 37*(1), 89–98. doi: 10.1007/s10834-015-9444-5.

Milevsky, A., Schlechter, M., Netter, S., & Keehn, D. (2007). Maternal and paternal parenting styles in adolescents: Associations with self-esteem, depression and life-satisfaction. *Journal of Child and Family Studies, 16*(1), 39–47. doi: 10.1007/s10826-006-9066-5.

Poasa, K. H., Mallinckrodt, B., & Suzuki, L. A. (2000). Causal attributions for problematic family interactions: A qualitative, cultural comparison of Western Samoa, American Samoa, and the United States. *Counseling Psychologist, 28*(1), 32–60. doi: 10.1177/0011000000281003.

Reitman, D., Rhode, P. C., Hupp, S. D. A., & Altobello, C. (2002). Development and validation of the Parental Authority Questionnaire – Revised. *Journal of Psychopathology and Behavioral Assessment, 24*(2), 119–127. doi: 10.1023/A:1015344909518.

Rinaldi, C. M., & Howe, N. (2012). Mothers' and fathers' parenting styles and associations with toddlers' externalizing, internalizing, and adaptive behaviors. *Early Childhood Research Quarterly, 27*(2), 266–273. doi: 10.1016/j.ecresq.2011.08.001.

Roman, N. V., Davids, E. L., Moyo, A., Schilder, L., Lacante, M., & Lens, W. (2015). Parenting styles and psychological needs influences on adolescent life goals and aspirations in a South African setting. *Journal of Psychology in Africa, 25*(4), 305–312. doi: 10.1080/14330237.2015.1078087.

Roman, N. V., Makwakwa, T., & Lacante, M. (2016). Perceptions of parenting styles in South Africa: The effects of gender and ethnicity. *Cogent Psychology, 3*(1), 1. doi: 10.1080/23311908.2016.1153231.

Shechory-Bitton, M., Ben David, S., & Sommerfeld, E. (2015). Effect of ethnicity on parenting styles and attitudes toward violence among Jewish and Arab Muslim Israeli mothers: An intergenerational approach. *Journal of Cross-Cultural Psychology, 46*(4), 508–524. doi:10.1177/0022022115576001.

Simons, L. G., & Conger, R. D. (2007). Linking mother–father differences in parenting to a typology of family parenting styles and adolescent outcomes. *Journal of Family Issues, 28*(2), 212–241. doi: 10.1177/0192513X06294593.

Sorkhabi, N. (2005). Applicability of Baumrind's parent typology to collective cultures: Analysis of cultural explanations of parent socialization effects. *International Journal of Behavioral Development, 29*(6), 552–563. doi: 10.1177/01650250500172640.

Stewart, S. M., & Bond, M. H. (2002). A critical look at parenting research from the mainstream: Problems uncovered while adapting Western research to non-Western cultures. *British Journal of Developmental Psychology, 20*(3), 379–392. doi: 10.1348/026151002320620389.

Trifan, T. A., Stattin, H., & Tilton-Weaver, L. (2014). Have authoritarian parenting practices and roles changed in the last 50 years? *Journal of Marriage and Family, 76*(4), 744–761. doi: 10.1111/jomf.12124.

Tur-Porcar, A. (2017). Parenting styles and internet use. *Psychology & Marketing, 34*(11), 1016–1022. doi: 10.1002/mar.21040.

Wel, F. (1994). "I count my parents among my best friends": Youths' bonds with parents and friends in the Netherlands. *Journal of Marriage and Family, 56*(4), 835–843.

Zhang, W., Wei, X., Ji, L., Chen, L., & Deater-Deckard, K. (2017). Reconsidering parenting in Chinese culture: Subtypes, stability, and change of maternal parenting style during early adolescence. *Journal of Youth and Adolescence, 46*(5), 1117–1136. doi: 10.1007/s10964-017-0664-x.

Eastern (collectivistic) parenting styles

4

Now that you have an idea of what the Western parenting style is, how it affects families in the Western world as well as in some Eastern countries, and an idea of how parenting is measured, let us us look at the parenting styles in the Eastern collectivistic world.

Comparatively, Eastern parenting styles have been researched and studied increasingly in recent decades in Western literature, in respect to the Western styles.[1] Because they have not been categorised as a whole, these styles are based on racial cultures instead; for example, Chinese parenting. Here the historical and cultural contexts behind them are mentioned first, backed up by studies in Eastern countries extracted from literature from the West. Some views on punishment and childrearing related to parenting styles from the Eastern viewpoint are also added in this chapter. The pros and cons of these parenting styles (see Table 4.1) finish the chapter for your reference and reading pleasure.

Very quickly, when an individualistic person is compared with the collectivistic person, for the latter the group comes first. For example, he or she will assess (either tacitly or openly) the group's thoughts, feelings, or actions before attempting an action. Thus, the group's aims and goals come before those of the individual. The belief here is that whatever is done is good for the group. Real-life examples come from cultural and institutional groups.

Eastern collectivistic parenting

Interestingly there is no simple answer in this topic, unlike the West, where four major parenting styles could be applied to families in assessing their parenting styles and outcomes. For the East, let us discuss Chinese, Indian, Japanese, Korean, and Muslim parenting, inter alia. I will try to summarise collectivistic parenting styles identified so far.

Note that there are many studies that have been done in the East on parenting, including those in the area's own languages; for example, Chinese, Indian, Japanese, and Korean. Thus, it is not possible to list them here, but I provide examples of a few to give the reader an idea of the topic in question. Readers may wish to consult established peer-reviewed sources for more information on Eastern parenting styles if desired.

Chinese parenting style

Chinese society (or wherever Chinese people are on earth) remains influenced by Confucian traditions, and *filial piety* is the guiding principle directing children's learning experiences. Filial teachings include obeying and honouring one's parents and lineage; in general, conducting oneself to bring honour to the family name, and not disgracing it. Traditionally, children in Chinese culture are expected to listen to adults, follow rules, self-monitor, and be alert to other people's evaluations and criticisms. It is the responsibility of parents to train and discipline children, and feel embarrassed or ashamed when children fail to obey them. Chinese fathers are typically stern disciplinarians, more concerned with propriety and feared by the children, and mothers are affectionate, protective, and lenient, and may be indulgent.

Apparently, there are two forms of filial piety: reciprocal and authoritarian. Reciprocal filial piety is defined by reciprocity and a natural, intimate, and affectionate parent–child relationship. Reciprocal filial actions from children include respecting and attending to one's parents, caring for them in their old age, and honouring them after death. The beliefs and behaviours of these children are grounded on gratitude to their parents and the desire to repay their efforts at nurturance. Thus, the consequences of reciprocal filial piety are positive (for example, enhanced interpersonal relationships, fewer parent–child conflicts). In contrast, authoritarian filial piety underscores submissiveness and a hierarchy. Thus, children are expected to subjugate their wishes to those of their parents, to maintain the family reputation, and to feel obliged to continue the family line. The filial actions of these children are driven by their parents and based on compliance with cultural norms. Thus, authoritarian filial piety has a negative effect on developmental outcomes—for example, higher levels of anxiety, depression, and aggression (Yeh & Bedford, 2003).

There exists an indigenous Chinese parenting aspect, called *chiao shun* (training), which involves training children early through continuous guidance and monitoring of behaviours, while providing care, concern, support, and involvement. Closely related to *chiao shun* is another parenting aspect, *guan* (to govern; to look after children closely and inculcate propriety in them), in the parent–child interaction. Here, I would like to add punishment to the description of Chinese training. The facet of punishment is seldom mentioned as Chinese people would like to keep their dirty linen at home. All forms of embarrassment or shameful stuff should not be exposed to the public. In reality, Chinese parents punish their naughty children by slapping the hand or face or caning the bottom. The *chiao shun* dimension is a little like the authoritative parenting style but leans more towards the authoritarian style. A study published in 1994 involving 50 Chinese immigrant mothers, comparing them with 50 European American mothers (Chao, 1994), testifies to the usefulness of this Chinese training parenting style. The results show that Chinese American preschool students still do well in school despite the authoritarian negativity.

There are five parenting dimensions identified in Chinese culture: encouragement of modest behaviour, parental protection, shaming/love withdrawal, directiveness, and maternal involvement (Huang, Cheah, Lamb, & Zhou, 2017).

> *Encouragement of modest behaviour* means behaving in a moderate, humble, and socially conforming way when interacting with others to maintain social and interpersonal harmony. *Parental protection*

refers to the parental desire to maintain a safe environment for their children, thus fostering children's dependency on adults. *Shaming* is a special socialisation practice for children to learn to be sensitive to the perceptions, feelings, and evaluations of others, in order to avoid future behaviours that are embarrassing or shameful for themselves and the family. *Directiveness* means that that parents take the main responsibility for regulating their children's behaviour and academic performance. *Maternal involvement* describes Chinese mothers' extensive involvement and devotion to their children's needs.

(pp. 796–797)

Filial parenting

As a result of discussions with parents, and many years of natural observation of Chinese parental behaviours, I believe there are indications of a fifth parenting style (compared to the four Western parenting styles) emanating from the dynamics of Singaporean Chinese families, and perhaps from families in similar conditions in other parts of the world—that of *filial parenting*. This refers to the almost unconditional devotion and care of both parents towards their one or two children. The word "almost" needs further interpretation here. *Almost* in terms of unconditional devotion and care means parents would include their demands of or expectations for their children. Due to having only one or two children in the family, being in the existing competitive environment, and because of affluence and modernisation, parents (grandparents as well) are doting on their children so that these children can be nurtured with the best care and support, and not hurt at all. The outcome of such a parenting style has concerned professionals (for example, teachers and policy makers; see Maddeaux, 2017; Moore & Abetz, 2019; *New Paper*, 2013) who have to deal with the resultant behaviours of the children.

The aims of filial parenting are twofold: first, to guarantee the future success of children; second, to develop reciprocal filial piety when the parents attain old age. The second aim is a hidden motive, which may be expressed or tacitly, sincerely wished for. This motive is not an appalling intention, but rather a loving wish between parents and their children. Preferably, filial parenting occurs from the time pregnancy is confirmed through the period of childhood, to young adulthood; up to 21 years of age at least. Filial parenting could go beyond this age whether or not the children are living with the parents, and obviously be well maintained if they are living together.

Many conditions are involved in parenting, but some are of prime importance for filial parenting: both parents present; one or two children; all in the family are normal healthy individuals; the presence of filial piety; the presence of face (reputation) and filial parental love; and a competitive environment. The biological parents in the family are married legally to each other, and committed to the household. One parent must be working. Either the father or mother is holding down a job with a steady income to sustain the family. What is essential is that the income is sufficient to meet the family's needs and provide excess if needed.

In summary, changing times have influenced Chinese cultural beliefs and actions. As familial interdependence is emphasised in the Chinese cultural context, Chinese adolescents' filial beliefs are related to the parenting they have experienced, and these beliefs may be associated with their psychosocial outcomes. Given the current economy of, say, Singapore, both parents are often employed. This constitutes a dual income and provides more for the indulgence of the children. The family has one or two biological children, who may be of any biological sex. As I have observed in my dealings with clients and families (in therapy sessions, talks, and visits to homes and institutions), filial parenting works ideally in a family of one or two children. With larger families or families of more children, there is a dilution of parental attention and care, sibling rivalry, and competition for fixed finances, among other issues. Presumably, everyone in the family is a growing and developing person according to societal norms, and they are healthy individuals. In other words, no one in the family has a permanent disability or illness or some other factor influencing the family dynamics. As I have observed in my dealings with families who have children with disabilities, if a child has, say, autism, the parenting style adopted will take on a different course. Chinese people of the past have been advocates of filial piety, though this virtue is losing its grip on present-day Chinese people due to environmental changes and the influences from other cultures. Ideally, both parents are brought up with Confucian teachings in filial piety. Or both parents must have at least been exposed to the features or practices of filial piety, like loving and caring for one's parents, and being respectful, considerate, loyal, dutiful, and obedient. Should one parent come from another culture, he or she would subscribe to filial piety practices of the other parent. To put it another way, the parent with strong beliefs in filial piety is dominant in filial parenting. Additionally, the two related values of filial piety, face and filial parental love, play significant roles in filial parenting, and have to be present in the dynamics of the small family. A competitive environment in which there is much emphasis on achievement and success in education, and the accumulation of wealth and material gains, serves to propagate filial parenting. Singapore is such a competitive environment. In a big way, the Singapore government behaves like a filial parent to the Singaporean population. Some other conditions are catalytic to filial parenting: the presence of a significant other, a metropolitan environment, governmental policies, and ease of communication. Depending on the financial abilities and situation of the family, a domestic helper may be present in the household to augment the parenting role. Most of the time, filial parenting is enhanced through the domestic helper. A grandparent too may be present in the household to augment the parenting role. In many ways, living in a city state, with few outdoor recreational areas for people, has an important effect on the lifestyles of the family and parenting behaviours. Coupled with hot humid weather, this means people choose to remain indoors in the comforts of cool air-conditioning. Given the strong allure of internet games, indoor activities are preferred. Parenting seems easier and comfortable with children staying at home rather than being elsewhere. At least filial parents feel their children are safer around them in the home, rather than outside. Presently, governmental policies greatly enhance filial parenting; for example, the practice of meritocracy in Singapore. Those who excel in education will be rewarded with top scholarships and prestigious positions in public service. Parents craving knowledge to put their children into the best spots for nurturance and grooming will find and put to full use the wealth of public information available in various forms and media made available through modern communication means.

Children brought up through the filial parenting style do have their pros and cons. These features may overlap with other parenting styles, but what are discussed here are the observed features of the filial parenting style. A noteworthy point is that continual adoption of this style by Chinese Singaporeans will serve to maintain the familial systems local parents are used to, and seen in the perspective of the present Singapore system, it may well characterise the image of Chinese Singaporeans. When the world consists of only small families, the filial parenting style may become a norm, and the pros and cons will become just normal features of family and parenting.

The pros of filial parenting are: children develop in accordance with filial parents' wishes, there is little or no sibling rivalry, and a sense of artificial filial piety is maintained. Children get to develop mostly according to parental desires, or according to the needs of society as perceived by their filial parents. For example, if both parents are doctors, the child may be groomed to be one too. If the society demands more lawyers and practising law is perceived as a lucrative job, parents will urge their children to take up law. Exceptions to the aforementioned development do occur; for example, if the children are sufficiently assertive to seek their own developmental path, or are supported by a scholarship to go through a special programme of choice—in the fine arts, say. On the whole, the child will grow up to be a respectable person in society. The disregarding of personal interests itself is a self-sacrificing trademark of being Chinese. For members of a collectivistic society this sacrifice is small in terms of the benefits of that society. If it is a one-child family, there is no sibling rivalry at all, and no need to vie for parental attention and care. The only child benefits wholly from both parents, and significant others present in the family or the familial circle. If it is a two-child family, there is some sibling rivalry, but there is one parent to one child, so a 50% sharing of parental time. If the two children are of different sexes, they will have equal but quite different attention accordingly. Perceptibly, filial parents believe and trust that if they look after their children to the best of their abilities, their children will look after them when they are old, just as they would with their own parents; the continuation of filial piety. Remember: parental love with a hidden motive. But, as many filial parents have found out, because of filial parenting they have produced a crop of human beings who will care for themselves and have problems maintaining their own needs and demands rather than being able to meet those of their parents, given the present environment—higher costs of living, and healthcare, among other issues.

The cons of filial parenting are: loss of natural childhood; loss of expression to develop the self; lack of awareness of and empathy for others; adopting of the entitlement attitude; loss of natural filial piety;

and lack of independence for parents and children. With the overzealous care and protection from filial parents, coupled with a lack of open spaces in Singapore, and then with a planned schedule of activities beginning in early childcare, children of filial parenting have to endure a childhood of a very different kind—the loss of natural childhood; in Britain, this is termed Nature Deficit Disorder. The conviction of filial parents is that with their style of parenting, with the inclusion of outdoor activities for their children among the regimen of activities, their children will still be getting wholesome activities. As with the loss of a natural childhood, most children of filial parents do not get the opportunity to develop into a personality of their preference. With so much indulgence and guidance, and indoctrination, the children will likely face difficulty identifying what they want to be in life; in other words, they cannot be true to their natural selves. Many children will grow up, having had a good education and a successful career, to find themselves asking later on, in or after the middle of their life, whether that is what they want in life. And given the rigid environment of Singapore, where only favourable jobs are frequently publicised, there is not much scope for one in trying to find the true-self path in life. For children of filial parenting, the self comes before anyone or anything else; in other words, they become self-centred. From the perspective of the filial parents or their children, they are not so. They are just not bothering others when they go about their activities. This self-centredness is difficult to change; it has become a trait. When the world of children is often provided for without a thought for payment and effort in obtaining goods and services, these children will develop an entitlement attitude. This is happening in many filial families, especially with the well-to-do families. Affluence is the cause of this disadvantage.

The parent–child relationship in the old Chinese way has been altered by filial parenting. It is unthinkable that children look after their parents as we did in the past, given their present conditions—being an only child or one of two, and having been cared for and nurtured all through their growing life. If they can sustain their own families, that is already a bonus. Given the continual care and nurturance of their parents, the children would not be able to stand up for themselves. They seldom make their own decisions, except perhaps for food and clothing, and material goods. To put it another way, the nurturance and care from their parents cause dependence on one another; a vicious cycle. Filial parents will claim that their children need them for care, love, and support, whereas the children will claim their parents need them for company. Overall, in the filial parenting style, parents expect their children to follow their guidelines and wishes, and to be their best in every aspect. Failure to do so regularly results in frustration on both sides. Filial parents are overly nurturing and communicative, and respond excessively, often mixing friendliness with assertiveness towards their children. Their disciplinary methods are weak. Filial parents are very attached to their children's lives. The adoption of the filial parenting style generally turns out children who are obedient and proficient, but are less happy, less socially competent, low in self-esteem, and less self-regulated (Foo, 2014).

Evidence for Chinese parenting

Many studies are available in research literature providing evidence for Chinese parenting. Below is a glimpse of some from Hong Kong, China, Singapore, and the US.

A study in Hong Kong (Shek, 1995) assessed 2,150 Chinese adolescents (secondary school students) on the perception of their parents' styles. The results show that concern and restrictiveness are present in parenting styles, with fathers perceived to be relatively more restrictive and showing less concern than mothers. Signs of gradual change in the parents' differences are appearing. Another Hong Kong study (Chan, Bowes, & Wyver, 2009) examined 189 Chinese mothers regarding the relationships among parental goals, parental beliefs, and parenting styles. The results show that these mothers embraced the Chinese parental belief of *guan*, filial piety, and harmonious social relationships. Mothers who embraced *guan* and filial piety report either an authoritarian or a psychologically controlling parenting style, whereas those who embraced *guan* and harmonious social relationships adopt an authoritative parenting style. A third study in Hong Kong (Chen, 2014) examined 395 university students regarding the relationship between perceived parenting style, filial piety, and life satisfaction. The results show that perceived authoritative parenting is linked with reciprocal filial piety, and contributes positively to the students' life satisfaction. Perceived authoritative and authoritarian parenting are linked with authoritarian filial piety, but authoritarian filial piety is not associated with the students' life satisfaction (Yeung, 2016).

A study in China (Xu et al., 2005) of parenting styles and mother–child interaction examined 97 Chinese mothers and their young children. The results show that mothers' adherence to Chinese values is linked to both authoritative and authoritarian parenting styles, particularly collectivism and conformity to norms, whereas emotional self-control and humility are linked to the authoritarian parenting style. Mother–child dysfunctional interaction is linked to mothers' heightened parenting distress, a lack of perceived social support, and perceptions of children's difficulty. Note that Mainland Chinese mothers' level of education is positively associated with their endorsement of an authoritative parenting style, and negatively associated with an authoritarian parenting style.

Another study in Beijing, China (Li, Putallaz, & Su, 2011), examined 670 mothers, 570 fathers, and their 671 children regarding the relationship between interparental conflict styles and child aggression. The results show that parental coercive and psychological control could lead to children's overt and relational aggression. Both maternal and paternal coercive control and maternal psychological control are positively correlated with males' overt and relational aggression, whereas paternal coercive control and psychological control are positively correlated with females' relational aggression. Notably, Chinese parents who use aggressive conflict-solving strategies within interparental relationships also increase the use of harsh parenting, especially in their treatment of their children's behaviours.

Another study in eastern China (Wang & Qi, 2017) examined 828 secondary students and their parents regarding the mediating role of child emotional dysregulation in the association between harsh parenting and Chinese adolescents' problematic internet use, and the moderating role of child forgiveness on this association. The results show that harsh parenting increases child emotional dysregulation, which in turn increases the use of the internet to cope, and decreases child forgiveness. That is, parents who endorse harsh disciplinary strategies tend to have children with more emotional dysregulation and a lower tendency to forgive other people once they have been unjustly hurt. More importantly, child forgiveness can help moderate the relationship between harsh parenting and child problematic internet use.

A study in China and the US (Li, Costanzo, & Putallaz, 2010) compared over 100 college students regarding the associations among perceived maternal socialisation goals (self-development, filial piety, and collectivism), perceived maternal parenting styles (authoritative, authoritarian, and training), and social-emotional adjustment (self-esteem, academic self-efficacy, and depression). The results show that Chinese students see higher maternal collectivism socialisation goals and more authoritarian parenting. And, training parenting mediates the positive association between their filial piety goal and academic self-efficacy.

A recent study (Tang, Li, Sandoval, & Liu, 2018) investigated over 226 pairs of Chinese 10th grade students and one parent on the influence of parenting styles on children's academic motivation. Some terms are defined first. *Intrinsic motivation* is taking a course of action with complete autonomy or self-determination. *External regulation* is doing something to obtain external rewards or to avoid punishment. *Identified regulation* occurs when one understands and endorses the personal value and significance of a given behaviour. *Introjected regulation* is doing something partially in accordance with regulations of behaviours to obtain pride and self-esteem or to avoid guilt or anxiety. The results show that mothers' authoritative parenting style is related to intrinsic motivation and identified regulation, whereas mothers' authoritarian parenting style is negatively related to introjected regulation and external regulation. And both mothers' and fathers' permissive parenting styles are positively related to external regulation.

As for filial parenting, I have conducted numerous research studies with my students at a Singapore university and found much truth in its existence; the list of studies is too lengthy to list here. Surprisingly, filial parenting seems to be present as well among non-Chinese people in Singapore, namely the Malays and Indians. This is probably due to close proximity or the small-family parenting system—as families become smaller, that is, with fewer children, filial parenting is likely to occur. My presentations on its existence at international conferences have received feedback informing me that filial parenting also exists in Malaysia, Philippines, and Russia, under similar childcare conditions. Russia is a surprise to me as I expect it to be more Western in culture. I was informed that Russian families have practised filial parenting for over 100 years without having a name for it. So I have given them one now. The outcome in Russia is that children are emigrating to avoid their parents sticking to them for old-age care—an outcome Singapore may wish to be aware of and prepare for.

Notably, the Chinese parenting style has been studied as a subset of the Western authoritarian style, referred to as the *ethnic minority* parenting style in the US. To the East, the Chinese parenting style is strong in parental demandingness (or control) and responsiveness, whereas in the West it is strong in demandingness but weak in responsiveness (Huang & Gove, 2015).

Indian parenting style

India is the second most populated country in the world, housing 16% of the global population. Almost 30% of its population is urban, comprising 54 million households (Sriram & Sandhu, 2013). It is a nation of cultural diversity and plurality at many levels. The deep group-oriented nature of Indians can be described as "familial self" or having a collective, interdependent orientation. Children grow up in a network of multiple interactions with members from within and outside the family. This inclusive arrangement is prevalent in joint/extended families in rural and semi-urban communities. In urban nuclear households, education and global interactions have provided parents with new concepts on childcare and development which they integrate with traditional wisdom and practices. The smaller family size is prevalent but does include the involvement of extended kin members. With mothers working, arrangements for alternative childcare and household management are made (Tuli, 2012).

Parents in India (and perhaps, also among Indians the world over) encourage in their children values and customs, and respect for other people. Children are taught to satisfy the wishes of elders in the family and society, and earn praise and rewards rather than internalising values. Respecting the family hierarchy and keeping distance between leaders and followers, superiors and inferiors, authorities and subordinates, is essential. Thus, the authoritarian parenting style is consistent with Hindu values of respect and duty towards parents and other elderly members of the society. Intergenerational dependence is seen in rural agrarian and urban societies with low socio-economic status where children contribute to the family's economy while adults look after their aged parents. Thus, independence is not valued (Karmakar, 2015).

Traditionally, the duty of the father (fathering) is to perform his *swadharma* (right course of action in life) for the family's welfare, and to fulfil the roles of provider, guide, mentor, and nurturer, and pass on *sanskar*. *Sanskar*, the most unique aspect of Hindu culture, refers to the purification and refinement of inner consciousness, acquired through childhood experiences when children absorb conduct and values that become part of the subconscious; this develops the ability to discriminate right from wrong, and makes him or her more dynamic, valuable, and responsible towards the self and society. The process focuses on three areas: purification of a person, making up for deficiencies, and enrichment of values (Sriram & Sandhu, 2013).

The behaviour of children needs to be regulated and learnt from observation. Mothers are the key figures for this behaviour regulation. To mothers, the involvement of too many carers may cause confusion for the child and should be avoided. The roles of fathers and grandparents are secondary; this was more so in the past. There is strong desire for children to be self-reliant, but this is situation- and domain-specific. For instance, food must be consumed without distraction (such as watching TV), but when elders are present children have to wait for their turn to eat. And mothers are aware of the nature of feeding practices to mediate unhealthy food consumption habits of children (Vohra & Soni, 2016). Mothers believe it is their duty to provide children with the right information and experiences at an early age. Because daughters and sons are considered inherently different by mothers, so their behaviours must be regulated differently. Within the family, physical proximity and contact through activities such as eating and sleeping together are encouraged (Tuli, 2012).

For grandmothers, though they now prefer a living arrangement independent of the joint household due to changing times, they would like to maintain strong familial bonds (Tuli, 2012).

In middle-class Indian families, having children is a socio-religious responsibility for couples. For mothers, becoming pregnant is an accomplishment, a fulfilment of a social role. After 30 is considered an old age for the birth of the first child. Not following the expected schedule to marry and procreate attracts unwelcome remarks from relatives and strangers. Breastfeeding is considered best for babies. The average duration of mothers breastfeeding their babies is between four and six months; the first-born child is usually being breast-fed for a longer time than the second-born. Mothers who are unable to breastfeed for various reasons do express feelings of guilt and inadequacy. When children are able to self-feed with food, mothers still feed them to ensure they eat right and well (Tuli, 2012).

Indian parents of today assign great importance to children's success professionally and personally, thus resulting in their increased focus on developing friendly relationships with children. Indian families are also confronted with new challenges of altered norms, and reduced time and support from the extended family or the state (Sriram & Sandhu, 2013).

As with pushy, concerned parents, academic stress is high among Indian students due to the expectations and pressure put upon them by their parents for them to do well in school (Deb, Strodl, & Sun, 2014). Surprisingly, immigrant Indians do attempt to maintain their culture while being in a culturally-different country (Sapru, 2006). Perhaps, when people are away from their country or a place where they are the majority, they might learn about themselves from the non-majority's viewpoint.

Evidence for Indian parenting

A study in urban Western India (Sriram & Sandhu, 2013) examined 132 middle-class fathers regarding their thoughts and feelings, and contributions to their children's success. The results show that the fathers highlight their notions of achievement, and the nature and extent of their involvement in different areas of their children's lives, namely providing, guiding, and mentoring; practical and emotional support; communication; education; and extracurricular activities. The fathers' visions of a successful child, the nature of their involvement, and their reasoning are in line with their desire for involvement in promoting the child's cognitive and social competence, and passing on *sanskar*.

Another study in Kolkata, India (Karmakar, 2015), examined 250 children and adolescents regarding the relationship between parenting styles (authoritative, authoritarian, and permissive) and internalisation of moral values. Four types of value regulation (external, introjected, identified, and integrated) were assessed.

> *External* regulation describes behaviours that are controlled by contingencies external to the individual; for example, earning a reward. *Introjected* regulation refers to behaviours controlled by demands or contingencies inside the person, such as self-esteem

contingencies. *Identified* regulation is acceptance of values by individuals after identification of their importance for their self-selected goals. *Integrated* regulation comes from the integration or reciprocal assimilation of identified values and regulations into one's coherent self.

(p. 440)

Thus, at the lower levels of internalisation (external and introjected), compliance with values is experienced as being controlled (either externally or internally), whereas at the higher levels (identified and integrated), value-congruent behaviour is seen as being more autonomous or self-initiated. The results show that for adolescents, the authoritarian parenting style is linked with external and introjected regulation, and the authoritative parenting style is associated with identified and integrated regulation. The reverse is true for children.

A recent study in Tripura, India (Debbarma & Bhattacharjee, 2018), investigated 1,200 adolescent students regarding the impact of caring and overprotecting parenting styles on the emotional intelligence and adjustment patterns of these students. The results show that a positive parental bonding style could enhance the emotional intelligence and reduce adjustment-related problems of adolescent students. Caring parenting provides positive encouragement and feedback to children, and thus enables them to develop positive feelings about themselves and deal effectively with the changing environment.

Japanese parenting style

Japan, a rather homogeneous country, went through five major eras. The first saw the restructuring by the Tokugawa shogunate, beginning in the mid-17th century; importantly, it included the spreading of Confucian ideas to the general public. The second saw progressive economic commercialisation nationally, increasing urbanisation of the population, and small-family dominance in the second half of the 18th century. The third saw political and social changes in the late 19th century, with a concerted Japanese effort to catch up with the West. The fourth saw maturation of its economy, industrial revolution, and the appearance of the urban middle-class families in the first twenty years of the 20th century. The fifth saw rapid economic growth (Kojima, 1996).

In the 16th century, training programmes for children appeared in Japan, while senior family members wrote childrearing documents for the next generation. By the mid-17th century childrearing documents became public, consisting of orthodox Confucian moral teachings. Childrearing in the 18th century theorised that children differed in innate moral character and intellectual abilities, and parents had a major part in these. Coupled with education, the goals were to maintain and faithfully perform one's assigned role in the society. The treatment of children would consist of proper guidance on being competent, the establishment of a suitable environment and proper role models for learning, and an emphasis on children's understanding of parental teaching and admonition as being effective for development and appealing to the children's sense of self as self-regulation. At the same time, people were encouraged to pursue their inclination through thrift, honesty, patience, humaneness, and family harmony. This became the motivation for adults and children in modern Japan (Kojima, 1996).

By the 19th century, childrearing and education in Japan were similar to those of the West. The emphasis was on personality and intellectual development of the child, and both over-stimulation and overprotection of the baby were discouraged. Mothers were told that their eagerness in childcare would enable children to grow healthy and wise, and contribute to a harmonious husband–wife relationship and to their own happiness. By the 20th century, many Japanese were attending school, in which fierce competition set in. Hence the need to have fewer children in the family, so that the fewer could be better (Kojima, 1996).

Evidence for Japanese parenting

A study in Japan (Machizawa-Summers, 2007) explored 45 adult female outpatients with borderline personality disorder regarding the relationship between this disorder and childhood trauma and perceived parental behaviours. Forty-five female patients with non-organic psychological disorders were used in comparison. Japanese borderline personality disorder patients generally have fewer manipulative suicide threats and substance abuse problems, but more derealisation and depersonalisation. They often have an enmeshed child–parent relationship and few of them are independent from their parents. The results show that the patients with borderline personality disorder report more severe forms of childhood traumas, including emotional, physical, and sexual abuse and emotional and physical neglect. Notably, the patients with borderline personality disorder recall both of their parents as being more overprotective/controlling and less caring.

Another study in Japan (Nakayama, 2011) investigated 286 pairs of junior high school students and their parents regarding the association between parenting style (responsiveness and control) and the parents' intention to use advanced information monitoring systems, like GPS devices and identity cards. The use of monitoring systems is a new form of parental monitoring. The results show that more than half of the parents had some degree of intention to use them. Thus, the predictor of parents' intention to use is their tendency towards control, and that of the children's intention is their perceived responsiveness.

Another study (Uji, Sakamoto, Adachi, & Kitamura, 2014) examined 1,320 Japanese people to see whether children's later mental health is influenced by parents' authoritative, permissive, and authoritarian parenting. The results show that the people evaluated their mothers as more authoritative than their fathers. Both maternal and paternal authoritarian parenting styles worsened their later mental health, including symptomatic problems, their risk to themselves and others, life functioning, and psychological well-being. Both maternal and paternal authoritative parenting had a beneficial impact on their later mental health. Notably, the older the person, the more he or she would perceive his or her maternal and paternal parenting as authoritarian and less permissive.

A recent study in Japan (Hirata & Kamakura, 2018) investigated 329 university students regarding the extent to which individual differences in personal growth initiative and self-esteem are affected by parenting styles. The results show that personal growth initiative and self-esteem are affected by the authoritative parenting style, but not the authoritarian parenting style or the permissive parenting style generally. For female students, readiness for change (a subscale of personal growth initiative) is affected by the authoritarian parenting style.

Korean parenting style

For this section, what data are available in the literature are mainly from South Korea, though *Korea* should be taken to mean both North and South Korea.

Although traditional family values and modern family values coexist, historically Korean parenting styles have been based on Confucian values such as *Hyo* (filial piety), *Samgang* (three bonds), and *Oryun* (five principal relationships), shame, and *Chemyon* (social face/respect), which together form a hierarchal, authoritarian, and patriarchal family system (Kim & Agee, 2018).

Hyo ideology postulates 12 virtues that govern parental responsibilities towards children, and children's reciprocal responsibilities towards parents. The virtue of parental attentiveness to children (*guan-sim*), the virtue of parental devotion and care to children, beginning while the baby is in utero (*jung-sung*), and responsibility for teaching children all they need to know to succeed in life (*chek-im*), mean that Korean parents are highly devoted to parenting. Group harmony is of paramount importance, self-effacement is more crucial than self-enhancement, and self-serving biases are smaller. Thus, one might also expect relatively less self-enhancement among South Korean mothers because of the concept of *gyeum-son*, which is respecting others by lowering yourself and not being assertive, emphasising self-effacement to some degree (Cote, Kwak, Putnick, Chung, & Bornstein, 2015).

Traditional parental roles in Korea dictate that mothers care for children and the household, and support their spouse's career. Thus mothers may find it difficult to achieve a balance among their multiple roles—as parents, spouses, co-workers, and friends (Cote et al., 2015). Particularly in middle- and upper-class Korean families, mothers are expected to sacrifice themselves and their careers for the sake of their children's education. Good mothers provide their children with day-to-day, close attention so that their children become capable and competitive, and do have profound knowledge of childrearing and the education system. Mothers are also expected to provide their children with emotional care and support on a daily basis. The ideal mother is one who sacrifices herself for her children and is judged by her children's accomplishments. Consequently, stay-at-home mothers who spend enough time and energy on their children's education are seen as better mums (Park, 2018). Mothers would rate an external attribution (their child's behaviour) as a cause of parenting successes and an internal attribution (their effort) as a cause of parenting failures. They may feel especially pressured to perform well as parents, affecting their feelings of competence (Cote et al., 2015). Interestingly, mothers who engage intensively in their children's education are often criticised for being so responsible for looking after all their children's needs that they are over-involved (Park, 2018).

In contrast, Korean fathers, regardless of class, are rarely accused of being over-involved in their children's education. They perform predominantly as providers for their families. Breadwinner fathers who financially support their children's education are often seen as fulfilling their paternal duties, whereas fathers who are, or who are willing to become, primary caregivers of their families often suffer the stigma attached to male nurturers. Notably, recent increases in time spent by Korean parents on childcare resulted much more from an increase in mothers' time than fathers' (Park, 2018).

As regards overseas Koreans, Korean American families, for example, have been found to be distinctly more oriented towards Korean culture than mainstream culture, with minimal parental acculturation. Although Korean immigrant parents largely preserve their traditional and core parenting values and behaviours, they do adopt new cultural traits. They continue to emphasise traditional etiquette and manners that symbolise the core tradition of respect for elders, including using two hands to hand things to them, and using honorifics for them. They also maintain traditional parenting practices such as co-sleeping (where children sleep in the same room, or in the same bed, as their parents) and using indirect expressions of affection. Simultaneously, they decrease their use of corporal punishment, reduce their endorsements of stern parenting, and place less emphasis on children's obedience to parents. From Chinese culture, *guan* (to govern/train and love) and *qin* (a child's feeling of closeness to parents or parental benevolence) blend direct control, close monitoring, and implicit parental affection through instrumental support, devotion, and support for education rather than physical, verbal, and emotional expressions. Korean virtues and manners include ideal parenting virtues (e.g., parents being role models to teach children the main values), centrality of the family, the family hierarchy, age veneration, and family obligations and ties (Choi et al., 2018).

Evidence for Korean parenting

A study in Korea (Seo & Choi, 2018) examined 2,378 early adolescents from elementary school to the middle school transition regarding the association between negative parenting and mobile phone dependency. The results show that negative parenting, including inconsistency, over-expectation, and over-intrusiveness in parenting, influences mobile phone dependency during early adolescence. Specifically, adolescents who perceive more negative parenting are more likely to be involved in the middle dependency-stability class and the high dependency-decreasing class. Over time, all adolescents show moderate level of mobile phone dependency.

Another study (Kang & Shih, 2018) questioned 25 Korean American youths on their perception and interpretation of the experience of their parents' parenting. The results show that these youths were appreciative of their parents for materials and services provided for their well-being and success. They understood that these fundamental aspects of their parents were shaped by the conditions of immigration. They aligned with the cultural understanding and perspective-taking of their parents as well.

A study of Korean immigrant parents in New Zealand (Lee, Keown, & Brown, 2018) examined 128 mothers and 79 fathers regarding their parenting styles and culturally-specific parenting practices. The results show that both parents indicated a high degree of devotion and involvement in the care and education of their child, with fathers more likely than mothers to use shaming/love withdrawal and modesty encouragement. Across the participants, there were contrasting relationships between authoritative parenting styles, devoted/involved parenting, modesty encouragement/shaming/non-reasoning parenting practices, and child behaviour problems. A blend of Western and Korean parenting practices were found being utilised after the Koreans settled in New Zealand.

Muslim parenting style

The Islamic world consists of Eastern and Western Muslim countries. Although they are distributed, they are quite homogeneous, except for refinements in actual practices—traditions that are upheld or have changed somewhat with time. Islamic teachings are based primarily on the Qur'an and traditions of the Prophet Muhammad. Their special emphasis is on the role of parents, the religious community, and the mosque in the religious upbringing of youths and children. Inferring from the teachings and practices of the earliest Muslim communities, young people and children are part and parcel of spiritual life, and present in the mosque as full participants in the Muslim community. This latter practice has been upheld to the present day in many Muslim countries, including Indonesia and Malaysia. Mosques, usually located within neighbourhoods, whether rural or urban, also act as educational institutions where young people assemble for religious classes. Schools play a central role for students to receive secular and religious lessons and engage in co-curricular activities. Thus, social and contextual factors are important contributors to Muslim adolescent religious development (Krauss et al., 2013).

Indonesia, an Asian country with the largest Muslim population in the world, has religion influencing its goals, strategies, emotional climate, and parenting practices. Religious beliefs shape socialisation goals and parenting strategies of Indonesian parents. Islam emphasises group harmony, and a strong respect for and deference to the authority of elders and parents in particular. The vast majority of Indonesian families therefore emphasise closeness and harmony (*rukun*), loyalty, obligation, respect (*hormat*), and voluntary cooperation (*gotong-royong*). It is an obligation for children to obey their parents and elders, and to preserve the family's honour.

Social relationships are strictly regulated towards maintaining a respectable distance from those in authority. The father, who is customarily the head of the family, makes most of the important decisions for the family. Indonesian fathers largely keep their distance from their children and are expected to punish any of their gross misconduct. Mothers spend more time with the children and are responsible for their care, discipline, and emotional support. Such a delineation of parental roles contributes to differences in the patterns of father– and mother–child interactions. Additionally, the child's sex may influence perceived parenting styles. Studies have indicated that sons report a higher score regarding authoritarianism than daughters (for example, Abubakar, Van de Vijver, Suryani, Handayani, & Pandia, 2015). Sons tend to seek more autonomy from parents than daughters. In spite of the father's leading position within the family, the mother is very influential. Older daughters are expected to take up some maternal responsibilities, such as household chores and sibling care. Parents' socialisation processes are therefore geared towards ensuring that children prepare to take up these responsibilities within the family and the larger society.

In the Arabic world, people live in an authoritarian and collective cultural system in which the family (nuclear and extended) is the priority. Independence and self-actualisation are viewed as egoism. Psychological individuation of adolescents is not accomplished and the individual's identity continues to be enmeshed in the collective into adulthood. There still exist physical and emotional abuses in parenting in Bahrain, Egypt, Jordan, Morocco, and Saudi Arabia; particularly among lower-class, uneducated parents and larger or dysfunctional families. Comparatively, females receive the harsher aspects of authoritarianism. The focus of their teaching is on modesty, mobility, and sexual behaviour. They have fewer choices and options in life. They live almost exclusively within the borders of home and family life. Conversely, the teaching of males focuses on social duties and responsibility; they enjoy more choices and options, and a wider space of mobility where they are able to manoeuver within social authority, and find paths for self-expression. In addition, females are punished more harshly too. In extreme cases, immodest females may be killed in the name of saving the so-called honour of the family. However, as females are more submissive, there are indications that authoritarian parenting and physical punishments are applied more towards the males (Abubakar et al., 2015).

In today's world, Arabic societies are diverse. The percentage of urbanisation varies from 23% in Yemen and 24% in Somalia to 91% in Qatar and 96% in Kuwait. Many urban Arab families continue to maintain an extended family structure where three generations or more live under one roof. Arab youths are exposed to the open and free lifestyle of the city, and the resulting demands for freedom challenge parental tradition. Arab parents in the US, for example, are much concerned about losing control over the behaviour of children influenced by mainstream American culture (Dwairy & Menshar, 2006).

Notably, Iranian immigrant patriarchal families in the US are characterised by a deep-seated sense of Iranian identity, including cultural morals, values, and familial dynamics. The father is the undisputed authoritarian and has the responsibility of disciplining the children, whereas the mother's power is subtle and indirect. Although she may try to curtail conflict when it arises, she does not undermine the father's authority. Mothers are turned to for survival needs, cultural socialisation, and love and affection. Parents may monitor their children to keep them on track academically and out of trouble. Conflict in Iranian families may result in the silent treatment (one form of psychological control) between family members. Shame is another psychologically controlling technique used by parents to ensure children do not embarrass the family, and act obediently. Autonomy and separation from the family unit are viewed as disrespectful and ungrateful. Hence, if Iranian youths try to loosen the ties from their traditional and familial norms and values, parents may assert their authority through psychological control (Frank, Plunkett, & Otten, 2010).

In summary, Muslim cultures have a tendency to adopt authoritarian styles regarding the upbringing of children (teaching respect and obedience at home; urging children to be good people), while being permissive about their outside activities, such as sports and their choice of career. And a Muslim child is likely to accept the incoming attitudes of his or her parents in a similar manner as religious values are embraced. This means that instead of internalising criticism that might have an impact on his or her self-compassionate attitude, it is accepted as part of a broader religious framework (Ahmed & Bhutto, 2016).

Evidence for Muslim parenting

A study in Indonesia (Abubakar et al., 2015) investigated 500 adolescent students regarding the association between maternal and paternal parenting styles and their psychological well-being. The results show that mothers are perceived to be authoritative, and fathers are perceived to be authoritarian. Both maternal and paternal authoritative parenting styles are positively associated with students' psychological well-being.

A study in Egypt (Dwairy & Menshar, 2006) investigated 351 adolescents concerning their mental health in relation to parenting styles and adolescent–family connectedness. The results show that in rural communities, the authoritarian style is predominant in the parenting of male adolescents, whereas the authoritative style is predominant in the parenting of female adolescents. In urban communities, the authoritarian style is predominant in the parenting of female adolescents. The connectedness of all female adolescents with their family is stronger than that of male adolescents. The connectedness of females is found to be more emotional and financial in villages, and more functional in the city. Female adolescents have a higher frequency of psychological disorders. Mental health issues are linked with authoritative parenting, but not with authoritarian parenting. It seems that authoritarian parenting within an authoritarian culture is not as harmful as within a liberal individualistic culture.

A study in Rawalpindi and Islamabad, Pakistan (Sartaj & Aslam, 2010), investigated 200 college students regarding the impact of authoritarian and authoritative parenting in the home and on health and emotional adjustment. The results show that students raised by authoritative parents have better homes, health, and emotional adjustment compared to adolescents raised by authoritarian parents. Authoritative parents have positive, and authoritarian parents negative, relationships with their home, health, and emotional adjustment.

Another study (Kauser & Pinquart, 2016) testifies that Western parenting styles work in Lahore, in Punjab, Pakistan. This study examined 1,140 adolescent students regarding parenting styles, and the associations between perceived parenting styles and juvenile delinquency. The results show that the authoritative parenting style is associated with lower levels of juvenile delinquency, whereas neglectful parenting is associated with higher levels of delinquency. Moreover, perceived maternal parenting styles show stronger relationships with juvenile delinquency than paternal parenting styles.

A study in Malaysia (Krauss et al., 2013) investigated 596 secondary school students concerning the influence of community engagement and parenting factors on religiosity. The results show that parental monitoring, mosque involvement, and school engagement helped in the development of a religious worldview, whereas parental religious socialisation, parental monitoring, mosque involvement, school engagement, and youth organisation involvement accounted for the development of a religious personality.

In a nutshell, Eastern collectivistic cultures place an emphasis on group harmony, cohesion, and common goals. Eastern families continually stress the sociocultural parenting characteristic of interdependence among family members as a predominant trait. Basically, family members fulfil different roles in a system of reciprocity, which is about caring and mutual obligation. In turn, parents and elders within the family hold considerable authority and responsibility, and are treated with great respect by the children. Interdependence begins early in childhood, where it has been reported that children as young as infants and toddlers learn to become oriented towards this interdependence (Otto, 2016).

Some concepts and perceptions of Eastern cultures need to be re-emphasised here. Of significance are the Confucian teachings and concept of filial piety among the Chinese, Japanese, and Koreans; the role of Indian fathers; and the influence of religion among the Muslims. Notably, modern-day people from Eastern cultures may be associated less with such descriptions, and many have taken up Christianity as their religious affiliation. Besides, East Asian parenting is often described as over-involved, overprotective, authoritarian, and emotionally distant. Parents are often stereotyped as children-focused when it comes to utilising family resources. In reality, Eastern cultural frameworks of parental authority over children reflect a strong family system and demonstrate strong parental love and concern. This is in contrast to Western frameworks and literature on parenting, which characterise this parental authority as harsh and stifling (Otto, 2016). In other words, Eastern collectivistic children would perceive strict parenting accompanying warmth as acceptable. Studies have shown that among Asians warm and strict parenting can coexist (Abubakar et al., 2015).

Punishment

Baumrind's parenting typology has often classified Chinese parenting[2] as more authoritarian (Fung, Li, & Lam, 2017). Chinese parents are inclined to chastise misbehaving children from the age of 2; though they are less developed cognitively, socially, and emotionally, they are deemed ready to learn properly. Of course, parental disciplining increases as the children grow, hopefully for the better, with parents accessing more of their thoughts and preferences about it. When disciplining children, in general, private and public settings are considered. As mentioned before, Chinese people like to keep their problems at home. Thus, parents are sensitive to disciplining children in public. At home, they are more relaxed, open, and direct with one another. In disciplinary encounters, parent–child conflict is inevitable. Given that harmony is a long-standing Confucian attitude, conflict violates this basic orientation; it is a stressful producer which may lead to embarrassment of the self and others. In real parent–child conflicts such as heated arguments, parents may choose strategies such as deliberate ignoring or acquiescence, or simply having no response to avoid confrontation, so as to achieve their goals more effectively. Five types of strategies of parents are power assertion, reasoning, conflict avoidance, isolation, and no reaction. Four uses of these strategies are single, simultaneous, contingent, and ratcheting (Fung et al., 2017).

A study in Canada (Maiter, Alaggia, & Trocmé, 2004) investigated nearly 30 parents of South Asian (Indian) descent regarding their attitude towards child discipline, maltreatment, and neglect. The results show that these parents, as with others, consider persistent and excessive use of physical discipline to be inappropriate, that parental behaviours as such may have negative emotional consequences on children, and that supervision of children is important. However, these parents are not willing to contact child protective services if they encounter families with abuse.

Notably, South Korea is a society where many parents endorse a strict approach to childrearing, including corporal punishment (Kim & Holloway, 2018).

Childrearing

As discussed above, childrearing is a priority in Eastern collectivistic families, and more important than parents' own desires. Generally, parents go to great lengths to ensure their offspring succeed in life. Full support comes from the parents, be it physically, emotionally, psychologically, or financially. It begins before birth and persists all the way to old age if children continue to live with their parents—an unimaginable move among Western children.

Chief among the principles and virtues of these people are power and control of religion or faith. Eastern parents can be adamant that their children adopt and stick to the faith they believed in, so much so that childrearing may be swayed by religious teachings—for example, having a son to maintain the family line, and performing circumcision on the male for health reasons.

As mentioned earlier, to ensure children uphold the family's honour with proper behaviours and ethics, parents may use punishment of various sorts, like caning, scolding, etc.

Application of Eastern collectivistic typology

Surprisingly, there is no study that investigates the use of Eastern collectivistic parenting styles on Western individualistic families. Perhaps, as word about Easterners doing well educationally and economically continues to spread, Western parents are more aware and are pushing their children to be more competitive, particularly in the area of education. Or, it is already happening but the Western world is yet to acknowledge it.

How are Eastern parenting styles measured?

As mentioned in Chapter 3, this section gives a glimpse of the measurement of the established parenting styles, Western and Eastern and others. Details of this topic can be found in Chapter 8.

As for measuring parenting in Eastern collectivistic countries, most Western-produced parenting scales or measures are translated for use in the country in question—for example, the commonly used Parental Authority Questionnaire (Reitman, Rhode, Hupp, & Altobello, 2002), which has found popularity in many parenting studies. Additionally, some Eastern countries have designed their own parenting questionnaires to suit their parenting conventions and own uses. For example, my filial parenting style has an accompanying questionnaire. I have conducted quite a few studies confirming the validity of the questionnaire, but more are needed to make it a valid one for universal use.

Conclusion

In summary (see Table 4.1), Eastern parenting is about upholding the traditions and customs of cultures while keeping up with the times. Family and lineage come before self, and collectivistic properties are more important but do allow for self-regulation and self-determination. Parents often exercise authoritarian-style parenting to the extent of being over-involved, demanding yet caring, nurturing, and supportive of their children.

Table 4.1 Pros and cons of Eastern-style parenting

	Pros	Cons
Chinese parenting	Concept: – Confucian filial piety, the guiding principle directing child's learning experiences. Filial teachings include obeying and honouring one's parents and lineage; in general, conducting oneself to bring honour to the family name and not disgrace it. – Two types: reciprocal and authoritarian. – Five parenting dimensions: encouragement of modest behaviour, protection, shaming/love withdrawal, directiveness, and maternal involvement. – *Chiao shun* involves training child early through continuous guidance and monitoring of behaviours, while providing care, concern, support, and involvement. – *Guan* or governing in the parent–child interaction; goes with punishment too: verbal, physical, and emotional. Parent: – Maintains authority over child, continues the family name and line. – Harmonious family and relationships. – Humility-oriented. Child: – Does as parent wishes and desires. – Strong emotional control.	Concept: – Considered as authoritarian parenting but with a twist; lots of demandingness and responsiveness. Parent: – Unable to perceive other parenting styles, which may be more suitable for upbringing of children. – Punishment may lead to more punishment. Child: – Trying to disregard this concept by being individual is unfilial or bad, dishonouring the family and clan. – Attempt at interracial marriage is discouraged. – May have relational aggression.

(*Continued*)

116 Eastern (collectivistic) parenting styles

Table 4.1 (Cont.)

	Pros	*Cons*
Filial parenting	A form of Chinese parenting that may be practised by other ethnic groups. *Filial parenting* refers to the almost unconditional devotion and care of both parents towards their one or two children. Two aims: to ensure future success of children, and to develop reciprocal filial piety, that is, respect, devotion, and care when the parents reach old age. Parent: – Considers this the ideal parenting style. Child: – Develops in accordance with filial parents' wishes. – There is little or no sibling rivalry. – A sense of artificial filial piety is maintained.	Parent: – Stressful trying to uphold traditions and virtues in the changing world. Child: – Loss of natural childhood. – Loss of expression in order to develop self. – Lack of awareness of and empathy for others. – Can adopt an entitled attitude. – Loss of natural filial piety. – Lack of independence for parents and children.
Indian parenting	Concept: – Collective, interdependent orientation, within family and outside it. Parent: – Respects family hierarchy. – Maintains power distance. – Satisfies wishes of elders in family and society. – Encourages values, customs, and respect for others. – Earns praises and rewards. – Fathers to perform *swadharma* (right course of action in life); fulfil the roles of provider, guide, mentor, and nurturer; and pass on *sanskar*	Concept: – Considered as authoritarian parenting but with a twist; lots of demandingness and responsiveness. Parent: – Unable to perceive other parenting styles which may be more suitable for upbringing of children. – Punishment may lead to more punishment. Child: – Trying to disregard this concept by being individual is unfilial or

(Continued)

Eastern (collectivistic) parenting styles 117

Table 4.1 (Cont.)

	Pros	Cons
	(purification and refinement of inner consciousness). - Mothers are key figures for behaviour regulation; strategies by mothers include persistent repetition, offering explanations, instilling fear, invoking guilt, and negotiating with rewards. - Within family, physical proximity and contact through activities such as eating and sleeping together are encouraged. Child: - Learns through observation. - Should be self-reliant but this is conditional on situation and domain. - Should be successful personally and professionally.	bad, dishonouring the family and clan. - Attempt at interracial marriage is discouraged. - May have relational aggression. - Does not internalise values into self.
Japanese parenting	Concept: - Confucian moral teachings. Parent: - Develops innate moral character and intellectual abilities. - Maintains close, harmonious interpersonal relationships. - Performs one's assigned role in the society. - Provides proper, competent guidance, and establishment of suitable environment and proper role models for learning. - Emphasis on children's understanding of parental teaching and admonition as effective for development, and appealing to the children's sense of self as self-regulation.	Concept: - Considered as authoritarian parenting but with a twist; lots of demandingness and responsiveness. Parent: - Unable to perceive other parenting styles which may be more suitable for upbringing of children. - Punishment may lead to more punishment. Child: - Trying to disregard this concept by being individual is unfilial or bad, dishonouring the family and race. - Attempt at interracial marriage is discouraged.

(Continued)

Table 4.1 (Cont.)

	Pros	Cons
	– People pursue their inclination through thrift, honesty, patience, humaneness, and family harmony. Child: – Learns through strict teaching and observation. – Should be self-reliant. – Should be successful personally and professionally.	– May have relational aggression.
Korean parenting	Concept: – From Chinese culture, *guan* (to govern/train and love) and *qin* (a child's feeling of closeness to parents or parental benevolence) blend direct control, close monitoring, and implicit parental affection via instrumental support, devotion, and support for education rather than physical, verbal, and emotional expressions. – *Hyo* ideology postulates 12 virtues governing parental responsibilities towards children, and children's reciprocal responsibilities towards parents. – Emphasises ideal parenting virtues (e.g., parents being role models to teach children the main values), centrality of the family, family hierarchy, age veneration, and family obligations and ties. – Makes virtues of parental attentiveness to children and of parental devotion and care to children, beginning while the baby is in utero.	Concept: – Considered as authoritarian parenting but with a twist; lots of demandingness and responsiveness. Parent: – Unable to perceive other parenting styles which may be more suitable for upbringing of children. – Punishment may lead to more punishment. Child: – Trying to disregard this concept by being individual is unfilial or bad, dishonouring the family and clan. – Attempt at interracial marriage is discouraged. – May have relational aggression. – May feel parents are over-involved in their lives.

(*Continued*)

Table 4.1 (Cont.)

Pros	Cons
- Parents have responsibility for teaching children all they need to know to succeed in life. - Group harmony is of paramount importance; self-effacement is more crucial than self-enhancement. - For mothers, respecting others by lowering yourself and not being assertive; emphasising self-effacement to some degree. Parent: - Maintains such traditional parenting practices as co-sleeping and using indirect expressions of affection. - External attribution (child behaviour) seen as cause of parenting successes, and an internal attribution (effort) as cause of parenting failures. - Fathers financially support their children's education. - Mothers consider children their priority, rather than their personal life. - Stay-at-home mothers are preferred. - Mothers are to provide their children with emotional care and support on a daily basis. - Transnational parents use their status to influence study and careers of children overseas. Child: - Learns through observation: be self-reliant (conditional on situation and domain); be successful personally and professionally.	

(*Continued*)

Table 4.1 (Cont.)

	Pros	Cons
Muslim parenting	Concept: – Islamic teachings are based primarily on the Qur'an and the traditions of Prophet Muhammad. – Special emphasis on the role of parents, the religious community, and the mosque in the religious upbringing of youth and children. – Young people and children are part and parcel of spiritual life and present in mosque as full participants in the Muslim community. Strong concept that is uniting Muslims across the world. Family: – Emphasise closeness and harmony, loyalty, obligation, respect, and voluntary cooperation. – Obligation for children to obey their parents and elders and to preserve family honour. – Social relationships are strictly regulated towards maintaining respectable distance from those in authority. Parent: – Father, head of the family, makes most important decisions; keeps his or her distance from child and punishes them for gross misconduct. – Mother spends more time with child, being responsible for their care and discipline. – Older daughters are to take up some maternal responsibilities, such as household chores and sibling care.	Concept: – Considered as authoritarian parenting but with a twist; lots of demandingness and responsiveness. Parent: – Will not perceive other parenting styles which may be more suitable for upbringing of children. – Punishment may lead to more punishment. Child: – By trying to go away from the Islam teaching, he or she will be disowned. – Attempt at interracial marriage is difficult; partner has to convert to Islam. – May have relational aggression.

(Continued)

Table 4.1 (Cont.)

	Pros	Cons
		Child: – Females receive harsher aspects of authoritarianism, including punishment. – Focus of teaching on modesty, mobility, and sexual behaviour. – Have fewer choices and options in life. – Live almost exclusively within the borders of home and family life. – Males focus on social duties and responsibility; enjoy more choices and options, with a wider space of mobility, and are able to manoeuver within social authority, and find paths for self-expression. – Authoritarian parenting and physical punishments are applied towards males, as females are more submissive.
Overall Eastern parenting style	Style: Eastern-oriented; collectivistic; interdependent; family-oriented; upholds religious tradition and cultural customs and practices. Socialisation goal: Emphasise collectivistic attributes (e.g., harmonious interpersonal relationships, obedience, modesty, dependence on the group). Childrearing: Mainly mother's role; father is supportive; directive; academia- and achievement-oriented; aims to fulfil parental wishes and goals. Punishment: May use corporal punishment, including caning, slapping, scolding, etc. Perception from West: Authoritarian; strict; controlling; involves training; unsuitable for bringing out the best of children; may cause mental illness and maladjustment in children.	

(*Continued*)

Table 4.1 (Cont.)

Pros	Cons
	Ongoing issues: How best to raise children without giving in too much but retaining one's culture? How many children are ideal? Is interracial marriage suitable?

Notes

1 In Eastern countries, parenting styles have been studied in their own languages but not translated into English for the consumption of the West; and certainly not compared to Western measurements of parenting.
2 I have just used *Chinese parenting* here; the discussion may refer to other Eastern cultures as well.

References

Abubakar, A., Van de Vijver, F. J. R., Suryani, A. O., Handayani, P., & Pandia, W. S. (2015). Perceptions of parenting styles and their associations with mental health and life satisfaction among urban Indonesian adolescents. *Journal of Child and Family Studies, 24*(9), 2680–2692. doi: 10.1007/s10826-014-0070-x.

Ahmed, N., & Bhutto, Z. H. (2016). Relationship between parenting styles and self compassion in young adults. *Pakistan Journal of Psychological Research, 31*(2), 441–451.

Chan, S. M., Bowes, J., & Wyver, S. (2009). Parenting style as a context for emotion socialization. *Early Education & Development, 20*(4), 631–656. doi: 10.1080/10409280802541973.

Chao, R. K. (1994). Beyond parental control and authoritarian parenting style: Understanding Chinese parenting through the cultural notion of training. *Child Development, 65*(2), 1111–1119. doi: 10.1111/j.1467-8624.1994.tb00806.x.

Chen, W. (2014). The relationship between perceived parenting style, filial piety, and life satisfaction in Hong Kong. *Journal of Family Psychology: Journal of the Division of Family Psychology of the American Psychological Association (Division 43), 28*(3), 308–314. doi: 10.1037/a0036819.

Choi, Y., Kim, Y. S., Lee, J. P., Kim, H., Kim, T. Y., & Kim, S. Y. (2018). Bilinear and multidimensional cultural orientations and indigenous family process among Korean immigrant mothers and fathers. *Asian American Journal of Psychology, 9*(2), 127–139. doi: 10.1037/aap0000097.

Cote, L. R., Kwak, K., Putnick, D. L., Chung, H. J., & Bornstein, M. H. (2015). The acculturation of parenting cognitions: A comparison of South Korean, Korean immigrant, and European American mothers. *Journal of Cross-Cultural Psychology*, 46(9), 1115–1130. doi: 10.1177/0022022115600259.

Deb, S., Strodl, E., & Sun, J. (2014). Academic-related stress among private secondary school students in India. *Asian Education and Development Studies*, 3(2), 118–134.

Debbarma, R., & Bhattacharjee, A. (2018). Impact of caring and overprotecting parenting style on emotional intelligence and adjustment of school students. *Journal of Psychosocial Research*, 13(1), 91–100.

Dwairy, M., & Menshar, K. E. (2006). Parenting style, individuation, and mental health of Egyptian adolescents. *Journal of Adolescence*, 29(1), 103–117. doi: 10.1016/j.adolescence.2005.03.002.

Foo, K. H. (2014). Filial parenting is not working! In P. Mandal (Ed.), *Proceedings of the International Conference on Managing the Asian Century: ICMAC 2013* (pp. 343–351). Singapore: Springer. doi: 10.1007/978-981-4560-61-0.

Frank, G., Plunkett, S. W., & Otten, M. P. (2010). Perceived parenting, self-esteem, and general self-efficacy of Iranian American adolescents. *Journal of Child and Family Studies*, 19(6), 738–746. doi: 10.1007/s10826-010-9363-x.

Fung, H., Li, J., & Lam, C. K. (2017). Multi-faceted discipline strategies of Chinese parenting. *International Journal of Behavioral Development*, 41(4), 472–481. doi: 10.1177/0165025417690266.

Hirata, H., & Kamakura, T. (2018). The effects of parenting styles on each personal growth initiative and self-esteem among Japanese university students. *International Journal of Adolescence and Youth*, 23(3), 325–333. doi: 10.1080/02673843.2017.1371614.

Huang, C., Cheah, C. S. L., Lamb, M. E., & Zhou, N. (2017). Associations between parenting styles and perceived child effortful control within Chinese families in the United States, the United Kingdom, and Taiwan. *Journal of Cross-Cultural Psychology*, 48(6), 795–812. doi: 10.1177/0022022117706108.

Huang, G. H. C., & Gove, M. (2015). *Asian parenting styles and academic achievement: Views from Eastern and Western perspectives*. Mobile: Project Innovation.

Kang, H., & Shih, K. (2018). "Actions speak louder than words": Korean American emerging adults' perceptions and meaning making of their parents' instrumental aspects of parenting. *Journal of Family Issues*, 39(3), 644–667. doi: 10.1177/0192513X16676856.

Karmakar, R. (2015). Does parenting style influence the internalization of moral values in children and adolescents? *Psychological Studies*, 60(4), 438–446. doi: 10.1007/s12646-015 0338 2.

Kauser, R., & Pinquart, M. (2016). Gender differences in the associations between perceived parenting styles and juvenile delinquency in Pakistan. *Pakistan Journal of Psychological Research*, 31(2), 549–568.

Kim, H., & Agee, M. N. (2018). "Where are you from?" Identity as a key to parenting by 1.5 generation Korean-New Zealand migrants and implications for counselling. *British Journal of Guidance & Counselling*. Online. doi: 10.1080/03069885.2018.1457770.

Kim, S., & Holloway, S. D. (2018). Parenting and young children's emotional self-regulation in urban Korean families. *Journal of Early Childhood Research*, 16(3), 305–318. doi: 10.1177/1476718X18775759.

Kojima, H. (1996). Japanese childrearing advice in its cultural, social, and economic contexts. *International Journal of Behavioral Development, 19*(2), 373–391. doi: 10.1177/016502549601900209.

Krauss, S. E., Ismail, I. A., Suandi, T., Hamzah, A., Hamzah, S. R., Dahalan, D., ... Idris, F. (2013). Parenting and community engagement factors as predictors of religiosity among Muslim adolescents from Malaysia. *International Journal for the Psychology of Religion, 23*(2), 87–102. doi: 10.1080/10508619.2012.670039.

Lee, B., Keown, L. J., & Brown, G. T. L. (2018). Relationships between parenting practices and perceptions of child behaviour among Korean immigrant mothers and fathers. *International Journal of Psychology, 53*(5), 402–410. doi: 10.1002/ijop.12398.

Li, Y., Costanzo, P. R., & Putallaz, M. (2010). Maternal socialization goals, parenting styles, and social-emotional adjustment among Chinese and European American young adults: Testing a mediation model. *Journal of Genetic Psychology, 171*(4), 330–362. doi: 10.1080/00221325.2010.505969.

Li, Y., Putallaz, M., & Su, Y. (2011). Interparental conflict styles and parenting behaviors: Associations with overt and relational aggression among Chinese children. *Merrill-Palmer Quarterly, 57*(4), 402–428.

Machizawa-Summers, S. (2007). Childhood trauma and parental bonding among Japanese female patients with borderline personality disorder. *International Journal of Psychology, 42*(4), 265–273. doi: 10.1080/00207590601109276.

Maddeaux, S. (2017, May 20). Sympathy for the li'l devils; why we shouldn't be so dismissive of spoiled little rich kids. *National Post*.

Maiter, S., Alaggia, R., & Trocmé, N. (2004). Perceptions of child maltreatment by parents from the Indian subcontinent: Challenging myths about culturally based abusive parenting practices. *Child Maltreatment, 9*(3), 309–324. doi: 10.1177/10775595042668.

Moore, J., & Abetz, J. S. (2019). What do parents regret about having children? Communicating regrets online. *Journal of Family Issues, 40*(3), 390–412. doi: 10.1177/0192513X18811388.

Nakayama, M. (2011). Parenting style and parental monitoring with information communication technology: A study on Japanese junior high school students and their parents. *Computers in Human Behavior, 27*(5), 1800–1805. doi: 10.1016/j.chb.2011.03.007.

New Paper (2013, May 13). Surveys, HR practitioners say Gen Y job seekers are asking for more, 6.

Otto, W. J. (2016). What teachers should know about why these students perform so well: An examination of Korean-American achievement through student perspectives of East Asian parenting beliefs, styles and practices. *International Electronic Journal of Elementary Education, 9*(1), 167–181.

Park, J. (2018). Public fathering, private mothering: Gendered transnational parenting and class reproduction among elite Korean students. *Gender & Society, 32*(4), 563–586. doi: 10.1177/0891243218771551.

Reitman, D., Rhode, P. C., Hupp, S. D. A., & Altobello, C. (2002). Development and validation of the Parental Authority Questionnaire – Revised. *Journal of Psychopathology and Behavioral Assessment, 24*(2), 119–127. doi: 10.1023/A:1015344909518.

Sapru, S. (2006). Parenting and adolescent identity: A study of Indian families in New Delhi and Geneva. *Journal of Adolescent Research, 21*(5), 484–513. doi: 10.1177/ 0743558406291766.

Sartaj, B., & Aslam, N. (2010). Role of authoritative and authoritarian parenting in home, health and emotional adjustment. *Journal of Behavioural Sciences, 20*(1), 47–66.

Seo, M., & Choi, E. (2018). Classes of trajectory in mobile phone dependency and the effects of negative parenting on them during early adolescence. *School Psychology International, 39*(2), 156–169. doi: 10.1177/0143034317745946.

Shek, D. T. (1995). Chinese adolescents' perceptions of parenting styles of fathers and mothers. *Journal of Genetic Psychology, 156*(2), 175–190. doi: 10.1080/ 00221325.1995.9914815.

Sriram, R., & Sandhu, G. K. (2013). Fathering to ensure child's success: What urban Indian fathers do? *Journal of Family Issues, 34*(2), 159–181.

Tang, J., Li, N., Sandoval, J. R., & Liu, Y. (2018). Parenting styles and academic motivation: A sample from Chinese high schools. *Journal of Child and Family Studies, 27*(10), 3395–3401. doi: 10.1007/s10826-018-1164-7.

Tuli, M. (2012). Beliefs on parenting and childhood in India. *Journal of Comparative Family Studies, 43*(1), 81–91.

Uji, M., Sakamoto, A., Adachi, K., & Kitamura, T. (2014). The impact of authoritative, authoritarian, and permissive parenting styles on children's later mental health in Japan: Focusing on parent and child gender. *Journal of Child and Family Studies, 23*(2), 293–302. doi: 10.1007/s10826-013-9740-3.

Vohra, J., & Soni, P. (2016). How do Indian mothers use feeding practices with children? *Journal of Children's Services, 11*(4), 283–299. doi: 10.1108/JCS-02-2016-0004.

Wang, M., & Qi, W. (2017). Harsh parenting and problematic internet use in Chinese adolescents: Child emotional dysregulation as mediator and child forgiveness as moderator. *Computers in Human Behavior, 77*, 211–219. doi: 10.1016/j. chb.2017.09.005.

Xu, Y., Farver, J. A. M., Zhang, Z., Zeng, Q., Yu, L., & Cai, B. (2005). Mainland Chinese parenting styles and parent–child interaction. *International Journal of Behavioral Development, 29*(6), 524–531. doi: 10.1080/01650250500147121.

Yeh, K.-H., & Bedford, O. (2003). A test of the dual filial piety model. *Asian Journal of Social Psychology, 6*, 215–228. doi: 10.1046/j.1467839X.2003.00122.x.

Yeung, J. W. K. (2016). Parenting discrepancies in the aggregate parenting context and positive child outcomes in Chinese parent–child dyads. *Personality and Individual Differences, 98*, 107–113. doi: 10.1016/j.paid.2016.03.064.

Other relevant parenting styles

5

By now, you have an idea of the major parenting styles from the West and East. Just a quick review: we have authoritarian, authoritative, permissive, and neglecting parenting styles from the Western individualistic world, and a general parenting style that is nurturing, motivational, and meaningful, yet controlling, from the Eastern collectivistic world, including my filial parenting style for Chinese Singaporean people.

Seemingly, there are other versions of parenting styles that are surfacing in the literature and media. In this chapter, we are going to discuss tiger parenting, helicopter parenting, positive parenting, and a few others, some of which are referred to as *parenting model* or *parenting practice* (see below). Finally, I'd like to introduce you to my proposed negotiation parenting style (Foo, 2015). The chapter finishes with a table summarising the pros and cons of these parenting styles (see Table 5.1).

Tiger parenting

Tiger parenting refers to a very strict or demanding form of parenting. Rightly so, it means *tiger mothering*. The term was coined by Yale law professor Amy Chua in her 2011 book *Battle Hymn of the Tiger Mother*.

Basically a Chinese American concept, the term parallels strict parenting styles typically enforced by families in the Eastern cultures. Tiger parenting became popular partly due to three shows: the 2015 Mainland China (Chinese) drama *Tiger Mom*, the 2017 Hong Kong series *Tiger Mom Blues*, and the 2015 Singaporean TV show *Tiger Mum*. The stereotypical character is a Chinese mother who relentlessly drives her children to study hard, to the destruction of the children's physical and social development and emotional well-being. To put it another way, tiger parents pressure their children to attain high levels of academic achievement, using authoritarian parenting methods.

The publication of Amy Chua's book found advocates and critics among the public. Amy claims that her strict and overly controlling form of parenting is the Chinese way, and that her daughters owe their successes to it. Undeniably, one of Chua's daughters attended Harvard and was invited to play the piano at Carnegie Hall. In comparison, Chua stated that the American emphasis on developing and enhancing children's self-esteem is the less effective strategy for bringing up children.

Tiger parenting has prompted scholarly discourse on this parenting style and its likely effects on families. Although tiger parenting may have probably been adopted in Chinese Confucian families in the past in China, it is extreme in the eyes of many Chinese families worldwide, who use the Eastern collectivistic parenting style discussed earlier. Possibly many do not admit it or they have already modified their parenting style over time, having recognised and considered that socialisation of children and their well-being are more important.

An eight-year longitudinal study (Kim, 2013) showed that tiger parenting was not a common parenting profile in a sample of over 400 Chinese American families. Tiger parenting does not relate to superior academic performance in children; the best developmental outcomes are found among children of supportive parents. Eight parenting dimensions are found among Chinese American parents: four positive (warmth, inductive reasoning, monitoring, and democratic) and four negative (hostility, punitive, psychological control, and shaming). High positive and negative dimensions create tiger parenting; high positive and low negative dimensions create supportive parenting; low positive and high negative dimensions create harsh parenting; and low positive and negative dimensions create easy-going parenting.

In summary, a moderate level of shaming may be an important factor in supportive, successful parenting among Chinese Americans. Furthermore, tiger fathers are also present in Chinese American families. Tiger mothering diminishes as children grow older, while tiger fathering increases. In earlier adolescence, mothers are likely to be the emotional caretakers of their children. As children grow and become more involved with the outside world, fathers take on a more active role.

Another investigation comprising four studies (Fu & Markus, 2014) showed that it was the models of the self that guided behaviour among four samples of over 200 high school Asian and European American students. These models are ingrained in divergent cultural assumptions about the role of others in the self, and provide different guidelines for the appropriate role of parents when their child fails. Depending on the model of the self being used, pressure by parents may take on different meanings and consequences. These studies found that Asian American high school students experience more interdependence with their mothers and pressure from them, but that the pressure does not strain their relationship. Furthermore, following failure Asian American students are more motivated and pressured by their mothers. Thus, with Asian Americans, given the cultural emphasis on interdependence, parents actively guide their children to meet expectations, and push them to succeed, particularly in school. In turn, even in adolescence, children expect their parents to be involved in their lives, and they take up their parents' goals for themselves as their own. Thus, when children struggle, pressure by parents may not produce resentment. In fact, at the point of failure, pressure from mothers may become an additional resource that children can draw on for motivation.

Helicopter parenting

Helicopter parenting is a style of upbringing in which an overprotective father or mother discourages a child's independence by being too involved in his or her life. This parental over-involvement in children's lives is described as the hovering of parents over their children, ready to take responsibility for their decisions and their problems. Parents adopting helicopter parenting use directive behaviours and withhold the granting of autonomy. From the Western viewpoint, helicopter parenting represents parenting that is strong on warmth and support, but also strong on control and weak on granting autonomy to the child. Surprisingly, it may involve benevolent intentions for the child's well-being, like guidance and emotional support. My take on this is that the child has resolved his or her cognitive dissonance on the situation or takes the let-fate/faith-decide-for-me attitude.

According to literature (Kwon, Yoo, & De Gagne, 2017), Korean students may experience higher levels of helicopter parenting than other Asian groups because their parents have higher expectations for children's academic success, are more actively involved in their children's school life and application process, and provide more resources than others. For example (see the section on Korean parenting in Chapter 4), Korean American parents put higher emphasis on their parental role and responsibility; they generally have a higher socioeconomic status than other Asian American groups, and are well educated too. Besides, Korean American children are likely to perceive that their parents from Korea put more academic pressure on children than others.

Helicopter parenting has been highlighted publicly because it is considered a developmentally inappropriate form of parental over-involvement in children's outcomes. Under the pressure of modernity and raised expectations for individual achievements in order to compete in an international job market, this phenomenon is believed to be prevalent, and may have seeped into middle-class parents in Western culture. Research on the effects of helicopter parenting suggests mostly negative outcomes in health and psychological adjustment such as lower levels of independence, emotional well-being, self-efficacy, and effective coping skills, and higher levels of anxiety, depression, and child behavioural problems (Bradley-Geist & Olson-Buchanan, 2014).

However, there are studies showing that helicopter parenting could lead to neutral or even positive outcomes for young adults, such as higher satisfaction and engagement with the college experience, and that helicopter parents provide high levels of emotional support (Gomes & Deuling, 2019).

A study in the US (Kwon et al., 2017) investigated 40 Korean college students on helicopter parenting and its effects. The results show that the students identified three important broad categories of helicopter parenting:

over-involvement and/or overprotection, strict over-control without granting autonomy, and benevolent intention. Negative consequences for the students were in the psychological, social, and emotional areas (for example, increasing levels of anxiety, risky behaviours, and family conflicts, undermining self-efficacy, confidence, and self-esteem). Some had experienced obesity and binge eating from the stress of helicopter parenting, as well as a lack of freedom, opportunities, decision-making and healthy development. Parents were ever-present in children's lives with strict controlling behaviours. Negative reactions from students involved disgust, disapproval, anger, embarrassment, rebellion, stress, and frustration. Benefits for the students included feeling loved and supported; receiving parents' guidance, close monitoring, and support that was needed, especially during the teen years; and parental protection from making mistakes, thus helping them in their academic work and school-related accomplishments. They would likely develop good work ethics, make the right choices (e.g., choosing a good group of friends), have a safer and healthier lifestyle, go on to prestigious schools, and obtain a good professional career.

Another study in Korea (Lee & Kang, 2018) investigated over 550 Korean adults regarding the relationship between parent–child affection, pressure caused by parental career expectations, and psychological adjustment (depressive symptoms and life satisfaction). The results show that higher levels of helicopter parenting are directly linked with greater depressive symptoms. Higher levels of helicopter parenting also have an indirect relationship with greater depressive symptoms through higher levels of pressure as a result of parental career expectations. However, higher levels of helicopter parenting are indirectly linked to better psychological adjustment (fewer depressive symptoms, greater satisfaction with life) through higher levels of parent–child affection. Thus, helicopter parenting could be related to both negative and positive psychological outcomes depending on the mediating factors.

A study in the US (Darlow, Norvilitis, & Schuetze, 2017) examined nearly 300 undergraduates (categorised as Caucasian/White, African-American/Black, Hispanic American, Asian-American, and Others) on the role of helicopter parenting and its effects on their anxiety, depression, self-efficacy, and adjustment. The results show that higher levels of helicopter parenting are associated with more symptoms of depression and lower self-efficacy, which in turn are linked with lower levels of academic and social adjustment to college. Thus, contrary to the goals of many parents who are over-involved in the lives of their college students, helicopter parenting may defeat what is likely to be its goal of improving student success by negatively impacting student mental health.

For Koreans (at home or overseas), helicopter parenting equals creating a robot, a person with no self-identity, and is reminiscent of authoritarian parenting. Korean American parents are likely to be helicopter parents because: one, they have higher expectations of, and stricter standards for, education; two, they are less flexible and lenient; three, they have limited experiences with diversity; four, they emphasise how they appear to others; and five, they feel they should be more involved in children's lives as an immigrant compared to non-immigrant groups. The benevolent intention of helicopter parents occurs or is perceived because the parents hover over their child to protect him/her from any foreseeable harm and believe that it is best for their child, or it is their parents' way of showing their love and affection. Perhaps it is also due to children's passive reactions to the behaviours involved in helicopter parenting. Even though they do not like such parenting, they often do not express their negative emotion explicitly, but are instead likely to succumb and do what they want secretly. This is well aligned with Koreans' traditional value of filial piety; Korean American students try to repress their negative emotions towards their parents and embrace the cultural value of obedience towards parents as an authority figure (Darlow et al., 2017).

In summary, as the entry into adulthood is delayed, parental involvement in young adults' lives is increased. The growth of autonomy and self-reliance becomes an important task, but supportive parenting remains important for children's well-being. Over-parenting hinders the development of coping mechanisms, leading students to feel that they lack control over their lives, resulting in a lack of volition. Hence, parents should heed children's desire for less parental intervention.

Positive parenting

Is this a particular parenting style or a generic term covering parenting that requires positive or good approaches and practices?

An article (Seay, Freysteinson, & McFarlane, 2014) worked through the existing literature on positive parenting and defined it as the continual relationship of parent and child that includes caring, teaching, leading, communicating, and providing for the needs of a child consistently and unconditionally. It specified that all of the key constructs within the relationship found in the definition should be addressed in proper positive parenting.

There is apparently no special write-up on positive parenting, but its practices are recommended and embedded in many parenting programmes. A special study in Melbourne, Australia (Whittle et al., 2014), analysed 188 adolescents on the effects of positive (warm and supportive) maternal behaviour on structural brain development during adolescence, employing longitudinal structural magnetic resonance imaging. The results show that higher frequency of positive maternal behaviour is linked to reduced growth of the right amygdala, and accelerated thinning of the left and right orbitofrontal cortex and right anterior cingulate cortex (males only) from early to mid adolescence. These structures shape the development of adolescents' ability to regulate emotion and behaviours, which otherwise could lead to the development of mental disorders. Another study in Brazil (Bartholomeu, Montiel, Fiamenghi, & Machado, 2016) analysed 202 children aged 7 to 10 regarding the relationship between parenting styles and children's social skills. The results show that positive parental styles are predictors of altruism, whereas negative parental styles are predictors of assertiveness, conversation, and social confidence. Yet another cross-cultural study (Pastorelli et al., 2016) examined over 1,000 mother–child dyads regarding the reciprocal relations between positive parenting (the quality of the mother–child relationship and the use of balanced positive discipline) and children's prosocial behaviour in Colombia, Italy, Jordan, Kenya, the Philippines, Sweden, Thailand, and the US. The results show that children with higher levels of prosocial behaviour at age 9 stimulate higher levels of mother–child relationship quality in the following year. This means that being prosocial in late childhood contributes to the enhancement of a nurturing and involved mother–child relationship in countries that vary widely on socio-demographic profiles and psychological characteristics.

An example of a programme on positive parenting is the Incredible Years Toddler Course, an effective intervention for South Asian families in the UK (Awan & Butterworth, 2017). Another is the Family Nurse Partnership, a programme of intensive support for teenage mothers and their babies, delivered by nurses in Scotland (Trueland, 2012).

Spain has a comprehensive positive parenting strategy covering regulations, policies, programmes, and actions (Arranz Freijo & Rodrigo López, 2018) to foster child development through the promotion of parenting competencies and family support. It consists of three sections. The first describes positive parenting support resources provided by institutions and non-governmental organisations. The second analyses prenatal and perinatal periods from a positive parenting perspective, and presents programmes encompassing the period from birth to 11 years of age, including an online programme for the period from birth to age 3, a support programme for family reunification after temporary foster care, and an analysis of family leisure time. The third focuses on the assessment of family contexts and parenting skills throughout childhood, and presents a proposal for promoting good professional practice and programme design.

In a nutshell, the positive parenting style is authoritative parenting with consistent parental support, guidance, and interaction throughout the developmental stages. Many proposals on positive parenting are available in the literature for reference for the interested reader.

Additional parenting models/practices/styles

Distal versus proximal parenting

These are the recommended alternative parenting strategies for early infants (Keller et al., 2009). Distal parenting, characterised by face-to-face contact and object stimulation—that is, communication through the distant senses—emphasises autonomy and separateness, which have been demonstrated as precursors of independent agency, and is prevalent in urban educated middle-class families of Western cultures in which competition, individual achievements, self-enhancement, and equality constitute the preferred socialisation goals. This parenting style is related to an early development of self-recognition. The proximal parenting style, characterised by bodily proximity and body stimulation, is predominant in traditional subsistence societies, like those of rural, poorly-educated farmer families, in which socialisation goals that embody relatedness, obedience, and hierarchy are preferred. This parenting style reinforces closeness and warmth, and is related to an early development of compliance. However, parents from urban educated families in cultures with a more interdependent history use both strategies.

The Nordic model

In contrast with the authoritative model, Swedish and Norwegian educators have adopted a neo-Rousseauian romanticisation of children as self-absorbed and self-gratifying. Parents are advised to empathise with their children's wishes and psychic needs and to constrain and inhibit them as little as possible. Swedish and Norwegian children remain in a play-oriented day-care setting, exposed to no formal learning, until they start school at age 7. In return for comprehensive, subsidised support for health care and day care, parents conform to (and most have internalised) a parenting model that puts a premium on persuasion and forbids spanking or other belittling disciplinary practices. The ban on corporal punishment in Sweden and Norway is often held up as a model for American families to emulate, although it has not yet been adequately evaluated, even within its own cultural context (Baumrind, 1997).

Norway is considered to be among the more egalitarian countries in the world; it has been relatively insulated from the recent crises in the world economy, and most sections of the population have improved their material level of living. A study (Elstad & Stefansen, 2014) examined 1,362 Norwegian adolescents' perception of parenting styles. The results showed that the adolescents' perceptions of their parents could be captured by four underlying dimensions: responsiveness, demandingness, neglecting, and intrusive. Parents in intact families are perceived as more responsive and demanding, and slightly less neglecting. Females saw their parents as demanding, while males saw them as intrusive. Parenting is perceived as being less responsive, demanding, and intrusive among older (ages 16 to 18) adolescents.

Harsh parenting

Harsh parenting refers to coercive parenting tactics, from frequent use of corporal punishment (perhaps, in a milder form) to escalated physical abuse and cruelty. What is considered harsh but normal in one culture may be viewed as abuse in another. Critically, would parents use this form of parenting if their children were well-behaved and obedient? Or, if it is used on badly-behaved children, is it appropriate then?

An example of a culture that uses harsh parenting is the Mexican family (Frías-Armenta & McCloskey, 1998)—largely traditional, where conformity to values and social norms is exalted. Discipline and respect for parents are upheld prominently. A common, convenient disciplinary approach used by Mexican parents is physical punishment. Corporal punishment is seen not only as necessary but also as a positive practice to produce good citizens. Undoubtedly, Mexican families promote positive and prosocial values among their members, such as solidarity, family loyalty, and friendship. However, Mexican families also display directive, authoritarian, and punitive tendencies in family relations. These patterns have been found in Mexico-born parents rearing their children in the US, who foster greater adherence to parental authority compared to US-born Mexican American parents (Frías-Armenta & McCloskey, 1998). These parenting beliefs and practices sometimes result in violent, abusive episodes against children, especially when stressful events are combined with the hierarchical structure of families.

A study in Sonora, Mexico (Frías-Armenta & McCloskey, 1998), identified the determinants of harsh parenting among 105 mothers. The results showed that the authoritarian parenting style directly affected the mothers' use of harshness: verbal and physical coercive tactics were applied on a regular basis. Apparently, it was the mothers' beliefs (likely the community's beliefs too) concerning the effective use of physical punishment and their lack of disciplinary skills that led to the use of harsh punishment in parenting. Also, family dysfunction (interspousal violence and parents' use of alcohol and drugs) had indirect effects via this parenting style. Additionally, the lower the occupational status of the father, the higher the dysfunction in the family; on top of that, the mother's history of abuse was also a factor. This is probably happening elsewhere in Mexico as well.

A study in the US (Waller et al., 2012) examined 731 multi-ethnic mother–child dyads regarding the relationship between parenting and the development of callous/unemotional behaviour in children. The results showed that harsh parenting contributes to the development of children's deceitful/callous behaviour.

Mobile parenting

Electronic technology has taken over the trends of communication in the 21st century. So much so that many adults cannot live without their mobile phone. And now this technology has crept into the hands of children, with their own phones and/or tablets. All because they provide a means of occupying or entertaining the child while the parent is busy. Hence, the media industries have decided to include children in their viewing targets. A recent article (Burroughs, 2017) investigated this aspect of growth. It is mainly about the development of the YouTube Kids app, with well over 10 million downloads, seeking to capture and monetise youth attention, particularly very young children and infants (aged up to 5 years). This trend is important because it is about parenting, particularly parenting practices involving the watching of televisual content by children on mobile phones and tablets. The YouTube Kids app corrals young children into a controlled space without unexpected participation and play.

Successful parenting includes good communication between parents and children, and getting children to be active for better health and growth. Parents are proud to show off their phone- and tablet-savvy children. No doubt the contents of the app are informative and enticing to the children. But if the use of these electronic devices is not properly controlled, it may just lead to another addiction which hinders proper development of the children, causing eyesight and posture problems, for example.

Nanny TV parenting

Surprisingly, the complexity of the world has taken many parents, old or new, back to school regarding parenting. It is like having to learn something new even though every parent has been doing it and could be seen openly doing it. The parent of today wants to be a pedagogical parent, and wants the best for their children, so they go through the extra effort to achieve that goal. Apparently, practices of parental learning operate throughout society, and involve a lifelong lesson. An article (Dahlstedt & Fejes, 2014) has identified this form of parenting, calling it *nanny TV (parenting)*, which attempts to construct the ideal parents through TV. For example, Swedish TV produced and broadcast its version of a parent-coaching series, called *SOS Family*, in 2008, based on the British *Supernanny* and the American *Nanny 911*. Family problems are presented and solutions are addressed. There is a consistently strong focus on emotions in the series. The ideal parent is a participant who, guided by the coach, is constantly endeavouring to achieve a makeover. The objective of this endeavour, however, is self-control, whereby the parents will in the end become their own coaches.

The question is, will this be the parenting trend of tomorrow for most countries? No amount of writing and talk can beat a four-dimensional medium called television in doing the parenting coaching. On top of airing parenting episodes, which can result from the endless list of issues parents grapple with daily, the nanny TV parenting programme can include a question-and-answer portion to involve the viewers in solving their pressing issues immediately, or to add to the planned episodes.

Negotiation parenting[1]

Raising a child in today's complex world is ever more challenging for parents; if they are not knowledgeable, the child can become a brat. Parents have to contend not only with illness, education, and finance, but also with food, competition from peers, teaching and learning, and the cyberworld. Today's foods are full of artificial chemicals that can harm the growing body and brain. Competition from peers reduces good education places. A mismatch of the child's learning type to the teacher's instructional style likely leads to a school dropout. The influence of the high-tech cyberworld makes information available at the touch of a button but seems to be more of a distraction and an interference if not well managed.

Families worldwide generally adopt the small-family parenting model, with three or fewer children. Negotiation parenting uses knowledge from business, the culture and family, sciences (cognitive neuroscience, food science, and medical science), smart parenting styles, strength models, teaching and learning, philosophy, and psychotherapy to inform parents on the know-how needed to nurture today's children. Essentially, the parents negotiate the journey for the child before it is able to contribute physically and cognitively. As soon as the child is ready, the parents join him or her in negotiating the journey through the world of people, objects, designs, and systems that impinge on the child's growth and development. Parenting becomes colourful but fun and manageable as both parents and child take the mysterious journey that unfolds before them. The journey for each child, however, is different. Family and culture form the backbone for it.

Conclusion

Table 5.1 summarises the pros and cons of other parenting styles. As a parent, one could be baffled by the numerous parenting styles available in the literature and media. It is really a tough call on what is best for a child. Of course, any parent will go for the best style recommended for parenting. But as one's living situation is different from another's and each child is again different, the choice of which parenting style to adopt is not easy. No doubt authoritative parenting seems to be the better single form among them, but given parents' expectations and goals, coupled with the abilities of the child, authoritative parenting may not be the choice of all parents. For a better-informed view on parenting, do consult the next two chapters on comparing the existing parenting styles discussed and knowing your own parenting style.

There is a lengthy list of descriptions of various parenting styles in the media too for the curious reader: affectionless control parenting, attachment parenting, child-centred parenting, dolphin parenting, free-range parenting, gentle parenting, idle over-parenting, mindful parenting, narcissistic parenting, nurturant parenting, persuasive parenting, slow parenting, snowplough parenting, strength-based parenting, supportive parenting, and toxic parenting.

Table 5.1 Pros and cons of other parenting styles

Types of parenting	Pros	Cons
Tiger parenting: – A very strict or demanding and controlling form of parenting. – Considered extreme authoritarian parenting in the West.	Parent: – Tiger mum in particular. – Pressures children to attain high levels of academic achievement. Child: – Grows up with multiple skillsets. – Has made a habit out of being productive. – Experiences more interdependence and pressure from mothers, but pressure does not strain relationship. – Pressure from mothers may become an additional motivational resource child can draw on.	Parent: – Could be stressful having to keep close watch on children. – Tiger mothering diminishes as children grow older, whereas tiger fathering increases. Child: – Lack of independence, and self-determination. – Loss of childhood. – Likely takes setbacks a lot harsher than peers. – May not know how to deal with failures.
Helicopter parenting: – A style of upbringing in which an overprotective, over-involved, strict father or mother discourages a child's independence by being too involved in the child's life	Parent: – Uses directive behaviours and withholds autonomy-granting. – Strong on warmth, support, and control, but weak on granting autonomy. – Provides guidance and emotional support. Child: – Higher satisfaction and engagement with education. – Feels loved. – Receiving parental guidance, close	Parent: – Take responsibility for child's decisions and problems. – Having to keep close watch on child could be stressful. Child: – They are fulfilling their parents' dreams. – Has to resolve cognitive dissonance on the parenting situation or take the let-fate/faith-decide-for-me attitude. – Lower levels of independence, emotional

(*Continued*)

140 Other relevant parenting styles

Table 5.1 (Cont.)

Types of parenting	Pros	Cons
	monitoring, and support needed, especially during the teen years, and protection from making mistakes. – Develops good work ethics, makes right choices (e.g., choosing friends). – Has a safer and healthier lifestyle. – Will not experience scarcity, and has a sense of comfort. – Goes on to prestigious schools, and obtains a good professional career.	well-being, and effective coping skills, and higher levels of anxiety, depression, and child behavioural problems. – Lower self-efficacy. – May rebel against parents.
Positive parenting: – The continual relationship of parent and child that includes caring, teaching, leading, communicating, and providing for the needs of a child consistently and unconditionally.	Parent: – Warm and supportive. – Strengthens bond between parent and child. – Easier for child to understand. – Encourages communication. Child: – Develops into a happier, healthier adult. – Altruistic later in life.	Parent: – Can be difficult to grasp. – Needs good parent–child interaction skills. – If it is done incorrectly, child may lack guidance. – Difficult to deal with child's bad behaviour quickly. Child: – Assertive, conversational, and has social confidence. – May find it hard to deal with challenges.
Distal parenting: – About face-to-face contact and object stimulation.	Parent: – High responsiveness and demandingness.	Parent: – Difficult to manage wilful, adamant child.

(Continued)

Table 5.1 (Cont.)

Types of parenting	Pros	Cons
– Prevalent in urban educated middle-class families of Western cultures. – Related to early development of self-recognition.	– Warm, reasonable, and flexible. – Emphasises autonomy and separateness. Child: – Becomes responsible, self-reliant, self-controlled, explorative, content, and responsible. – Independent, high-achieving, friendly, and cooperative.	– More roles and responsibility (e.g., making and reviewing rules). Child: – May still feel parents are controlling, leading to low self-esteem.
Proximal parenting: – About bodily proximity and body stimulation. – Predominant in rural, low-educated farmer families. – Related to an early development of compliance.	Parent: – High responsiveness and high demandingness. – Controlling, directing, strict with standard of conduct. – Embodies relatedness, obedience, and hierarchy. – Assigns family responsibilities. – Reinforces closeness and warmth. Child: – Fulfils parent's demand and wishes.	Parent: – May be stressful having to maintain style. – Cannot really express love and care openly. Child: – Discontented. – Withdrawn. – Not much of choice in life. – Low in social responsibility and competencies. – High in social assertiveness.
Nordic model: – Romanticisation of children as self-absorbed and self-gratifying.	Parent: – Empathises with child's wishes and psychic needs and aims to constrain and inhibit them as little as possible.	Parent: – Might be anxious if other children are better trained earlier. – How to manage out-of-control child?

(Continued)

Table 5.1 (Cont.)

Types of parenting	Pros	Cons
(Note: The model is propped up by a capitalist economy that encourages creative destruction. While the laws make it easy for companies to shed workers and implement transformative business models, employees are supported by generous social welfare programmes.)	– Uses persuasion and forbids spanking or other disciplinary practices. – Ban on corporal punishment. Child: – Remains in a play-oriented day-care setting, exposed to no formal learning, until they start school at age 7.	Child: – Will he or she lose out in some formal education?
Harsh parenting: – Coercive parenting tactics, from frequent use of corporal punishment to escalated physical abuse and cruelty.	Parent: – Corporal punishment is seen as necessary, and a positive practice to produce good citizens. – Verbal and physical coercive tactics applied on a regular basis. Child: – Obedient and conforming. – Learns self-control. – May be high-achieving.	Parent: – Seen as authoritarian, if not cruel to child. – Hard to distinguish abuser from punisher. – Needs to be role model first. Child: – May be passive-aggressive. – May lie to look good or right. – Low self-esteem. – May have mental health issues.
Mobile parenting: – Use of mobile phone and tablets with children.	Parent: – Can continue to do tasks while keeping children busy. – Can use phone/tablet to track child.	Parent: – Needs to spend on buying and maintaining electronic devices. – Needs to be computer-savvy too.

(Continued)

Table 5.1 (Cont.)

Types of parenting	Pros	Cons
	Child: – Becomes tech-savvy early.	Child: – May be addicted. – Uncertain information on health problems related to use of electronic devices (e.g., eyesight, posture). – May be bad for hand-writing and craft work.
Nanny TV parenting: – Teaching parenting through TV series.	Parent: – Gains a role model from programme. Child: – Gains a role model from programme.	Family: – It is not yet interactive for the family. – Cannot be dependent on it for life. – May produce couch potatoes.
Negotiation parenting: – Use knowledge from business, culture, family, sciences (cognitive neuroscience, food science, and medical science), smart parenting styles, strength models, teaching and learning, philosophy, and psychotherapy to inform parents regarding the know-how needed to nurture today's children.	Parent: – Authoritative parenting with skills. Child: – More of an all-rounder. – Can be good negotiator?	Parent: – Needs knowledge and skills in many areas. Child: – Overwhelmed by knowledge?

Note

1 Based on Foo (2015).

References

Arranz Freijo, E. B., & Rodrigo López, M. J. (2018). Positive parenting in Spain: Introduction to the special issue. *Early Child Development and Care, 188*(11), 1502–1512. doi: 10.1080/03004430.2018.1501565.

Awan, N., & Butterworth, R. (2017). Positive parenting. *Community Practitioner: The Journal of the Community Practitioners' & Health Visitors' Association, 90*(4), 38.

Bartholomeu, D., Montiel, J. M., Fiamenghi, G. A., & Machado, A. A. (2016). Predictive power of parenting styles on children's social skills: A Brazilian sample. *SAGE Open, 6*(2). doi: 10.1177/2158244016638393.

Baumrind, D. (1997). The discipline encounter: Contemporary issues. *Aggression and Violent Behavior, 2*(4), 321–335. doi: 10.1016/S1359-1789(97)00018-9.

Bradley-Geist, J. C., & Olson-Buchanan, J. (2014). Helicopter parents: An examination of the correlates of over-parenting of college students. *Education + Training, 56*(4), 314–328. doi: 10.1108/ET-10-2012-0096.

Burroughs, B. (2017). YouTube Kids: The app economy and mobile parenting. *Social Media + Society, 3*(2). doi: 10.1177/2056305117707189.

Dahlstedt, M., & Fejes, A. (2014). Family makeover: Coaching, confession and parental responsibilisation. *Pedagogy, Culture and Society, 22*(2), 169–188. doi: 10.1080/14681366.2013.812136.

Darlow, V., Norvilitis, J. M., & Schuetze, P. (2017). The relationship between helicopter parenting and adjustment to college. *Journal of Child and Family Studies, 26*(8), 2291–2298. doi: 10.1007/s10826-017-0751-3.

Elstad, J. I., & Stefansen, K. (2014). Social variations in perceived parenting styles among Norwegian adolescents. *Child Indicators Research, 7*(3), 649–670. doi: 10.1007/s12187-014-9239-5.

Foo, K. H. (2015). *Negotiation parenting: How not to raise a brat in today's complex world.* Singapore: Marshall Cavendish.

Frías-Armenta, M., & McCloskey, L. A. (1998). Determinants of harsh parenting in Mexico. *Journal of Abnormal Child Psychology, 26*(2), 129–139. doi: 10.1023/A:1022621922331.

Fu, A. S., & Markus, H. R. (2014). My mother and me: Why tiger mothers motivate Asian Americans but not European Americans. *Personality and Social Psychology Bulletin, 40*(6), 739–749. doi: 10.1177/0146167214524992.

Gomes, S. B., & Deuling, J. K. (2019). Family influence mediates the relation between helicopter-parenting and millennial work attitudes. *Journal of Managerial Psychology, 34*(1), 2–17. doi: 10.1108/JMP-12-2017-0450.

Keller, H., Borke, J., Staufenbiel, T., Yovsi, R. D., Abels, M., Papaligoura, Z., ... Su, Y. (2009). Distal and proximal parenting as alternative parenting strategies during infants' early months of life: A cross-cultural study. *International Journal of Behavioral Development, 33*(5), 412–420. doi: 10.1177/0165025409338441.

Kim, S. Y. (2013). Defining tiger parenting in Chinese Americans. *Human Development*, *56*(4), 217–222. doi: 10.1159/000353711.
Kwon, K., Yoo, G., & De Gagne, J. C. (2017). Does culture matter? A qualitative inquiry of helicopter parenting in Korean American college students. *Journal of Child and Family Studies*, *26*(7), 1979–1990. doi: 10.1007/s10826-017-0694-8.
Lee, J., & Kang, S. (2018). Perceived helicopter parenting and Korean emerging adults' psychological adjustment: The mediational role of parent–child affection and pressure from parental career expectations. *Journal of Child and Family Studies*, *27*(11), 3672–3686. doi: 10.1007/s10826-018-1193-2.
Pastorelli, C., Lansford, J. E., Luengo Kanacri, B. P., Malone, P. S., Di Giunta, L., Bacchini, D., ... Sorbring, E. (2016). Positive parenting and children's prosocial behavior in eight countries. *Journal of Child Psychology and Psychiatry*, *57*(7), 824–834. doi: 10.1111/jcpp.12477.
Seay, A., Freysteinson, W. M., & McFarlane, J. (2014). Positive parenting. *Nursing Forum*, *49*(3), 200–208. doi: 10.1111/nuf.12093.
Trueland, J. (2012). Positive parenting. *Nursing Standard (Through 2013)*, *26*(47), 18–19.
Waller, R., Gardner, F., Hyde, L. W., Shaw, D. S., Dishion, T. J., & Wilson, M. N. (2012). Do harsh and positive parenting predict parent reports of deceitful-callous behavior in early childhood? *Journal of Child Psychology and Psychiatry*, *53*(9), 946–953. doi: 10.1111/j.1469-7610.2012.02550.x.
Whittle, S., Simmons, J. G., Dennison, M., Vijayakumar, N., Schwartz, O., Yap, M. B. H., ... Allen, N. B. (2014). Positive parenting predicts the development of adolescent brain structure: A longitudinal study. *Developmental Cognitive Neuroscience*, *8*, 7–17. doi: 10.1016/j.dcn.2013.10.006.

Comparing parenting styles 6

Chapters 3 and 4 look at the major parenting styles from the East and West available on social media and in literature, formally and informally. Chapter 5 includes some up-and-coming parenting styles that need to be substantiated by research evidence. This chapter seeks to compare some of the Eastern and Western parenting styles that have been studied in research to give the reader an idea of which is more suitable for his or her child.

This is a difficult topic to present as the number of studies comparing parenting styles is large, and the comparisons are across different styles, racial/ethnic groups, and countries, using different parameters, variables, and methods. I will try to summarise the select few and group them accordingly for understanding and discussion.

A little theory on attribution serves to organise the thoughts for this chapter. After which, comparisons of Western and Eastern parenting styles are presented, with their outcomes.[1] Each outcome has a heading (for example, "Parental love"); its context, with evidence from related studies; and a learning comment. To broaden the comparison, parenting styles as perceived by parents and children are included. A little twist to the chapter involves snippets on immigrant parenting, consequences of punishment, and young versus older parents. This chapter attempts to consider the compatibility of Western and Eastern parenting styles.

First of all, let us touch on the topic of attribution, which is often used in explaining parenting and many other human behaviours. Simply put, attribution is the act of regarding something as being caused by a person or thing. A lot of blame in parenting is attributable.

Attribution

An interesting study (Poasa, Mallinckrodt, & Suzuki, 2000) discussed attribution in individualistic and collectivistic cultures. Remarkably, two assumptions of Western studies in attribution could be flawed when applied to collective cultures: one, that people have a need to judge themselves favourably; and two, that positive self-image and self-esteem are derived from attributions related to the individual self. Thus, in Western cultures, people enthusiastically accept acclamation when told they have succeeded (attributing success to their ability and effort), but nonetheless would attribute failure to external factors such as bad luck or the difficulty of the task. In Eastern cultures, mutual support and effort towards group goals are more important than individual achievements. For example, university students from India, South Africa, the US, and Yugoslavia tend to take more responsibility for success than failure, and attribute success to their own efforts (Poasa, Mallinckrodt, & Suzuki, 2000). Japanese students would have the most internal attributions for failure, and few internal attributions for success. In general, people from collectivistic cultures tend to give more attribution to external factors for both positive and negative events.

Attributional bias also functions at the group level (Poasa, Mallinckrodt, & Suzuki, 2000). Losers of competitions tend to attribute their opponents' success to causes internal to the opponents, whereas winners would attribute their opponent's failures to causes external to those opponents. Winning Asians (Easterners) would attribute their success mainly to luck and only slightly to their ability, whereas in losing they attribute their failure mostly to their ability and only slightly to luck. This pattern is the opposite to that found in the US (Westerners), in which the failure of one's opponent is attributed to traits of the opponent, whereas the success of one's opponent is attributed to external factors. Asians' attribution patterns may come from a motivation to enhance an opponent's self-esteem in the case of success, and protect an opponent's self-esteem in the case of failure.

For members of collective cultures, personal opinions and attributes are likely to be situation-specific, and are less likely to regulate behaviour across situations than for members of individualistic cultures, especially if the behaviour has an effect on others. In contrast to the values of self-expression and self-disclosure in individualistic cultures, voluntary control of the self is the essence of what constitutes maturity in collective cultures.

Now that you have an idea of how people make attributions—frequently without sufficient evidence but on gut feeling and general belief—let us move on to some select outcomes of parenting.

Select outcomes of parenting

Some significant outcomes of parenting, desirable or undesirable, are discussed next. Each is given a heading or grouped under a heading for ease of consumption.

Acceptance and rejection of children

One of the measures of parenting, or, should I say, one of the ways in which parents care about their children, is accepting or rejecting them. As parents naturally love their children with warmth, acceptance is the word. At the same time, parents may reject their children for reason of disability, because of a disordered mind, or depending on their situation.

A study (Schwartz et al., 2009) investigated an ethnically diverse sample of 1,728 college students in schools in the Northeast, Southeast, Midwest, West, and Southwest of the US regarding the association of perceived parenting with health-risk behaviours. The results show that college students' feelings that they are accepted by their parents (especially their fathers) as adolescents appear to be strongly protective against health-risk behaviours. These behaviours include illicit drug use (marijuana, hard drugs, and inhalants, and misusing prescription drugs), casual sex, driving under the influence of alcohol or drugs, and riding with a driver who has been drinking or using drugs. Notably, perceived acceptance from fathers makes a considerable unique contribution to many of the health-risk behaviours, way above any acceptance by mothers (which only influences sex-related behaviour).

Another study in Voorschoten, Netherlands (Muris, Meesters, Merckelbach, & Hülsenbeck, 2000), investigated 159 primary school children concering the relationship between perceived parental rearing behaviours, attachment style, and worry. The results show that children who perceived their parents as more rejecting of them and anxious reported higher levels of worry. Furthermore, self-reported attachment style appeared to be related to worry. Specifically, children who referred to themselves as avoidantly or ambivalently attached displayed higher levels of worry than did children who referred themselves as securely attached.

Another study (Putnick et al., 2012) assessed 998 families in 10 communities in nine countries (China, Colombia, Italy, Jordan, Kenya, Philippines, Sweden, Thailand, and the US) on whether parental reports of acceptance/rejection, warmth, and hostility/rejection/neglect of their preadolescent children differed cross-nationally, and relative to the sex of the parent and child. Parents from countries where an authoritative parenting style predominates (e.g., Italy, Sweden, and the US) are expected to be more accepting and warmer than parents from countries where a more authoritarian parenting style is more common (e.g., China, Jordan, Kenya, the Philippines, and Thailand). Parents from countries that stress obedience and conformity in children (e.g., China, Jordan, and Kenya) are expected to score lower on acceptance and higher on hostility/rejection/neglect than parents from countries that stress child agency and children's rights (e.g., Italy, Sweden, and the US).

The results show that both parents in all countries reported a high degree of acceptance and warmth, and a low degree of hostility/rejection/neglect, with some variation. Greater acceptance of children came from mothers than fathers in China, Italy, Sweden, and the US. Greater warmth came from mothers than fathers in China, Italy, Philippines, Sweden, and Thailand. Greater warmth came from fathers than mothers in Kenya. Analysis in detail by country from the study (Putnick et al., 2012) is mentioned next.

China

Chinese parents rated themselves as low in acceptance and warmth (with higher ratings from mothers) and high in hostility/rejection/neglect. In the socialisation of Chinese children, preschool children are parented in a lenient, indulgent manner by their mothers, whereas school-aged children are controlled and disciplined because of pressure from academic competition beginning from primary schools. Chinese parents exercise strong parental control, especially in the academic domain, while parenting attitudes in urban China are more progressive than authoritarian. In Chinese parenting, warmth and control are expressed more via material and physical means than psychological or affective expressions. The period of childhood covered in the present study (7–10 years) may be characterised by relatively less parental warmth and more hostility/rejection/neglect because parenting at this age started to focus on academic issues (Putnick et al., 2012, pp. 206–207).

Colombia

Colombian parents rated themselves as high in acceptance and warmth, and low in hostility/rejection/neglect. Colombia is a collectivist culture where authoritarian parenting predominates, and where sex roles influence parenting (i.e., traditionally fathers are the economic providers and mothers are the primary source of care for the entire family, with the responsibility for rearing younger children). However, contemporary Colombian parents are holding more progressive views. In the past 20 years, women's increased participation in the work force and high levels of education, and men's increasing participation with their children, may have led to more authoritative parenting styles. Both mothers and fathers rate their parenting role more positively than their work and marital roles, indicating a strong focus on parenting (Putnick et al., 2012, p. 207).

Italy

Italian parents rated themselves as high in acceptance (with mothers higher than fathers), mothers rated themselves as high in warmth (higher than fathers), and both parents rated themselves as low in hostility/rejection/neglect. The Italian paternal style is considered to be strict and authoritarian, with the maternal style as exceedingly warm, protective, and family focused. Italian parents place importance on children's emerging social skills and on dyadic affect-laden exchanges in which parents and children can experience physical and emotional closeness, warmth, and security. Similarly, Italian mothers believe the key task for them is to care for their children and rear them in a safe and protective family environment (Putnick et al., 2012, pp. 206–207).

Jordan

Jordanian mothers rated themselves as low in warmth, and both parents rated themselves as low in acceptance and high in hostility/rejection/neglect. Honesty, politeness, good habits, respecting elders, and obedience are valued by Jordanian mothers for instilling in their children. Traditionally, the Muslim view is for the child to be protected and cherished, and in return, the child is expected to be obedient and subject his or her will to the parents (Putnick et al., 2012, p. 208).

Kenya

Kenyan parents rated themselves as low in acceptance and warmth and high in hostility/rejection/neglect. This is one country where fathers rated their warmth higher than mothers. Kenyan parents have different parenting responsibilities. Mothers are responsible for all aspects of childrearing. They may report lower warmth with children because they are handling the most challenging aspects of childrearing. Notably, public displays of affection are viewed by parents as ineffective parenting techniques that could make good children disobedient. Therefore, Kenyan parents display their affection by giving tangible benefits such as extra food, material goods, and privileges. Hence, the lower level of warmth found in Kenyan mothers could be because they may be expressing their love and affection for their children in different ways (Putnick et al., 2012, pp. 208–209).

Philippines

Filipino parents rated themselves as high in warmth (with mothers higher than fathers), and average in total acceptance/rejection and hostility/rejection/neglect. Filipino parents are strongly family-oriented, and, in general, childrearing among them is affectionate, indulgent, and supportive, in spite of the high expectations for children to obey parental authority. Other research has found that from Filipino children's viewpoint, their mothers are more nurturant and involved than their fathers (Carunungan-Robles, 1986). Mothers also give directives and organise children's activities more than fathers, but children did not perceive differences in discipline between their parents (Putnick et al., 2012, p. 209).

Sweden

Swedish parents rated themselves as high in acceptance and warmth (with mothers higher than fathers), and mothers rated themselves as low in hostility/rejection/neglect (and lower than fathers). Although Swedish progressive parenting attitudes are equal between couples, they still adopt traditional roles in the family. This explains why Swedish mothers are warmer and display less hostility/rejection/neglect than fathers. Sweden's social structure respects equal rights between adults and children, and promotes sex equality—for example, its laws provide similar childcare benefits to mothers and fathers (such as paid time off from work following childbirth) (Putnick et al., 2012, pp. 209–210).

Thailand

Thai parents rated themselves average in all ways, and mothers rated themselves as low in warmth (but warmer than fathers). Thai families are traditionally hierarchical, with children encouraged to be compliant and obedient. Thai fathers tend to be less involved in childcare, and mothers discipline their children more. Furthermore, Thai women have total power for decision making about children. Perhaps having this power and the responsibility that comes with it leads mothers to feel somewhat less warm with their children. Notably, some Thai parents are more progressive than authoritarian in parenting attitudes (Putnick et al., 2012, p. 210).

The US

US parents rated themselves as high in warmth, low in hostility/rejection/neglect, and high in acceptance (with mothers more accepting than fathers). Generally, parents in the US are progressive in their parenting attitudes, with mothers committing high levels of investment in the parental role (Putnick et al., 2012, p. 210).

Learning: Overall, the researchers of these studies contend that acceptance of one's child is a cornerstone of adaptive and positive parenting. Rejection may lead to health-risky behaviours and worrying in children. Interestingly, acceptance and rejection are opposite poles, yet they can occur together.

Anxiety in children

Another frequently studied issue is anxiety in children brought about by undesirable parenting. Anxiety is one of the significant mental health issues in our life, with many causes, and affects us to varying degrees, whether singly or with other psychological or organic disorders. Anxiety caused by parenting stays with us for a long time.

A study (Mousavi, Low, & Hashim, 2016) examined 227 students (13–18 years of age and from Arab, Caucasian, Chinese, Indian, and Malay cultures) regarding the relationship between perceived parenting style and their anxiety. The results show that Malay and Chinese students reported the highest level of anxiety, whereas Indian and Caucasian students reported the lowest level. On emotional warmth, Chinese students were lowest and Caucasian students highest. On over-controlling/protection, Arab students were highest and Caucasian students lowest. Social phobia was the most common type of anxiety among the students. Thus, parental rejection, anxious childrearing, and control/overprotection are correlated with higher anxiety irrespective of cultural group, but these associations are stronger for Caucasian students.

Possible explanations are that: Chinese parents express less emotional warmth and are less accepting of their children's ideas; Malay parents are likely to encourage anxious cognitions and avoidance behaviours in relation to their children (anxious childrearing) and be more judgemental and critical (high rejection) compared with others; and Arab parents are likely to be overprotective and obsessed about the safety of their children, thus displaying emotional warmth and intimacy more directly. Parental warmth may neutralise the negative effect of high parental control. Parental overprotection may be interpreted by the students as expressions of care, concern, and parental love; but it leads to vulnerability to anxiety symptoms.

Learning: Parenting styles as predictors of anxiety are cross-culturally different. The elevation of anxiety symptoms in adolescents might be due to negative parenting behaviours such as greater rejection, anxious childrearing, and less direct expression of emotional warmth (similar to authoritarian parenting) by their parents. Another study (Segrin, Woszidlo, Givertz, & Montgomery, 2013) shows that parental anxiety is positively associated with overparenting, and that parental regret has an indirect effect on overparenting through greater anxiety. Thus negative parenting behaviour produces negative outcomes in children;

apparently, this effect is strongest in Western cultures. Social phobia scores are high as social anxiety symptoms increase in the adolescence period due to the developmental characteristics and changes of this period, in which adolescents tend to be emotionally separate from their parents and become more peer-focused. Consequently, uncertainty about the future, fear of rejection, and existing peer group pressure in adolescence may lead to social anxiety.

Child effortful control

Among the constructs of self-control is self-regulation, which is management of one's thoughts, behaviours, and actions before they are seen openly. It is very important for a child to learn self-regulation with proper understanding, learning, and practice; otherwise, many a child will get into hot water sooner or later in life.

A study (Huang, Cheah, Lamb, & Zhou, 2017) examined the associations between parenting styles and parentally perceived child effortful control (that is, higher-order control for self-regulation) of over 100 Chinese mothers from the UK, the US, and Taiwan. The results show that, generally, mothers used more Chinese-specific parenting with older children. Taiwanese mothers used more authoritarian parenting than US Chinese mothers. Perceived child effortful control is positively linked to Chinese-specific parenting in the US Chinese mothers. It is positively linked to authoritarian parenting in the UK Chinese mothers, and is positively associated with Taiwanese mothers' use of authoritative parenting. First-generation Chinese immigrant mothers in the US would like to maintain parenting beliefs and practices from their heritage culture (for example, a focus on education) while adjusting to and incorporating parenting practices endorsed by the larger societal context (for example, decreasing coercive practices and increasing autonomy-promoting practices).

Learning: Different parenting styles seem to produce the same result in child effortful control.

Compliant children

Parents would definitely like to have obedient children, which makes nurturing easier. Occasionally, parents may consider obedient children unintelligent if they are not lively and active. Well, parenting is a two-way phenomenon. No doubt parents initiate the moves in the first few years because of the lack of verbal communicative language from the child. But we know that children shape their developmental paths, and their temperaments moderate the relationship between parenting practices and compliance.

A study (Huang & Lamb, 2014) compared mothers (30 Chinese in Taiwan, and 30 Chinese immigrants and 29 non-immigrant white English in the UK) and their 5- to 7-year-old children regarding maternal control of children's compliance. Compliance is initially maintained externally by parental requests and directives, and is increasingly facilitated by internal factors as children mature. The responsibility for regulating children's behaviour gradually shifts to the children themselves with parents increasingly assuming the role of distant monitors. Three dimensions of temperament are surgency, negative affectivity, and effortful control. Children high in surgency tend to be active, impulsive pleasure seekers. Children high in negative affectivity tend to experience more negative emotions (such as sadness, fear, anger, and frustration), and they are less easily soothed when distressed. Children high in effortful control display more attentional and inhibitory control, and are likely to be vigilant. Notably, Chinese culture emphasises compliance more emphatically than do Western cultures, and Chinese children are also taught to comply with authority from a very young age. Compliance is a significant predictor of children's later social adaptation and maladaptation.

The results of the study show that the English mothers used less negative control and were more responsive than the Chinese immigrant mothers, and that the English mothers also showed more positive affect than both the Chinese immigrant and Taiwanese mothers. The Taiwanese children showed more situational compliance than the Chinese immigrant children. Committed compliance, moderated by surgency, appeared to increase as children grew older and was negatively influenced by maternal negative control. In an Etch-a-Sketch task, noncompliance was accounted for by the child's age and temperament, whereas opposition in a clean-up task was associated with maternal use of force. Situational compliance could be predicted by the child's age, temperament, and cultural group, and maternal control.

Another study in the US (Vuk, 2017) examined 5,935 eighth-grade students regarding parenting styles and gang membership. The results show that the authoritative parenting style is a healthy style which reduces the likelihood of gang involvement, whereas authoritarian, permissive, and neglectful styles are pathological parenting styles that increase the likelihood of participation in a gang by students. High levels of demandingness and responsiveness in authoritative parenting promote healthy emotional and behavioural responses in children, meaning that these children will manage their daily tasks and issues utilising prosocial coping mechanisms, rather than problem behaviours such as drug use or delinquency. Poor parenting leads to more opportunities for association with delinquent peers as such parenting either lacks supervision, which increases the opportunities to associate with delinquent peers, or it lacks emotional bonding, so children escape the rigid and cold family environment by associating with peers.

Learning: Parents and children shape one another's attitudes and behaviours, inter alia.

Children's behaviour could be shaped by rewards externally and internally; it is better if they are able to internalise their actions to go with their temperament. Parental control may be handy but when used negatively it turns children off regarding compliance and internalisation. Poor parenting may lead to delinquency or gang membership by children.

Homework

A study in the US (Cooper, Lindsay, & Nye, 2000) surveyed 709 student–parent pairs about parental involvement in their child's homework. Three dimensions of homework involvement are autonomy support, direct involvement, and elimination of distractions. A fourth dimension, parental interference, differentiated itself from autonomy support for students in higher grades. The results show that parents with students in higher grade levels reported giving students more homework autonomy and less involvement of all other types. Parents in poorer families reported less support for autonomy and more interference. Parents reported less elimination of distractions when an adult was not at home after school and, for elementary school students, when there was more than one child living in the home. Parents of elementary school males reported more direct involvement in homework, while parents of high school females reported more direct involvement. More parental support for autonomy was linked with higher standardised test scores, higher class grades, and more homework being completed. More positive parent involvement was linked with lower test scores and lower class grades, especially for elementary school students. Student attitudes towards homework were unrelated to parenting style for homework.

Learning: Seemingly, specific parental participation in a child's homework is crucial in the outcome of the child's academic performance. Supportive involvement, removal of distractions, and granting of autonomy are better than direct involvement and interference from parents.

Maternal parenting stress

Having a child when ready and desired is a blissful yet stressful episode in life. The blissful part is to see a life procreated, growing, and flourishing. But this journey is never smooth. Undesirable issues encountered include injuries and sickness, even death. Worrying issues include the child's whereabouts, safety, and friends. The list is endless as long as the parents care about the child. In all, parenting is stressful too.

A longitudinal study (Nomaguchi & House, 2013) investigated 11,324 children, their primary parents, teachers, and school administrators about racial/ethnic differences in maternal parenting stress during a child's early elementary school years. Parenting stress is a sense of difficulty experienced in the parenting role because the demands associated with the parenting role exceed the resources available to meet those demands. It is expected that parents with structural disadvantages (such as being a young parent, having more children, single-parenthood, a lower income, a lower education) and those from an authoritarian parenting style are more stressed. Because authoritarian mothers are less tolerant of children's disrespectful behaviour, they are more likely to have more frequent conflict with their children, which is a major source of parenting stress. This study is important because parenting stress has negative consequences for the quality of parenting and the well-being of children.

Results of the study are divided into three parts. First, in kindergarten, US-born black mothers, foreign-born Hispanic mothers, and foreign-born Asian mothers report higher levels of parenting stress than US-born white mothers due to structural disadvantages and authoritarian parenting values. Despite structural disadvantages, American Indian mothers report less stress—this is not explained, but I suspect it is their cultural beliefs, values, and customs that make a difference. Second, the black–white gap increases from kindergarten to third grade, and in third grade US-born black mothers' higher stress than white mothers' persists. As children get older and are able to understand the social meaning of race/ethnicity, black mothers are more likely than others to be concerned about their children's encounters with racial/ethnic prejudice and discrimination; thus the higher stress level. Third, foreign-born Hispanic and Asian mothers report more stress than white mothers at both ages due to structural disadvantages and authoritarian values.

Learning: Parents better be of adult age; have children within their means; be married in an intact family; have a good, steady source of income; and be better educated. Adopting the authoritarian parenting style may stress the parents out, if not well managed.

Parental love

This is one interesting aspect of parenting. Parental love is natural for parents to radiate through and with their children. But if used conditionally, it is a weapon for the parents. The consequence can be imagined and it may run a long way through the child's life.

A mixed-method study (McNeely & Barber, 2010) examined several thousand adolescents aged 14 to 17 regarding perception of parental behaviours. This study used the Cross-National Adolescent Project, which consisted of urban centres in Africa (black, coloured, and white samples in Cape Town, South Africa), Australia (Adelaide), Asia (Dhakka, Bangladesh; Beijing, China; Bangalore, India), the Balkans (Sarejevo, Bosnia), Europe (Darmstadt, Germany), the Middle East (Gaza, Palestine), North America (Ogden, Utah, in the US), and South America (Bogotá, Colombia). The results show that adolescents in all 12 settings confirmed supportive parenting behaviours, which included providing comfort, attention, physical affection, companionship, help, and money and things, both desired and needed. Though the proportion of adolescents naming these behaviours varied across the sites, they were perceived as loving by adolescents. Notably, when parents provide a rare and valued commodity, it is perceived as love. Varying across cultures were parental quality time, basic necessities, and support for education. Adolescents also extended the list of parental behaviours that made them feel loved, including moral guidance and advice.

Learning: Supportive parenting is a desired style. Love between parents and children comes in many forms, particularly when a valued thing desired by the adolescent is given by the parent.

Parenting styles perceived by parents

The following discussion looks at parenting as seen by parents, a normal phenomenon, as parents often perceive that they are right and proper in raising their children, according to the children's growth and behaviour.

A study (Bornstein et al., 1996) investigated 102 mothers (36 Argentine, 25 French, and 41 American) about their perception of parenting regarding social interactions, didactic interactions, and limit setting. All mothers came from urban Western settings. Argentine culture adopts the authoritarian style, directing the child to behave positively and stressing dependency and obedience. French culture emphasises cognitive stimulation, emotional support, and psycho-affective security. US culture places values on individual achievement, self-confidence, and autonomy in children, and gives weight to innate ability. The results show that all mothers perceived they were more sensitive to and stimulating of their children than their husbands. Both parents set limits on their children. US mothers rated themselves as more sensitive, affectionate, and didactic than Argentine and French mothers; their actual and ideal behaviours were close. French mothers considered the cognitive stimulation their husbands provided closer to their ideal than Argentine and US mothers.

Learning: The home environment reflects culture in terms of values, beliefs, and customs. Notably, parents' ideas are just one factor that mediates parenting behaviours and adjustment, and exerts direct and indirect effects on children's development.

Another study (Keller et al., 2005) investigated the parenting styles (specifically, early social experiences of infants between 2.5 and 3 months) among two agricultural societies, Indian Rajput and Cameroonian Nso, and German urban middle-class families. A similarity between the Rajputs and Nso is that their parenting pattern supports the development of cooperation and relational harmony. The differences between the two agrarian communities are related to emotional expressivity (e.g., caressing) and health status. The German caregiving pattern is towards the development of agency. Analysis in detail by country from the study is mentioned next.

Nandesari, Gujarati, India

The Rajputs have low socio-economic status here. Healthcare for women is provided by traditional birth attendants or government-trained staff. Families are nuclear or joint families. Nuclear families do have relatives living in the same compound or close by. Women's daily chores in the patrilocal households include fetching water, caring for cattle, preparing meals, washing clothes, and cleaning the house. The youngest daughter-in-law of the family is assigned work by her mother-in-law and elder sisters-in-law. For her first delivery, a woman returns to her family of origin to be cared for by her mother and free from household obligations. Otherwise, women work in the fields. During daily routines, the mother either leaves the child in somebody's care or takes him or her to the field, where he or she is cloth-cradled in the shade. Beliefs are in fate, horoscopes, and destiny. Socialisation of children is in the patriarchal joint family system. Social values and beliefs concerning the Hindu family in India are exemplified in Sanskrit texts—absolute moral authority of parents over children, that is, the duty of children towards complete conformity and obedience to parents. The mother's love for her child is not for public display and remains invisible to outsiders. The presence of a new baby is not the focus of attention, as too much attention would spoil the child. Indian Hindu culture celebrates special ceremonies at 3 months, in which the baby is exposed to the sun and the moon for the first time (Keller et al., 2005, 517–518).

Kikaikelaki, Cameroon

Rural Nso villages here are steered by ancient values, norms, customs, and conventions that are based on Catholicism, Protestantism, and Islam. Most women deliver their babies at the local health centre with the help of a nurse or a traditional birth attendant, whereas some go to the large American-run hospital. Most households are monogamous other than ranked persons with traditional titles, who are polygamous. Close contact is maintained with relatives and neighbours living in the same lineage or family land. Subsistence is through communal efforts and endeavours by family members, with farming being the responsibility of women. Men bring home the produce from the distant farms, and some weave, carve and fabricate furniture from local bamboo, and tap palm wine. The aim of childrearing is to inculcate the moral values of obedience, respect for authority, and conformity to the group. The child is regarded as the reincarnation of a deceased ancestor and a gift from God; infants' expressive behaviours (such as giggling or body movements) are messages from ancestors. Socialisation of children in accepting responsibility, commitment, and involvement for the communal good such as harmony and group stability is entrenched in expressive interactional exchanges. Mothers have primary responsibility for childcare. They only leave young infants with female elder siblings or relatives to perform household chores. Women return to work on the farm when the baby is 3 months of age. The infants are then left in a bowl at the edge of the field or with a young caregiver to be within hearing distance of the mother, who will react immediately to the needs of the infant (Keller et al., 2005, pp. 515–517).

Osnabrueck, Saxony, Germany

Here, both parents are highly educated and pursue independent careers before having children. After childbirth, women have a paid two-month maternity leave, which most extend to one year unpaid. Few fathers take paternity leave. Fathers work outside the home, earning money for the family income; the practical chores of childcare are done by mothers. Healthcare is fully covered by the social security system. Infants are expected to spend time alone or entertain themselves with toys in order to give the mother some free time for herself. Caregivers are hard to come by because relatives do not live in the neighbourhood and baby sitters have to be paid. Independence from the parent is thus the major socialisation goal of infancy. In German middle-class families, 3 months of age represents a pivotal developmental phase. Parent–infant interactions are characterised by a peak in mutual eye contact, an early outcome in relational development. Infants are expected to reach the first steps of autonomy at this time, including sleeping through the night and the establishment of a mature circadian rhythm (Keller et al., 2005, pp. 518–519).

Another study (Atzaba-Poria & Pike, 2008) examined 125 families (59 English and 66 of Indian origin in Great Britain) regarding the relations between child characteristics, contextual factors, and mothering and fathering. The results show that children's negative emotionality is positively linked to parental use of harsh discipline, and negatively linked to parental warmth. Mothers tend to be warmer to girls than to boys. At the contextual level, socio-economic status is positively linked to parental warmth, and marital relationship quality is negatively associated with maternal and paternal use of discipline. Raised levels of negative job spill-over and lower socio-economic status are linked to increased use of harsh discipline only for the English fathers, whereas paternal marital satisfaction is negatively related to paternal use of discipline only for the Indian fathers.

Learning: This study focused on middle childhood, as by age 7 children are aware of their ethnicity, and still within the bounds of the family home. Notably, a child's temperament and the context of marital relations of the parents (socio-economic status and quality of marriage) have great influence on parenting, as alluded to in Chapter 1.

Another study (Li, Costanzo, & Putallaz, 2010) compared 137 college students (79 Chinese college students from a university in Northern China, and 58 European American college students from a university in the southeastern United States) on the associations among perceived maternal parenting styles (authoritative, authoritarian, and training), perceived maternal socialisation goals (self-development, filial piety, and collectivism), and the social-emotional adjustment (self-esteem, academic self-efficacy, and depression). The results show that European American students perceived more maternal self-development socialisation goals, whereas Chinese students perceived more maternal collectivism socialisation goals and authoritarian parenting. Both groups were similar in the associations between perceived maternal authoritative parenting and socio-emotional adjustment (e.g., higher self-esteem and higher academic self-efficacy). However, perceived maternal authoritarian and training parenting styles were related to Chinese students' adjustment (e.g., more academic self-efficacy and less depression). Furthermore, authoritative parenting mediates the positive links between the self-development, collectivism goals, and socio-emotional adjustment for both groups. And training parenting mediates the positive link between the filial piety goal and students' academic self-efficacy for the Chinese students.

Another study (Graf, Röder, Hein, Müller, & Ganzorig, 2014) compared 120 parents (40 immigrant Mongolian parents in Germany, 40 Mongolians in their native country, and 40 German parents) on parenting practices and socialisation goals in a cultural context. The results show that regarding parenting, Germans use less corporal punishment and monitor the activities of children more closely than both Mongolian groups, whereas power assertion is used less by Mongolians in their native culture than

Mongolians and Germans in Germany. However, Mongolians in Germany rated socialisation goals more similarly to Germans than Mongolians in their native culture, indicating a change under new cultural influences.

In Germany, most people are Christians. Their main cultural context is independence, and less value is placed on obedience. German parents direct their parenting behaviours towards the development of self-regulation and autonomy, starting from infancy. For example, parents encourage their children to sleep in a separate room on their own, they communicate with their children about decisions, and they use non-impulsive parenting behaviour (Graf, et al., 2014, p. 1318).

In Mongolia, most people live in urban areas and the most widespread religion is Buddhism. Modern Mongolian culture is autonomous, in which educated middle-class families live in a society with interrelated cultural heritage. The family is important for Mongolians. They bring their tent-living nuclear family to the cities. Mongolian parents adopt the authoritarian stance towards their children, which emphasises respect towards elders and obedience. Mongolian children are confronted with physical force and use of corporal punishment by their parents, which is perceived as acceptable parenting behaviour (Graf, et al., 2014, pp. 1318–1319).

Overall, as expected, parenting styles, goals, and outcomes go generally according to Eastern or Western styles described in earlier chapters. In cases where parents have adopted a different approach than that expected of their culture, the goals and outcomes are similar to that parenting style, and their perceptions. For example, the Nso and Rajput infants are often in their caregivers' view, and cared for by different persons for more time than German infants. German infants spend more time alone; otherwise, they are within their mothers' reach. With respect to body stimulation, Nso and Rajput caregivers provide infants with substantial amounts. In the case of Chinese college students, they face authoritarian and training parenting and cultural-specific socialisation goals, whereas the European American college students face authoritative parenting and self-development goals. Notably, when authoritative parenting is adopted by either cultural group, the outcome is the same, indicating the universality of this parenting style. Interestingly too, regarding the maternal collectivism socialisation goal, the European American students perceived it as related to authoritarian parenting. In contrast, with maternal collectivism socialisation goals, the Chinese students perceived it as independent from authoritarian parenting as they reaped its benefits. In the case of Mongolians and Germans, immigrants had assimilated themselves with the mainstream people in Germany, adopting their parenting and socialisation goals too.

Parenting styles perceived by children

Now that you have read how parents perceived themselves in the roles of parenting, it is time to read how children perceive parenting from their own viewpoints, an issue that is often ignored or unnoticed. Fortunately or unfortunately, children are on the receiving end of parenting most of the time, until they are able to survive on their own. It is like giving feedback for improvement in a communication or a product sale. If feedback is not accepted, then communication or production is one-way, which may not be right. Nevertheless, children do view their parents in the light of whether their authority is appropriate, proper, and just (called parental legitimacy), and whether to trust and obey them (Trinkner, Cohn, Rebellon, & Van Gundy, 2012).

A study (Quoss & Zhao, 1995) investigated 82 children (9–11 years old; 50 Chinese and 32 Americans), and 137 parents (85 Chinese and 43 Americans) in urban China and the United States respectively regarding children's perception of and satisfaction with parenting styles. The results show that the Chinese children perceived their parents to be authoritarian, whereas these parents perceived themselves to be democratic in their parenting style. Both US children and parents perceived their families to be characterised by democratic parenting. In general, children from both cultures were satisfied with the parent–child relationship regardless of parenting style, but American children were highly satisfied with what the family did together, family decision- and choice-making, and ways of punishment.

Learning: Chinese parents today may be more open to Western cultural ideas than previous generations, who grew up when traditional values of parental power and authority dominated the society. Many studies, however, still point the finger at the authoritarian parenting of Chinese people (Huang et al., 2017; Quoss & Zhao, 1995). Therefore, contemporary Chinese parent–child relationships may be changing with the times.

Another study (Barnhart, Raval, Jansari, & Raval, 2013) examined 226 college students in India and 517 college students in the US concerning their perceptions of parenting styles. The results show that

Indian college students considered permissive parenting more effective and helpful than US college students. In contrast, the US students considered authoritative and authoritarian parenting to be more effective, helpful, and caring than the Indian students. A majority of Indian and US college students chose authoritative parenting similar to their own parents', and as the type of parent they wish to be.

Learning: These results are not in line with the said parenting styles of the East and West.

Indian students viewed permissive parenting as the choice they would take as parents after what they had gone through with their parents' authoritarian style, and after globalisation had influenced them. Also, permissive parenting indicates a low level of explicit parental control combined with lots of warmth, which the Indian students may prefer.

Another study (Olivari, Hertfelt Wahn, Maridaki-Kassotaki, Antonopoulou, & Confalonieri, 2015) compared 702 adolescents' retrospective perceptions of parenting styles in Sweden, Italy, and Greece. The results showed that the authoritative style, as perceived by the adolescents, was the most frequently adopted by parents. In these countries, legislation and policies concerning the family role in educating and caring for children emphasise the importance of parents raising children by treating them with respect, supporting and protecting them, and prohibiting the use of physical punishment. Mothers, as compared to fathers, were perceived as more authoritative, authoritarian, and permissive. Males perceived their parents as more authoritarian and more permissive than females. Swedish parents were perceived as less authoritarian than Italian and Greek parents, and more permissive than Italian parents. Greek parents were perceived as less authoritarian and more permissive than Italian parents.

Learning: This study provides an interesting contribution to the parenting styles literature, showing how countries' legislation concerning family matters and socio-economic status is related to the perception of parenting behaviours.

Overall, parenting styles may not go in accordance with the beliefs and understanding that parents have adopted and applied on their children. Children do have their views on what parenting is like for them now, and what they would like to adopt in the future. This is like doing therapy with clients with issues.

There are two takeaway lessons here.

First, people often perceive life situations from their understanding at one time, and may change their perception at a different time. This equates to experiencing matters as a child and then as an adult, and seeing things from one's own and another's viewpoint. Second, one generation is definitely quite different from the next; thus, we cannot do the same as before.

Immigrant parenting

With globalisation, people are moving around the world to enjoy life, work, live, and retire, among other purposes. So are parents, because of job transfers or a change of lifestyle, among possible reasons. Many parents are working overseas for a better life at home, without their spouses or children. Similarly, many families have immigrated to give children a better schooling experience. However, moving into another country or culture is not as simple as going next door to buy groceries. The following discussion highlights two aspects of immigrant parenting: parenting cognitions and family conflict.

Parenting cognitions

A study (Cote, Kwak, Putnick, Chung, & Bornstein, 2015) compared 179 mothers (73 South Koreans, and 50 Korean immigrants and 56 European Americans in the US) of 20-month-old children on two types of parenting cognitions: attributions and self-perceptions. The results show that Korean immigrant mothers' attributions for parenting resembled European American mothers in the US, whereas their self-perceptions of parenting closely resembled those of mothers in South Korea. Notably, European American mothers agreed with ability attributions as explanations for their parenting success, as did Korean immigrant mothers; but not mothers in South Korea. This is called *enhancing bias*, that is, giving themselves credit for their positive outcomes versus self-effacement. South Korean mothers acknowledged levels of ability and internal effort attributions as explanations for their lack of success at parenting tasks, whereas Korean immigrant and European American mothers acknowledged child behaviour as the explanation for their lack of success at parenting tasks. Additionally, South Korean mothers claimed to be more invested in parenting than either Korean immigrant or European American mothers. Both European American and Korean immigrant mothers reported feeling more satisfied with, and a greater sense of competence in, parenting than South Korean mothers.

Learning: Settling in another country, among many issues, brings about role conflict for immigrants who have to maintain their own cultures while trying to live with the mainstream culture. The acculturation model has discussed whether immigrants assimilate, integrate, marginalise, or separate. In the end, most modify their attitudes and behaviour somewhat, while maintaining some of their own. Integration happens more so with those born outside of the immigrated country, whereas those born in the immigrated country usually are assimilated. Thus, one's cognition and attribution of the self are also affected; hopefully, to better suit the environment—otherwise, problems arise.

Family conflict

No family is without conflict of any sort. As a minimum, parents could have minor bickering over choices of food, furniture, colours for walls, and more. Then, more arguments when children are present in the family, on choices of parenting styles, schools, household chores, etc. More arguments still if people immigrate to another country while trying to acculturate or stay the same.

A study (Farver, Xu, Bhadha, Narang, & Lieber, 2007) examined 360 adolescents and their parents (180 Asian Indian and 180 European American) in the US regarding their parental childrearing beliefs on adolescent psychological well-being. Family conflicts have been found to occur frequently over the routine details of family life: doing chores, getting along with siblings, regulating activities, doing homework, and being concerned about appearance. Parents see conflicts in terms of being pragmatic, social conventions, or rules, whereas adolescents tend to interpret them in terms of personal autonomy, jurisdiction, and choice. Asian Indian adolescents specified more family conflict, ethnic identity achievement, and anxiety, and their parents endorsed training and shaming childrearing beliefs more than European American families. Asian Indian parents who have an integrated or assimilated acculturation style approximated the European families' family conflict and their childrearing beliefs. With exposure to situations that challenge their ways of thinking, immigrant parents develop childrearing beliefs that function in both cultures.

In the US, conflict in Asian Indian families typically revolves around parental disapproval of mainstream American attitudes towards dating and adolescents' desire for independence, especially with regard to career choice and marriage. Notably, Asian Indian cultural values are not compatible with the fairly open style of Western parent–child communication. Asian Indian parents do not usually recognise their adolescents' ability to make sound decisions, and are negative about independent and autonomous behaviour. The socialisation of Asian Indian children tends to focus on sociocultural continuity. Thus, Asian Indian immigrant families may adapt to changes pragmatically, such as celebrating Western holidays, but they resist alterations in values surrounding arranged marriages, dating, and so forth.

Learning: Immigrant parents often have to grapple with managing the family in two cultures; that of the mainstream and theirs. Reconciling both means giving up some of one's traditions and practices and adopting some of those from the other culture. Family conflict arises if parents are not really prepared to immigrate and are not ready for changes, even for a working stint in the new country. But for the success of the family, most immigrant families have to become accustomed to changes in their lifestyle or face periods of unhappiness until moving back to their own society.

Punishment

As mentioned in earlier chapters, punishment is part of parenting in some cultures and a no-no in others. Mainly, punishment, whether minor or not, produces negative outcomes for the children if not well managed. Noteworthy is the fact that, as I have observed and experienced, punishment, if used appropriately, has its benefits.

A study (Shechory-Bitton, Ben David, & Sommerfeld, 2015) examined 374 mother–daughter dyads (155 native-born Jewish Israelis, 133 Jewish Mizrahi immigrants from Muslim countries, and 86 native-born Arab Muslim Israelis) regarding corporal punishment. Israeli laws forbid the use of corporal punishment. The results show that Muslim women scored lower on authoritative styles and higher on both authoritarian and permissive styles than Jewish women. They were also more tolerant of corporal punishment than the Jewish women. The Jewish Mizrahi mothers had parenting styles more similar to the native-born Jewish

Israelis mothers than to the native-born Arab Muslim Israeli mothers, despite coming from a similar cultural background. Possibly, Jews who immigrated to Israel from Muslim countries are more influenced by Israeli culture prevalent in the absorbing population. Analysis in detail by dyads from the study is mentioned next.

Native-born Jewish Israelis/Jewish Mizrahi immigrants

The Jewish population consists of different cultural groups defined according to their countries of origin or their level of religiosity (secular or ultra-orthodox). The majority of the Jews who were born in Israel were Ashkenazim. In the 1950s, large waves of Jews immigrated from Western countries (Europe, America, and Anglo-Saxon countries) and Muslim countries (the Middle East and North Africa). From 1990, large numbers of Jews immigrated from Russia and Ethiopia. Thus, the Jewish population is divided into two main categories: those from Western countries, called Ashkenazim, and those from Muslim countries, called Mizrahim or Sephardim. Much of the Jewish sector is characterised by Western family values. As a whole, Jewish society in Israel tends to be Western-oriented, with democratic, liberal, and individualist values. Jewish Israeli parents tend to encourage their children's individuality and independence. Children are often given a central place within the family, and equal relationships are formed that encourage children to freely pursue their independence, as well as their own interests and aspirations (Shechory-Bitton, et al., 2015, p. 509).

Native-born Arab Muslim Israelis

Among these people the majority are mostly Sunni, residing in small towns and villages, and maintain a conservative ideology that stresses traditional and Muslim beliefs. The Arab population is characterised by higher rates of poverty and unemployment compared with the Jewish majority. They have a distinct religious, cultural, historical, and national identity, and share a common heritage and cultural values that differ from those of the mainstream Jewish population. The Muslim Arab population is largely characterised by traditional patriarchal and authoritarian family values. Muslim Arab societies are considered more traditional, collective, and authoritarian, and children in Arab families are socialised to obey their parents and submit to their demands that advance the benefit and harmony of the collective. Arab mothers can be more physically punitive as well as non-punitive with children (Shechory-Bitton, et al., 2015, p. 509)

Another study (Meyer et al., 2015) examined 295 parents and 3-year-old children regarding the relationship between parenting style during early childhood and children's error-related negativity. Error-related negativity is a negative deflection in the event-related potential occurring approximately 50 milliseconds after error commission at frontocentral electrode sites, and is considered to reflect the activation of a generic error-monitoring system. The results show that hostile parenting and an authoritarian parenting style predicted a larger error-related negativity in children three years later. Error-related negativity magnitude mediates the relationship between harsh parenting and child anxiety disorder. Possibly, parenting may shape children's error processing through environmental conditioning, and thereby the risk of anxiety.

Learning: Despite the public's image of Jews and Arab Muslims, the facts tell a different story with respect to their parenting styles and attitudes towards corporal punishment. Many people are at least influenced by modernisation for the betterment of their families and cultures, and possibly their survival. With regard to the brain, harsh parenting hurts it and may cause anxiety in children.

Where punishment is concerned, Westerners were more influenced by attributes of the actors and the deed, whereas Easterners were more influenced by information about the actors' role relationship to others in the scenario. Thus, Westerners would choose sanctions that isolate the individual; Easterners are likely to choose sanctions that emphasise restitution and maintaining relationship roles (Poasa et al., 2000).

Younger versus older parents

We all know that being a parent at an age where one is ready or prepared is better than being caught off guard. For example, having a like-minded partner, a home, a steady income, and childcare services and amenities around, to name a few variables, would put any new parent at ease about having a child. This is possibly a major reason why married couples are not having children soon after marriage (Chin

Heng, 2006; Li, Lim, Tsai, & O, 2015). It is expected that younger mothers are not fully ready for parenting.

A past study (Reis, 1989) investigated 150 young adolescent mothers, 260 older adolescent mothers, and 242 adult mothers regarding their determinants of parenting. The results show that young adolescent mothers differed from adult mothers in terms of their knowledge of child development, punitive attitudes towards childrearing, and levels of depression. Specifically, black mothers were more punitive towards childrearing, had less knowledge of developmental milestones, perceived themselves as getting less social support, and were more depressed. Older mothers, regardless of ethnic groups, had achieved the highest level of knowledge of child development, were the least punitive, perceived themselves as getting the greatest amount of social support, and were the least depressed.

Learning: Thus, it is preferable to be a mother at a mature age than earlier. This is indicated by teenage pregnancy and motherhood and their accompanying parenting problems.

Compatibility of Eastern versus Western parenting styles

The authoritarian parenting style is associated with positive parental characteristics in collectivistic cultures and negative parental characteristics in individualist cultures. Thus, culturally, authoritarian parents who may be restrictive or demand obedience without question (as in Western parenting) may not be rejecting and lacking in warmth, and unlikely to attribute negative dispositions to their children for their behaviour (as in Eastern parenting).

Training is a culture-specific form of parenting that is distinct from Baumrind's typology and parenting dimensions of warmth and control. As a culture-specific model of Chinese parenting, training is defined by the concept of *chiao shun*, which entails organisational control, and the concept of *guan*, which entails parental investment and involvement. The factors of *chiao shun* and *guan* render training distinct from authoritarian and authoritative parenting styles. The organisational control of training emphasises self-discipline, hard work, achievement, obedience, and family honour. Besides, the responsiveness of authoritative parents or the parenting dimension of warmth is covertly expressed by Chinese parents' support of child achievement, and is distinct from the expressions of affect and non-contingent praise of Western parents.

The positive and negative perceptions of adolescents in collectivistic and individualist cultures respectively mediate and enhance the negative effects of authoritarian parenting. When adolescents from collectivistic and individualist cultures perceive a lack of warmth, use of shame, psychological intrusion, or authoritarian parental control that arbitrarily curtails legitimate autonomy, they would perceive such a hierarchy as undesirable and hostile, rather than a necessity for the preservation of harmony. Indeed, such perceptions are linked to conflict and the absence of harmony or cohesion, and related to negative psychosocial outcomes and feelings of isolation and depression.

A possible reason for the success of authoritative parenting found in cross-cultural studies may be that these parents employ more effective ways or means of obtaining goals by balancing demanding and responsive practices, being more flexible and rational, and by being able to choose from the variety of parenting practices. For example, the goal of happiness for Chinese children is significantly determined by their academic competence. Throughout development, authoritative parents pursue goals in any area (e.g., social, academic) by balancing different forms of control with different ways to support autonomy (supporting children's ability to meet their obligations without external control or parental assistance) (Sorkhabi, 2005).

Conclusion

We have looked at Eastern and Western parenting styles, and compared them to some extent based on available literature. Personal experiences of readers, I am sure, will result in the same, or you will have more to add to the discussion. Let us put all the mentioned parenting styles side by side to get a better picture of them (see Table 6.1 below).

In summary, although any inconsistency between parenting styles tends to be damaging to the child, the benefits of having at least one authoritative parent outweigh the negative effects of inconsistent parenting styles (Abubakar, Van de Vijver, Suryani, Handayani, & Pandia, 2015).

Table 6.1 Analysis of parenting styles

Parenting styles	Dimensions					Children				Remarks
	Parents									
	Demandingness/control	Responsiveness to child's needs	Responsiveness to child's interests	As source	As role model	Self-control	Academic performance	Social competence	Mental health	Extended family inclusion
Western										
Authoritative	Medium to high; conform to group standards; clear, firm directions	High	High; Encourage child's efforts	Always	Warm; Accepting; Reciprocal; Flexible	Medium to high; self-reliant	High	High; self-assertive; responsible; agentic; explorative	Good		Ideal style; Tough on parents if children are difficult
Authoritarian	High; strict; assign household duties	Low	Low; parent's wishes	Basics	Preserve tradition and order; value obedience; detached	Low; Discontented; be obedient; poor self-control	Low to medium	Low; distrustful; withdrawn	Poor, may have problematic behaviours; higher levels of depression		Punishment is used
Permissive/indulgent	Low	Medium to high	High	Available	Relatively warm; non-active agent	Low; higher self-esteem	Medium to low	Medium	Poor, misconduct; problematic; Low levels of depression		Parent does consult with child

(*Continued*)

Table 6.1 (Cont.)

Parenting styles	Dimensions					Children				Extended family inclusion	Remarks
	Parents										
	Demanding-ness/control	Responsive-ness to child's needs	Responsive-ness to child's interests	As source	As role model	Self-control	Academic performance	Social competence	Mental health		
Western											
Neglecting/uninvolved	Low	Low; dismissive	Low	Basics	Little emotional involve-ment	Poor; low self esteem; aggressive	Low	Low; may be Problematic	Depends; may be Problematic		Child on own mostly
Chinese parenting	High; strict; training; governing	High; protective	Low; parent's wishes	Filial piety; family eat, sleep together	Modest behaviour, harmonious relationship	Low; lack developed self	High	Medium to low	Medium; relational aggression	Medium; inter-generational dependence	Punishment is used; parent–child dependence
Filial parenting	High	Very high; very protective; over-involved	Low; parent's wishes	Filial piety; good income; family eat, sleep together	High achieving	Low; lack developed self; self-centred; entitlement attitude	High	Medium to low	Medium	Low to medium; inter-generational dependence	Over-nurturance; parent–child dependence
Indian parenting	High	Low; protective	Low; parent's wishes	Family eat, sleep together	Father is authority; mother is behaviour regulator;	Low	High	Situation-specific	Medium; relational aggression	High; inter-generational dependence	Uphold tradition and customs

Table 6.1 (Cont.)

Parenting styles	Dimensions					Children					Remarks
	Parents										
	Demandingness/control	Responsiveness to child's needs	Responsiveness to child's interests	As source	As role model	Self-control	Academic performance	Social competence	Mental health	Extended family inclusion	
Western	High	Low	Low		high achieving						
Japanese parenting	High	Low	Low	Confucian ethics and morality	Highly motivating	High	High	High	Low to medium; relational aggression	Low	Homogeneous culture
Korean parenting	Very high; Strict; training	Low; protective; over-involved	Low	Filial piety; High Socioeconomic status	High	Low	High	Medium to low	Low to medium; relational aggression	Low	Punishment is used
Muslim parenting	High	High	High	Qur'an and tradition of Prophet Muhammad	Father is authority; mother is emotional support; group harmony	Low to medium	Medium	Medium	Medium; relational aggression	High; intergenerational dependence	Home teaching; punishment is used

Note: evaluations in boxes are based on existing standards of Eastern and Western parenting styles compared. These may vary depending on different schools of thoughts and orientation, and personal opinions.

Note

1 Comparisons between two entities can be made using either their features, processes, or outcomes. Here, outcomes is chosen because, I believe, parents (performance- or result-oriented) would like to know more about them than the others.

References

Abubakar, A., Van de Vijver, F. J. R., Suryani, A. O., Handayani, P., & Pandia, W. S. (2015). Perceptions of parenting styles and their associations with mental health and life satisfaction among urban Indonesian adolescents. *Journal of Child and Family Studies, 24*(9), 2680–2692. doi: 10.1007/s10826-014-0070-x.

Atzaba-Poria, N., & Pike, A. (2008). Correlates of parenting for mothers and fathers from English and Indian backgrounds. *Parenting, 8*(1), 17–40. doi: 10.1080/15295190701665698.

Barnhart, C. M., Raval, V. V., Jansari, A., & Raval, P. H. (2013). Perceptions of parenting style among college students in India and the United States. *Journal of Child and Family Studies, 22*(5), 684–693. doi: 10.1007/s10826-012-9621-1.

Bornstein, M. H., Tamis-LeMonda, C. S., Pascual, L., Haynes, O. M., Painter, K. M., Galperln, C. Z., & Pecheux, M. (1996). Ideas about parenting in Argentina, France, and the United States. *International Journal of Behavioral Development, 19*(2), 347–367. doi: 10.1177/016502549601900207.

Carunungan-Robles, A. (1986). Perceptions of parental nurturance, punitiveness, and power by selected Filipino primary school children. *Philippine Journal of Psychology, 19*, 18–28.

Chin Heng, B. (2006). Delayed motherhood through oocyte and ovarian tissue cryopreservation: A perspective from Singapore. *Reproductive BioMedicine Online, 12*(6), 660–662. doi: 10.1016/S1472-6483(10)61077-2.

Cooper, H., Lindsay, J. J., & Nye, B. (2000). Homework in the home: How student, family, and parenting-style differences relate to the homework process. *Contemporary Educational Psychology, 25*(4), 464–487. doi: 10.1006/ceps.1999.1036.

Cote, L. R., Kwak, K., Putnick, D. L., Chung, H. J., & Bornstein, M. H. (2015). The acculturation of parenting cognitions: A comparison of South Korean, Korean immigrant, and European American mothers. *Journal of Cross-Cultural Psychology, 46*(9), 1115–1130. doi: 10.1177/0022022115600259.

Farver, J. M., Xu, Y., Bhadha, B. R., Narang, S., & Lieber, E. (2007). Ethnic identity, acculturation, parenting beliefs, and adolescent adjustment: A comparison of Asian Indian and European American families. *Merrill-Palmer Quarterly, 53*(2), 184–215. doi: 10.1353/mpq.2007.0010.

Graf, F. A., Röder, M., Hein, S., Müller, A. R., & Ganzorig, O. (2014). Cultural influences on socialization goals and parenting behaviors of Mongolian parents. *Journal of Cross-Cultural Psychology, 45*(8), 1317–1327. doi: 10.1177/0022022114537702.

Huang, C., Cheah, C. S. L., Lamb, M. E., & Zhou, N. (2017). Associations between parenting styles and perceived child effortful control within Chinese families in

the United States, the United Kingdom, and Taiwan. *Journal of Cross-Cultural Psychology, 48*(6), 795–812. doi: 10.1177/0022022117706108.
Huang, C., & Lamb, M. E. (2014). Are Chinese children more compliant? Examination of the cultural difference in observed maternal control and child compliance. *Journal of Cross-Cultural Psychology, 45*(4), 507–533. doi: 10.1177/0022022113513652.
Keller, H., Abels, M., Lamm, B., Yovsi, R. D., Voelker, S., & Lakhani, A. (2005). Ecocultural effects on early infant care: A study in Cameroon, India, and Germany. *Ethos, 33*(4), 512–541. doi: 10.1525/eth.2005.33.4.512.
Li, N. P., Lim, A. J. Y., Tsai, M., & O, J. (2015). Too materialistic to get married and have children? *PloS One, 10*(5), e0126543. doi: 10.1371/journal.pone.0126543.
Li, Y., Costanzo, P. R., & Putallaz, M. (2010). Maternal socialization goals, parenting styles, and social-emotional adjustment among Chinese and European American young adults: Testing a mediation model. *Journal of Genetic Psychology, 171*(4), 330–362. doi: 10.1080/00221325.2010.505969.
McNeely, C. A., & Barber, B. K. (2010). How do parents make adolescents feel loved? Perspectives on supportive parenting from adolescents in 12 cultures. *Journal of Adolescent Research, 25*(4), 601–631. doi: 10.1177/0743558409357235.
Meyer, A., Proudfit, G. H., Bufferd, S. J., Kujawa, A. J., Laptook, R. S., Torpey, D. C., & Klein, D. N. (2015). Self-reported and observed punitive parenting prospectively predicts increased error-related brain activity in six-year-old children. *Journal of Abnormal Child Psychology, 43*(5), 821–829. doi: 10.1007/s10802-014-9918-1.
Mousavi, S. E., Low, W. Y., & Hashim, A. H. (2016). Perceived parenting styles and cultural influences in adolescent's anxiety: A cross-cultural comparison. *Journal of Child and Family Studies, 25*(7), 2102–2110. doi: 10.1007/s10826-016-0393-x.
Muris, P., Meesters, C., Merckelbach, H., & Hülsenbeck, P. (2000). Worry in children is related to perceived parental rearing and attachment. *Behaviour Research and Therapy, 38*(5), 487–497. doi: 10.1016/S0005-7967(99)00072-8.
Nomaguchi, K., & House, A. N. (2013). Racial-ethnic disparities in maternal parenting stress: The role of structural disadvantages and parenting values. *Journal of Health and Social Behavior, 54*(3), 386–404. doi: 10.1177/0022146513498511.
Olivari, M. G., Hertfelt Wahn, E., Maridaki-Kassotaki, K., Antonopoulou, K., & Confalonieri, E. (2015). Adolescent perceptions of parenting styles in Sweden, Italy and Greece: An exploratory study. *Europe's Journal of Psychology, 11*(2), 244–258. doi: 10.5964/ejop.v11i2.887.
Poasa, K. H., Mallinckrodt, B., & Suzuki, L. A. (2000). Causal attributions for problematic family interactions: A qualitative, cultural comparison of Western Samoa, American Samoa, and the United States. *Counseling Psychologist, 28*(1), 32–60. doi: 10.1177/0011000000281003.
Putnick, D. L., Bornstein, M. H., Lansford, J. E., Chang, L., Deater-Deckard, K., Di Giunta, L., ... Bombi, A. S. (2012). Agreement in mother and father acceptance-rejection, warmth, and hostility/rejection/neglect of children across nine countries. *Cross-Cultural Research, 46*(3), 191–223. doi: 10.1177/1069397112440931.
Quoss, B., & Zhao, W. (1995). Parenting styles and children's satisfaction with parenting in China and the United States. *Journal of Comparative Family Studies, 26*(2), 265–280.

Reis, J. (1989). A comparison of young teenage, older teenage, and adult mothers on determinants of parenting. *Journal of Psychology, 123*(2), 141–151. doi: 10.1080/00223980.1989.10542970.

Schwartz, S. J., Zamboanga, B. L., Ravert, R. D., Kim, S. Y., Weisskirch, R. S., Williams, M. K., ... Finley, G. E. (2009). Perceived parental relationships and health-risk behaviors in college-attending emerging adults. *Journal of Marriage and Family, 71*(3), 727–740. doi: 10.1111/j.1741-3737.2009.00629.x.

Segrin, C., Woszidlo, A., Givertz, M., & Montgomery, N. (2013). Parent and child traits associated with overparenting. *Journal of Social and Clinical Psychology, 32*(6), 569.

Shechory-Bitton, M., Ben David, S., & Sommerfeld, E. (2015). Effect of ethnicity on parenting styles and attitudes toward violence among Jewish and Arab Muslim Israeli mothers: An intergenerational approach. *Journal of Cross-Cultural Psychology, 46*(4), 508–524. doi: 10.1177/0022022115576001.

Sorkhabi, N. (2005). Applicability of Baumrind's parent typology to collective cultures: Analysis of cultural explanations of parent socialization effects. *International Journal of Behavioral Development, 29*(6), 552–563. doi: 10.1177/01650250500172640.

Trinkner, R., Cohn, E. S., Rebellon, C. J., & Van Gundy, K. (2012). Don't trust anyone over 30: Parental legitimacy as a mediator between parenting style and changes in delinquent behavior over time. *Journal of Adolescence, 35*(1), 119. doi: 10.1016/j.adolescence.2011.05.003.

Vuk, M. (2017). Parenting styles and gang membership: Mediating factors. *Deviant Behavior, 38*(4), 1–20. doi: 10.1080/01639625.2016.1197011.

The role of significant others   7

As parents are working people, there will be times when parenting has to be performed by others. Fortunately, parents can be assisted by close relatives like grandparents, uncles, and aunties; neighbours and friends; and paid helpers like maids or baby sitters. "Nannying" is the term used to refer to such assistance in parenting. Whoever is the nanny, it is a matter of caregiving or baby-sitting of the child.

This chapter examines the roles of the significant others described above, and discusses whether they make a difference to the parenting provided by the child's parents. Most published literature on parenting by significant others focuses on general childcare by nannies; some focuses specifically on childcare by grandparents and maids or domestic helpers. This chapter first looks at discussion on the use of nannies, then the parenting of children by grandparents and by maids. It ends with a summary of the pros and cons of using the significant others to help parent one's children (see Table 7.1).

General comments on childcare

Experiences or interactions with people and the environment mould a child's mind and personality. Thus, caregiving is fundamental to child development, whether the caregiver is a parent, a grandmother, a relative, or a teacher in a childcare centre.

Research has found that early exposure to childcare can foster children's learning and enhance their lives, or it can leave them at risk of troubled relationships. The outcome depends greatly on the quality of the childcare setting. Responsive caregivers who surround children with language, warmth, and chances to learn are the key to good outcomes. In the US, diversity and variability are hallmarks of childcare. Children whose families are not maintained by a good income or government support are the ones frequently exposed to poor-quality care (Phillips & Adams, 2001).

Parents seeking a balance between providing economic resources for their families and providing nurturance for their children face great dilemmas—sacrificing income for one parent to stay at home full-time with the child, or organising jobs so that the parents can combine employment and childcare without relying on other support, or both finding employment so they can afford non-parental childcare. Consequently, different parents face these decisions with differing resources, values, and available options. Nevertheless, they share a concern for the well-being of their children, and many experience anxiety and uncertainty as they begin to juggle their roles as employees and parents of a new baby (Phillips & Adams, 2001).

The outcomes of having childcare can run both ways: it may enhance the lives of young children and foster their development, or it puts children at risk and undermines their development. It also depends on the reactions of the family. Whatever happens, research shows that parents and the home environment remain the predominant influences on young children's well-being and adjustment. The question today is not whether childcare affects development or which environment is better, but rather how childcare interconnects with what happens at home to affect early development. Beneficial child outcomes are most likely when caregivers are responsive, warm, and sensitive to the children and surround them with verbal and non-verbal communication that does not involve "motherese" or "baby talk". Caregivers' qualifications also matter for infants and toddlers.

A word from neuroscience research. Such research has shown that the baby's brain needs to be tidied after birth because it has excess neurons and is also not well connected for carrying out its functions. It is natural that the brain wants to reach out to the environment in order to do so. It needs the baby to interact with the environment. So, the baby has to act and react with environmental stimuli, like human beings and objects, and things of all kinds. Every action and reaction provides feedback to the baby's brain to trim the excess neurons and make more neuronal connections throughout it. The more connections within the brain, the tidier the brain is, and the better the child is (Lomanowska, Boivin, Hertzman, & Fleming, 2017). Neglecting the baby or failing to stimulate him or her will lead to a duller personality (Lomanowska et al., 2017). Interested readers should look at material on developmental neuroscience on humans for more information. Remember, we can shape our brain by our actions, and this goes on through life.

In summary, the growth and developmental effects of childcare derive primarily from the quality of the interactions and experiences it provides for young children. Childcare can come from the parents, their relatives, nannies (baby sitters, maids, or domestic helpers, and anybody who is a caregiver), a childcare facility/crèche, or family care.

Research has found that global migrants are increasingly mothers who leave their families in the villages of the Southern Hemisphere to take up jobs caring for families in the Northern Hemisphere. Importantly, the focus is on the working conditions that such migrant mothers face in the north or on the children they leave in the south; a reorganisation of roles in the family (Isaksen, Devi, & Hochschild, 2008). For example, a Filipina mother works in the US while leaving her children behind for her sister to look after. So, what of the children left behind by their migrant mothers? Most children understand that their parents abroad will add to the family funds and improve their own education opportunities. But most view their parents' departure with a sense of loneliness and sadness. Notably, children living with both parents earned higher grades and a higher rank in class than children with absent parents. So, what of the migrant mothers? They still wanted to be the ideal mother when at home, but felt badly about the separation with their children when away. They tried to make up for the missing motherly love through money and material gifts. The children may see these gifts as a mother's way of apologising to them. Both migrant mothers and their children often felt obliged to the caregivers. Some children felt like a guest in the house, or a burden. So, some older children tried to behave like little mothers to younger siblings. Hence, this was an emotional challenge for children left behind, though it was not the same for all of them. Looking at the bigger picture, the effect of migrant mothers and their children will be a shift in childcare to their community and society (Isaksen et al., 2008).

Childcare by nannies

Children may be cared for by any suitable or qualified adult other than their own parents; in which case a nanny (often a female) is the chosen one. A nanny is any adult, who could be the grandparent, a maid, or a paid helper from anywhere; a responsible woman with childcare experience is usually preferred.

To almost all parents, getting a good nanny is akin to a matter of life and death—a very real issue as this has to do with a life, that of a baby or child, the precious priceless offspring. For one thing, it involves finding a skilled and trusted nanny; for another, it means keeping her in the job or role. A high turnover of nannies is very disruptive to the family's health (Millward Purvis & Cropley, 2003). Every pair of parents who has used a nanny will surely testify 100 per cent to this statement.

A big difference exists between inexperienced and experienced parents and nannies. Experienced nannies and parents will talk about expectations of the nanny's role before a contract is signed. Important expectations involve the handling of the children; reliability; energy levels; parenting style; housekeeping; discipline; managing problems; financial and other rewards; feedback; and the nanny's autonomy and need for support; communication; going the extra mile; age, qualifications, experience; and safety. Studies have found that matters discussed openly often include remuneration and conditions, and matters implied are often how the nanny and parent work with each other on caring for the children, and emotional and value-laden considerations. The more explicit the discussion about the expectations, the more likely a feeling of mutual trust and understanding, and perception of reciprocity, are achieved between parents and the nanny. If the implied expectations are made explicit, the better will be the parent–nanny relationship (Millward Purvis & Cropley, 2003).

If you take some time and surf the internet regarding nannies, you will find an abundance of articles on the problems parents faced with hiring them, though good outcomes with nannies are highlighted less. It is not the aim of this book to go into this here.

An interesting study (Yakeley, 2017) looks at the psychoanalytic aspect of nanny caregiving for a child. Simply put, psychoanalysis is a branch of psychology that deals with the human unconscious affecting and affected by life. The study is about the impact of early caregivers or nannies, other than the biological mother, on the psychic development of a child. It involves a nanny–child–mother relationship and an internalised image of this in the child's mind. It is about the role of the nanny in the family she works in, how she becomes involved in unconscious phantasies and unwanted projections of the child, and the affected attachment of the mother–child relationship. It is believed that both mother and nanny influence the child's behaviour and personality.

One way in which wealthier countries deal with labour shortages in childcare and aged care is to make use of migrants. So migrants have become a major source of nannies for children; sort of a surrogate parent, especially for parents who are at work full-time. Countries like Australia have produced special policies and rules for migrant nannies, protecting the parents and children, with oversight by the state largely focusing on the need to improve accessibility, flexibility, and affordability (Adamson, Cortis, Brennan, & Charlesworth, 2017).

Relevant matters include the need for more childcare places, increased funding and commitment to quality standards across service types, and extending subsidies to families using nannies.

Using migrants for childcare and aged care brings to mind the experiences I have observed among many families in Singapore, which uses a large force of foreign maids doubling as nannies for their children. Many stories have been told and have surfaced in courts and the media highlighting the good and bad outcomes of such a move. Good outcomes include the nanny going the extra mile for the child under her care, with many nannies gaining repeated employment contracts as a result. Bad outcomes include mistreating or even killing the child in her charge, though these cases are rare. All in all, it is a matter of managing cultural differences between parents and nannies, and laying out clearly the expectations of both parties.

Some experts have advocated that children above the age of 1 be exposed to non-parental care by adults (preferably other parents) other than the child's parents, relatives, and friends of the parents (Gheaus, 2011). Such exposure ensures that the well-being of the child and parents is considered, that is, the child's needs are met, and allows opportunities for employment of childcare professionals and institutions;

additionally, the children can better deal with the greater world of strangers as they grow up.

Childcare by grandparents

In extended/joint family living, grandparents are often found helping out in looking after the grandchildren as part of their aging role; this is termed "grandparenting". Most grandparents are willing partners in parenting grandchildren, especially in collectivistic cultures. In individualistic cultures, grandparents may adopt the hands-off principle in parenting grandchildren. This can happen in collectivistic cultures too. This kind of move is attributed to leaving parenting to the parents (as they like it or know best), or the "I don't interfere" policy. Of course, there are grandparents who would not want any more parenting after what they have gone through looking after their own children. Even in nuclear families, many grandparents would happily lend a hand in parenting grandchildren. For many families, grandparents live apart from their grandchildren. Thus, their relationship is a part-time one in which the grandparent imparts wisdom, recites children's and family stories, comforts the grandchildren, provides gifts, serves as a role model, and functions as a temporary childcare provider (Sands & Goldberg-Glen, 2000).

In joint families, children's behaviour is shaped not only by parents but also by grandparents. That is, grandparents share the responsibility of socialisation of grandchildren with the parents. Grandparents serve as bases of information and affection, and their emotional closeness and warmth towards their grandchildren may act as a buffer against any negative family conditions. Research has shown that grandchildren who have a close and warm relationship with their grandparents experience less psychological distress. Furthermore, emotional closeness with grandparents has also been shown to moderate the negative effects of the family context (Akhtar, Malik, & Begeer, 2017).

For example, adolescents internalise the effects of parenting that they perceive, which is in turn manifested in their development of social competence and adjustment. And authoritarian and permissive parenting decrease the social competence of children, whereas authoritative parenting increases that social competence. Such children may benefit from other opportunities, that is, support from peer groups, schools, and families, including grandparents. Thus, their emotional closeness to grandparents moderates the effect of parenting styles on components of social competence (i.e., social skills, involving impulsiveness, withdrawal, assertiveness, and overconfidence). This happens because the grandchildren usually discuss their concerns with their grandparents, who in turn would provide the grandchildren with social and emotional support, filling in gaps in communication between parents (especially fathers) and children (Akhtar et al., 2017). Additionally, strong grandparent support would augment that partner support in co-parenting (Poblete & Gee, 2018).

We frequently find grandchildren being looked after by Grandma rather than Grandpa; similar to the parenting of one's children where the mother does most of the caring, while the father does the playing. So Grandpa likes to play with grandchildren, while Grandma looks after them wholeheartedly and full-time, depending on the situation. To many grandparents, raising grandchildren is parenting a second generation of children. Some grandmothers perceive themselves as wiser, more relaxed, and more involved with their grandchildren. They also perceive such challenges as having limited energy, negotiating changing family roles, and parenting in a tough social environment. In terms of behaviours and emotional bonds, some grandmothers see similarities in parenting their children and grandchildren (Dolbin-MacNab, 2006).

The age of the grandparents may affect their caregiving of grandchildren. Older adulthood is a time of reflection; thus, older grandparents may find the responsibility of full-time parenting stressful due to a decline in their health or having to provide care for their spouse. On the other hand, looking after a grandchild may rejuvenate oneself, and offer a new source of meaning in life. In contrast, younger or middle-aged grandparents may be stressed by parenting grandchildren too. Factors causing stress for grandparents may be financial insecurity, health problems, employment issues, and family conflict.

Is there stress in looking after grandchildren, particularly full-time? Caring for a grandchild with psychological and/or physical problems, and having low family cohesion, are linked with the primary caregiving grandparent's stress. In addition, a lack of support from family and community can account for stress (Sands & Goldberg-Glen, 2000).

Is there satisfaction in looking after grandchildren? Possibly, higher socio-economic status, a higher level of physical health, and lower grandparent distress would lead to satisfaction in grandparenting.

Moreover, maternal grandparents might perceive more challenges and threats than would paternal grandparents; and grandfathers may perceive higher dysfunctional interaction with a grandchild (seeing grandparenthood more as compensation for parenthood, and perhaps harbouring more negativity about the grandparent role) than would grandmothers (Ben Shlomo, 2014).

Topics of discussions by grandchildren are commonly education, family, friends, leisure, and current events. And topics of discussions by grandparents are commonly education, family, leisure, friends, and occupations. Grandchildren report that current events is a topic substantially more often than grandparents, and the grandparents report talking about occupations substantially more than grandchildren (Lin, Harwood, & Bonnesen, 2002). This raises fascinating prospects for scrutinising the links between grandparent and grandchild concerning talking about family issues, perceptions of a shared identity, and relationship satisfaction. Notably, talking about the older person's age is less frequent than talking about the younger person's age as the latter is more acceptable as a relevant conversational issue.

Childcare by maids or domestic helpers

In today's world where both parents are working, and setting up a family on their own, with grandparents living away from them, a maid can come in handy when children are present. This mode of domestic help calls for attention and concern as a maid is often someone new and a stranger to the family, and could bring in lots of difficulties and worries if not well managed. Difficulties could include differences in language and culture, particularly regarding the methods of bringing up children. Of most concern to parents and grandparents alike is allowing another adult to nurture your children while you are not at home and away in the workplace. Trust and faith are all that matters; but how easy are they to come by now?

Numerous stories published in the media have said that parents have to be cautious when hiring maids or domestic helpers for their homes (*New Straits Times*, 2014; *Straits Times*, 2017). Preferably, as suggested in Muslim society, raising children and instilling in them life's core principles should solely be the mother's duty, and domestic helpers' skills should only be used for the housework roles of cleaner, cook, and nanny to children (*Gulf News*, 2015). They may likely outdo the parents. Many are parents themselves. Some have treated their charge as their own child. Many personal and interesting stories on this topic are available for your reading pleasure elsewhere; some are in the sections below.

So much has been said about parenting by nannies in general, and specifically by grandparents and maids. Let us now turn to some examples of childcare in different countries to broaden the understanding of this topic.

Examples of childcare

Grandparenting in China

In individualistic societies, like the US, intergenerational ties have become more central to individuals as a reaction to marital instability and demographic shifts. In collectivistic China, strong relationships between parents and children have persisted, despite a dramatically changing national socio-economic context. Grandparenting grandchildren is an increasingly common experience for many families in both urban and rural China.

Notably, many grandchildren live with their grandparents, in their homes, for childcare purposes. When the children's parents are absent due to work, grandparents spend seven hours more in childcare per week than those living in households with the parents present. Grandmothers in particular spend almost as much time in childcare as the mother (except for children in their first year of life). And paternal grandparents increase grandparents' time spent on childcare. In households with younger children, grandparents spend significantly more time in childcare than those with older children. Even with the widespread availability of day-care centres, grandparents' childcare involvement does not decrease (Chen, Liu, & Mair, 2011).

Thus, the concept of filial piety, which traditionally emphasised the responsibility of children for parents, is now well-adjusted with reciprocal or altruistic help from aging parents. It seems that working parents in China often rely on help from grandparents to balance the needs of work and childcare. The intergenerational solidarity and functionality are strong in China. The amount of childcare provided by grandparents adjusts to suit the needs of the family, yet is reflective of the cultural climate (Chen et al., 2011).

Health-wise, grandparents exhibit different status depending on their grandparenting situation. For example, grandparents who live in skipped-generation households (without the presence of the parents) do not suffer from poorer or deteriorating health compared with those who do not live with grandchildren. Compared with older adults who do not live with their grandchildren, grandparents living in three-generation households experience a steeper decline in health with age, despite their initial health advantage. Apparently, the high intensity of caring for younger grandchildren accelerates declines in health, whereas a lighter level of care has a protective effect. Paternal grandparents who co-reside with their son and grandson have a better level of health and slower rate of health decline than maternal grandparents in three-generation households; this is probably a protective effect associated with the culturally preferred type of living arrangement. In addition, rural grandparents and grandfathers engaging in high-intensity care have worse self-reported health status (Chen & Liu, 2012).

Grandparenting in South Africa

South African black grandparents in the present-day family play a key role in raising their grandchildren and giving parental support. For one, black parents view grandmothers as a primary source of support, and rely on them frequently. For another, grandmothers play a crucial role in the parenting support networks of black fathers. Grandparents are increasingly assuming parenting responsibilities for their grandchildren (Nkosinathi & Mtshali, 2015).

Grandparenting in South Africa takes different forms. There are grandparents assuming full childcare without a parent in the household (termed "custodial" grandmothers), and those grandmothers assisting their adult children by housing one or more parents and grandchildren ("co-parenting" grandmothers). Grandparenting occurs in response to a family crisis or divorce, or work demands, or school commitments of the parents.

Grandmothers play an influential role regarding parental competencies among urban black adolescent mothers in the early stages of the adolescent's transition to parenthood. Since few black adolescent mothers marry the father of their baby, the maternal grandmother often assumes some of the more traditional supportive paternal roles and responsibilities, while she simultaneously performs the role of mother for the adolescent mother. Basically, the grandmother's role is the central force in the parental adaptation of the young mother. Grandparents may provide assistance in advice or emotional support and contribute to the well-being of the children by serving in a parenting role themselves (Nkosinathi & Mtshali, 2015).

Caring for grandchildren is associated with financial strain and economic hardship for many grandparents. Childcare restrictions by employers on their workers' children mean that grandparents may be needed in bringing up their grandchildren. This in turn reinforces the customary practices of multi-generation households. Additionally, grandmothers perceive themselves as important in building families, educating younger generations, and providing generational continuity, and are proud of adopting the traditional male role of provider for the family if their men are unemployed (Nkosinathi & Mtshali, 2015).

Traditionally, in South African settings, interdependence and reciprocity have been more valued than independence as individuals, though there is evidence that this may be changing. Nevertheless, the presence of influential grandparenting styles in black families is not only a response to family difficulties but also reflects a way of thinking and organising family relationships that drives grandmothers to take the lead in parenting support (Nkosinathi & Mtshali, 2015).

Grandparenting in Western Europe

European societies are affected by aging and new family diversity. State policies and family customs influence and support each other. European countries (Sweden, Denmark, Netherlands, Belgium, France, Germany, Austria, Switzerland, Spain, Italy and Greece; see Igel, Brandt, Haberkern, & Szydlik, 2009) differ a lot in cultural dimensions and societal institutions. For example, northern family ties are weak, in Mediterranean countries obligations towards family members are strong, welfare state institutions in southern European countries rely on strong familism, and Nordic welfare states rely on universalism and state responsibilities for people in need. In northern countries and France, more grandparenting occurs than elsewhere in Europe.

Old people with higher life expectancy and better health in Western Europe contribute to intergenerational solidarity. Thus, grandparents play a central role in family networks, strengthening the parents' child-caring and employment; particularly when parents have fewer resources themselves. Young mothers are in favour of grandchildren being cared for by their parents, considering it the best childcare arrangement with emotional closeness between them. Grandparenting for a grandchild aged 6 or older requires less time than for a younger grandchild (Igel et al., 2009).

Childcare in Singapore

In Singapore, most mothers do not assist in raising their child's academic performance in their spare time; instead, they use private tutors or invest in other activities to do so. Many parents also choose to employ foreign domestic maids to do menial tasks at home and take care of their children, in order for them to continue working. Fortunately, the presence of a domestic helper in the home has an insignificant negative impact on academic grades of the children (Cheo & Quah, 2005). This could be due to the fact that time spent on academic work at home by the children is not time spent with the domestic helper.

Childcare in Hong Kong

Also in Hong Kong, due to the decreasing popularity of the extended family, many dual-earner families are having difficulties in coping with the demands of paid work and childcare. Consequently, maids (or "foreign domestic workers", as they are called) are hired to help working mothers look after the household. Most of these live-in maids are responsible for looking after elderly people over 65 or children under 12, and menial household chores. Thus, many Hong Kong children spend more time with their maids than with their parents. These maids are responsible for taking the children to after-school classes, eating with them at convenient food outlets, taking them to the park, watching television with them, and playing games and reading stories with them. Most of the children sleep in their maid's room. English-speaking and better-qualified maids, like those from the Philippines, also act as tutors, playmates, and confidants for the children under their care, thereby engaging in emotional support as well. As a result, many children develop a strong bond with them, and are spoilt by them. This intimate relationship could potentially cause discomfort in the parents, especially in the mother (Chan, 2005).

Having the maids, however, allows the mothers to work, and the parents to spend time with each other, contributing to a better marital relationship. The maids also buffer negative emotions that arise out of the daily domestic life. Despite the indispensability of maids, parents are reluctant to let them take up certain childcare and parenting roles. Leaving childcare wholly to them is not a preferred option for most Hong Kong families; apparently, there is a lack of trust between parents and maids, particularly when it comes to the caring of infants, a task that requires dedication and attention. Specifically, parents would like to be present at occasions for their children (such as when their children are giving a public performance or receiving awards), even if that means taking time off work. Parents retain for themselves tasks regarded as core parts of their relationship with their children, and those which symbolise their status as parents or as heads of the family; for example, going to a child's school performance, quality bedtime story reading, cooking up an impressive meal at family gatherings, visiting the doctor, shopping for new clothes, and supervision of computer usage and packing of school bags and homework (Chan, 2005).

Mothers are more likely than fathers to be jealous of the close relationship between their children and the maids for fear of their parental role being undermined.[1] Most maids get to see their families once every two years; thus, it is not unusual that some of them may project their emotional needs for family life onto their host families. Having a maid is like having a stranger in the home, which raises all kinds of issues, such as privacy and security. It is not easy to maintain consistency in how children are disciplined. Maids are the main caregivers but they do not have authority over discipline strategies. This generates concerns for parents regarding the quality of parenting they are contributing for their children. Overall, the maids, coming from a different culture and background, do contribute to different problems for the host families (Chan, 2005).

Childcare in South Africa

In many traditional African cultures, childrearing is a collective endeavour. The traditional Vhavenda childrearing practices in South Africa are interesting. Children are brought up in families following rules, norms, and values based on traditions of that society. They focus on modelling respect, perseverance as a virtue, and children working hard and actively participating in household chores. Traditional leaders contribute to foster the culture and traditional childrearing practices. Thus, children are guided by everyone in the family and community; an expression is that "another person's child is your child". The core of traditional childrearing practices is a belief that children who are brought up properly should have good morals and be respectful, must be responsible citizens, and should have the capacity to endure difficult situations. For example, the child is expected to be silent in the presence of adults, and to show respect to elders by kneeling when greeting them, receiving with two hands, and saying "Thank you". Children are disciplined through different methods, one of which is spanking.

With cultural evolution, however, most parents have abandoned the traditional childrearing practices (*nyaluso ya vhana*) in which grandparents take care of children, and now use maids and crèches to raise children. These modern ways could be a reason why many children are involved in acts of ill-discipline, substance abuse, inappropriate sexual activities, and so on (Murovhi, Matshidze, Netshandama, & Klu, 2018).

Childcare in Peru

Mobility has been a feature of Andean populations since the 16th century. This high degree of migration to urban centres is motivated by economic needs, a desire for education, or, as in the 1980s and early 1990s, an exodus from violence. This transnational migration is coupled with migrants' persistence and tenacity in maintaining and nourishing ties with relatives and friends in their homeland. Sex equality in migration suggests that both members of a couple may migrate. The transitory destiny of their children becomes a concern. But child fostering in the Andes is the answer (Leinaweaver, 2010).

Children are greatly desired in the Andean region, partly because even the smallest children are contributing members of the household, running errands, feeding animals, or gathering firewood. They are also desired to confirm and concretise one's status: full adult status is conferred only on persons with children. Child fostering in the Andes involves weighing different parties' needs and desires: a young person may benefit from moving to a socio-economically better-off setting, a biological parent may welcome the relief from the economic burden a child can represent, and a receiving household may need an extra pair of hands to help with housework or the comforting presence of another. Furthermore, the physical exchange of children strengthens network relations between distant kin (Leinaweaver, 2010).

Migration from Peru has increased dramatically over the past decade. Child fostering makes it possible for parents to migrate in search of better work opportunities, a unique strategy for socialisation of the child. It also prevents loneliness for the child if his or her parents are overseas as the child could be company for elderly parents and non-relative elders, and it reduces the responsibilities of parents (for example, the need to care for the child in the migrant country). Thus, for Peruvians engaging in labour migration, child fostering tempers some of the challenges of continuing to participate in established social networks from a distance (Leinaweaver, 2010).

Conclusion

Parenting is a crucial aspect of a child's growth, development, and life. Given the spread of available childcare in person (e.g., a nanny) or by an organisation (e.g., a childcare centre), it is often a difficult decision on the part of the parents to choose one from among them. Experience tells us that it is a matter of trust and faith when picking one and, fingers doubly crossed, nothing will happen to the child under their care. That said, it is not uncommon to find parents using all sorts of devices to track and monitor the movements and behaviours of the significant other with their child, like closed-circuit cameras hidden in inconspicuous places or cameras within computers. Hopefully, all will turn out well for both parents and the child, as it often does, in spite of the few cases mentioned in the media of abuse or even the killing of the child in care.

In summary, depending on significant others to parent one's child will be a thing of today and tomorrow given the dynamics of the changing world and its people. We must live with that. So let us summarise the pros and cons of using select significant others for parenting one's child (see Table 7.1).

Table 7.1 Pros and cons of parenting by significant others

Significant others	Pros	Cons	Remarks
Grandparent	Own parents. More trustworthy. Less worrying for parents, if same parenting style desired. Unlimited time if they are willing to take up parenting once more and living as extended family.	May spoil the children. May not keep up physically with child. May have to pay them as a token of appreciation. Prolonging the same parenting style they used. Need to travel to them if not living together.	Generally, grandparents spoil the grandchildren, who provide rejuvenation for them.
Maid or domestic helper	May have received proper training on childcare. Will do as instructed as a full-time paid job. May treat child as her own. Gives child a chance to socialise with her, culturally.	An outsider to the family or culture. Less trust at first; need to build up relationship. Child may be bonded to her more than own parents. Have to look after her welfare, e.g., annual leave, according to rules. May have to provide her with accommodation and food.	Generally, very supportive of parents' desire. Some may nurture children under care as theirs. Note: some maids or domestic helpers are from parents' own culture or country.
Nannies in general	May be qualified and experienced in childcare. Some countries demand proper training for them.	May be from another culture. Less trust at first; need to build up relationship. Childcare methods may be different.	Generally, they are experienced caregivers. Note: nannies may be from parents' own family circle or culture.

(Continued)

Table 7.1 (Cont.)

Significant others	Pros	Cons	Remarks
	Easier if they are from same culture. Gives child a chance to socialise with her.	Needs acculturation to desired parenting style of parents. May be limited by paid hours. May have to travel to her if not residential.	

Note

1 In psychology, this constitutes bonding, a strong attachment between an adult and a child, particularly in the first few years of life. The bonding will last throughout the child's life. Notice that a frightened child will turn to the person he or she has most bonded with. I have noticed many children run to the arms of the maid rather than the mother.

References

Adamson, E., Cortis, N., Brennan, D., & Charlesworth, S. (2017). Social care and migration policy in Australia: Emerging intersections? *Australian Journal of Social Issues, 52*(1), 78–94. doi: 10.1002/ajs4.1.

Akhtar, P., Malik, J. A., & Begeer, S. (2017). The grandparents' influence: Parenting styles and social competence among children of joint families. *Journal of Child and Family Studies, 26*(2), 603–611. doi: 10.1007/s10826-016-0576-5.

Ben Shlomo, S. (2014). What makes new grandparents satisfied with their lives? *Stress and Health, 30*(1), 23–33. doi: 10.1002/smi.2492.

Chan, A. H. (2005). Live-in foreign domestic workers and their impact on Hong Kong's middle class families. *Journal of Family and Economic Issues, 26*(4), 509–528. doi: 10.1007/s10834-005-7847-4.

Chen, F., & Liu, G. (2012). The health implications of grandparents caring for grandchildren in China. *Journals of Gerontology Series B: Psychological Sciences and Social Sciences, 67B*(1), 99–112. doi: 10.1093/geronb/gbr132.

Chen, F., Liu, G., & Mair, C. A. (2011). Intergenerational ties in context: Grandparents caring for grandchildren in China. *Social Forces, 90*(2), 571–594. doi: 10.1093/sf/sor012.

Cheo, R., & Quah, E. (2005). Mothers, maids and tutors: An empirical evaluation of their effect on children's academic grades in Singapore. *Education Economics, 13*(3), 269–285. doi: 10.1080/09645290500073746.

Dolbin-MacNab, M. L. (2006). Just like raising your own? Grandmothers' perceptions of parenting a second time around. *Family Relations, 55*(5), 564–575. doi: 10.1111/j.1741-3729.2006.00426.x.

Gheaus, A. (2011). Arguments for nonparental care for children. *Social Theory and Practice, 37*(3), 483–509.

Gulf News (2015, December 9). Parents warned against relying on housemaids when raising children.

Igel, C., Brandt, M., Haberkern, K., & Szydlik, M. (2009). Specialization between family and state intergenerational time transfers in Western Europe. *Journal of Comparative Family Studies, 40*(2), 203–226.

Isaksen, L. W., Devi, S. U., & Hochschild, A. R. (2008). Global care crisis: A problem of capital, care chain, or commons? *American Behavioral Scientist, 52*(3), 405–425. doi: 10.1177/0002764208323513.

Leinaweaver, J. B. (2010). Outsourcing care: How Peruvian migrants meet transnational family obligations. *Latin American Perspectives, 37*(5), 67–87. doi: 10.1177/0094582X10380222.

Lin, M., Harwood, J., & Bonnesen, J. L. (2002). Conversation topics and communication satisfaction in grandparent–grandchild relationships. *Journal of Language and Social Psychology, 21*(3), 302–323. doi: 10.1177/0261927X02021003005.

Lomanowska, A. M., Boivin, M., Hertzman, C., & Fleming, A. S. (2017). Parenting begets parenting: A neurobiological perspective on early adversity and the transmission of parenting styles across generations. *Neuroscience, 342,* 120–139. doi: 10.1016/j.neuroscience.2015.09.029.

Millward Purvis, L. J., & Cropley, M. (2003). Psychological contracting: Processes of contract formation during interviews between nannies and their "employers". *Journal of Occupational and Organizational Psychology, 76,* 213–241.

Murovhi, A., Matshidze, P., Netshandama, V., & Klu, E. (2018). Traditional child rearing practices in Vhavenda families South Africa. *Journal of Gender, Information & Development in Africa, 7*(1), 21–37.

New Straits Times. (2014, November 2). Indonesian maids too costly. Retrieved from www.nst.com.my/news/2015/09/%E2%80%98indonesian-maids-too-costly%E2%80%99.

Nkosinathi, M., & Mtshali, G. (2015). The relationship between grandparents and their grandchildren in the black families in South Africa. *Journal of Comparative Family Studies, 46*(1), 75–83.

Phillips, D., & Adams, G. (2001). Child care and our youngest children. *The Future of Children, 11*(1), 35–51.

Poblete, A. T., & Gee, C. B. (2018). Partner support and grandparent support as predictors of change in coparenting quality. *Journal of Child and Family Studies, 27*(7), 2295–2304. doi: 10.1007/s10826-018-1056-x.

Sands, R. G., & Goldberg-Glen, R. S. (2000). Factors associated with stress among grandparents raising their grandchildren. *Family Relations, 49*(1), 97–105.

Straits Times (2017, June 24). Make maids get consent before leaving S'pore. Retrieved from www.straitstimes.com/forum/letters-in-print/make-maids-get-consent-before-leaving-spore.

Yakeley, J. (2017). Mind the baby: The role of the nanny in infant observation. *International Journal of Psychoanalysis*, 98(6), 1577–1595. doi: 10.1111/1745-8315.12631.

Assessing your parenting style   8

By now you have had a good look at parenting styles. You may likely be happy with one or two and unhappy with others, and may be wondering what style is yours.

This chapter, hopefully, provides an answer to your query. To start, five of the prevalent theories and models that underpin the measurement of Eastern and Western parenting styles are mentioned. Next come common measurements (often called questionnaires or scales in the literature) used in parenting research. But as these measurements often examine either parenting styles or parenting outcomes, and due to space constraints, only select measurements regarding the former are briefly outlined. A list of the varied measurements of parenting outcomes is added thereafter, and one of the important outcomes that parents desire, that of academic achievement of children, is highlighted.

Finally comes the section you are waiting for: assessing your parenting style. Here, I have compiled a list of items into a table for your own check (see Table 8.1). Most of the items come from the Parenting Authority Questionnaire (Reitman, Rhode, Hupp, & Altobello, 2002), and from my previous research and work experience. Scoring is included. Whatever comes out of your assessment of your parenting style, do refer to the final chapter for suggested solutions of changes for the better, or for an overview.

Theories/models used in measuring parenting styles

Darling and Steinberg's contextual model of parenting style

Parental goals and values influence parenting practices and style, which affect the development of a child. Parenting practices directly affect the development of child behaviours and characteristics. In other words, parenting practices are the mechanisms for parents to have their child achieve parental socialisation goals. Parenting style influences child development by regulating the relationship between parenting practices and developmental outcomes, thereby increasing the child's acceptance of parental socialisation. In other words, the parenting style (a contextual variable) transforms the nature of the parent–child interaction, moderating the parental practices and child outcomes, and influencing the child's personality, especially in regard to his or her acceptance of parental influence. The child's openness to socialisation, in turn, moderates the association between parenting practices and child outcome (Darling & Steinberg, 1993).

Keller's integrative model

According to Heidi Keller (2013), a developmental psychologist, human parenting is a dynamic network consisting of different systems that integrate the interactive experiences of the child with his or her caregivers. The care systems that make up human parenting include: basic care, body contact, body stimulation, object stimulation, face-to-face exchange, and the narrative envelope. Notably, object stimulation and face-to-face exchange, which are called distal parenting, are prevalent in urban, educated middle-class families of Western cultures; and body contact and body stimulation, which are called proximal parenting, are prevalent in rural, low-educated farming families (Keller et al., 2009).

The system of basic care focuses on the provision of food, shelter, and hygiene. Its function is to ensure the child's survival and growth and a reduction in discomfort. Keenness in basic care gives the child a sense of safety and trust in the caregivers, which is linked to its self-development. The system of body contact is about the practice of carrying babies close to the caregiver's body. It provides attachment and protection against danger. The system of body stimulation involves the movement experiences between the child's body and parental behavioural responses. Its function is to build body awareness and effectiveness through environmental influences. The system of object stimulation for the child is meant to help him or her acquire knowledge about the physical world, encouraging cognitive development and releasing the child from dependency on social relationships.

In the face-to-face exchange system, eye contact is encouraged and accompanied by use of language in conversations with the baby. It stimulates perception of uniqueness, self-efficacy, and causal agency. The narrative envelope consists of the use of language by caregivers. Conversations with the child assist in the cultural appropriation of the self and others. This system is highly influenced by the mother's style of verbal communication with the child, who is also part of the cultural group to which he or she belongs (Seidl-de-Moura et al., 2014).

Self-determination theory

According to psychologists Edward L. Deci and Richard M. Ryan, self-determination theory is an empirically-based theory of human motivation, development, and wellness. It focuses on autonomous motivation, controlled motivation, and amotivation as predictors of performance, relational, and well-being outcomes. Autonomous motivation comprises intrinsic motivation and extrinsic motivation in which people have identified with an activity's value. When autonomously motivated, people experience a self-endorsement of their actions. Controlled motivation consists of both external regulation, in which one's behaviour is a function of external contingencies of reward or punishment, and introjected regulation, in which the regulation of action has been partially internalised, and is energised by factors such as an approval motive, avoidance of shame, contingent self-esteem, and ego-involvements. When people are controlled, they experience pressure to think, feel, or behave in particular ways. Both autonomous and controlled motivation energise and direct behaviour, and they stand in contrast to *amotivation*, which refers to a lack of intention and motivation.

The self-determination theory also covers the social conditions (autonomy, competence, and relatedness) that affect motivation. Additionally, it examines people's life goals or aspirations, showing differential relations of life goals to performance and psychological health. In other words, the theory covers basic issues of personality development, self-regulation, universal psychological needs, life goals and aspirations, energy and vitality, non-conscious processes, the relation of culture to motivation, and the impact of social environments on motivation, affect, behaviour, and well-being. This theory is applicable in the domains of work, relationships, parenting, education, virtual environments, sport, sustainability, health care, and psychotherapy (Deci & Ryan, 2008).

The family alliance model

The family alliance model is designed to conceptualise the relational dynamics in the early family. It is about the coordination a family can achieve when fulfilling a task, such as playing a game or having a meal. A coordinated family depends on four interactive functions: participation (of all members), organisation (members assuming differentiated roles), focalisation (family shares a common theme of activity), and affect sharing (empathy between members). The functions are operationalised through the spatio-temporal characteristics of non-verbal interactions, that is, distance between the partners, orientation of their bodies, congruence within body segments, signals of readiness to interact, joint attention, and facial expressions. Several standardised observational situations have been designed to assess the family alliance: Lausanne Trilogue Play, in which mother, father, and baby interact in all possible configurations of a triad, and the Picnic Game for families with several children. Studies using this model have found different types of family alliance: disorganised, conflicted, and cooperative. The type of family alliance in a given family is stable through the first years and is predictive of developmental outcomes in children, such as psycho-functional symptoms, understanding of complex emotions, and theory of mind development (Favez, Frascarolo, & Tissot, 2017).

Wendi Otto's East Asian Parenting Model

Wendi Otto, an academic, proposes the East Asian Parenting Model, which builds upon the combination of Chinese training and the contextual parenting style model by Darling and Steinberg, which directly affect the developmental outcomes of children. Basically, the model looks at East Asian ideologies with their parenting styles and practices and at why East Asian children are doing well academically. The themes identified in parenting ideology about child development and learning are: belief in children's self-control and good behaviour by age 5; use of effort in learning; a preference for children to be with adults for modelling; spanking for behavioural reasons or moral misbehaviour; mothers to be emotionally and physically close with children; fathers assisting with school through active participation and presence in children's lives; and parents as primary decision-makers, providing a happy, comfortable home, meeting children's expectations as best they can, and, in return, expecting parental requests to be responded to immediately (Otto, 2016).

In summary, the reader will find in studies the frequent use of the aforementioned theories/models and variables, operationalised or defined in concrete terms, in measuring parenting styles and outcomes.

Measuring parenting and child outcomes

Next, we'll go through how parenting and child outcomes are measured. There are two main ways of measuring in research: the quantitative and qualitative methods. The quantitative method uses fixed-choices lists called questionnaires, scales, instruments, inventories, or checklists, to use the main names for them. The qualitative method uses open-ended questions generally to elicit responses from participants. Many other qualitative approaches are available—for example, artefacts, anecdotes, bibliographies, films, narrations, pictures, tapes, videos, and any form of write-up or depiction. Some researchers combine these methods in research, calling them mixed-method studies.

For discussion, I will stick to *questionnaires* and *scales*. Note that some researchers use one or more questionnaires wholly (using all items) or partially (using some relevant items) or in combination to assess their objectives (e.g., types of parenting, outcomes of children), validate their designed questionnaires psychometrically, or to prove a point of contention, which are among their main uses.

The above theoretical section has given you an idea of parenting and child outcomes. However, the translation of theory into measures has been inconsistent, particularly when applied to different cultures. Some difficult situations include: use of typologies versus dimensions; parenting styles versus practices; having a limited number of items in a questionnaire/scale as opposed to the high number in practice areas; and methods being used to assess the validity of parenting practices in different cultures.

Typologies describe qualitatively diverse combinations of parental attributes. Such configurations would provide more of an aggregate, natural occurrence of parenting than would single, linear dimensions, such as acceptance versus rejection. The latter, however, is more concrete in measuring parenting, and could be universal too, but unrealistic—just one or two aspects is insufficient in describing parenting. As an illustration, adolescents internalise the effects of parenting that they perceive which, in turn, are manifested in their development of social competence and adjustment (Akhtar, Malik, & Begeer, 2017). How would you design a study to measure this?

Parenting questionnaires/scales

Many parenting questionnaires or scales have been designed and used in measuring parenting and outcomes. Quite a few are mentioned here briefly, and the commonly used ones in detail, for a better understanding of their scope and coverage.

Alabama Parenting Questionnaire

This questionnaire (Esposito, Servera, Garcia-Banda, & Del Giudice, 2016; Maguin, Nochajski, De Wit, & Safyer, 2016) is based on information on parenting, child disruptive behaviour, and delinquency in literature. It consists of a global version and brief report version; each comprises a parent form and a child form. The parent global report version consists of 35 items grouped into five scales—parental involvement (10 items), positive parenting (six items), poor monitoring/supervision (10 items), inconsistent discipline (six items), corporal punishment (three items)—and seven heterogeneous items on practices such as reasoning, ignoring, loss of privileges, time-out, and extra work. The items are focused on behaviour and meant for children in the 6- to 13-year-old age range.

Block's Childrearing Practices Report

This report (Chen, Dong, & Zhou, 1997) consists of 91 items that analyse different types of parenting practices such as encouragement of independence, punishment, induction, emphasis on achievement, inhibition of affection, and emphasis on conformity.

Chinese Paternal/maternal Overparenting Scale

This scale (Leung & Shek, 2018) consists of 44 items covering the following eight dimensions: close monitoring, intrusion on child's life and direction, strong emphasis on academic performance, frequent comparisons of child's achievement with peers, anticipatory problem-solving, overscheduling of child's activities, excessive care, and excessive affective involvement. A sample item is, "My development is under my father's/mother's meticulous plan."

Controlling Parents Survey

This survey (Dreher, Feldman, & Numan, 2014) is a 16-item scale measuring the influence of perceived parental control on personal development of college students. It covers the intrusive actions of parents (micromanaging, excessive control of students' lives) and students' emotional reactions (insecurity, helplessness, low personal control).

"Intrusive Parents" statements are:

> I find it hard to disagree with my parents. My parents called a campus office to make an appointment for me. My parents helped choose my classes. My parents called a professor or administrator to help me. My parents help manage my college schedule. When I was a child, my parents laid out my clothes for me. My parents did my homework for me. My parents will intervene if I have a problem with a professor.

"Emotional Immaturity" statements are:

My parents helped choose my classes. I feel uncomfortable or helpless when alone. I now consider myself an adult (r). It's easy to work independently, begin my own projects (r). I am often uncomfortable in social situations. I am confused when making decisions on my own. I enjoy challenging tasks (r). I am eager to handle adult responsibilities (r). I am often stressed when with people I don't know. r = reverse scoring.

Differentiation-of-self Scale

This scale (Schwartz, Thigpen, & Montgomery, 2006) is a 43-item self-report inventory assessing aspects of the differentiation-of-self construct. Differentiation of self is the ability to balance emotional and intellectual influences in cognitive functioning, and intimacy and autonomy in relationships. *Fused* people are unable to distinguish their emotions and intellect from those of others; they are less flexible, less adaptable, and more dependent on the people around them. *Differentiated* people are more flexible, adaptable, autonomous, and better able to cope with stressors. Higher differentiation is related to fewer psychological symptoms, greater marital satisfaction, less marital discord, fewer physical complaints, less life stress, greater autonomy, less chronic anxiety, greater health-related behaviours, and higher levels of identity and intimacy resolution.

This scale consists of four subscales: emotional reactivity, I position, emotional cut-off, and fusion with others. *Emotional reactivity* measures emotional lability, emotional flooding, or hypersensitivity. *I position* reflects a clearly defined sense of self. *Emotional cut-off* reflects feeling threatened by intimacy, which often leads to interpersonal distancing. *Fusion with others* reflects emotional over-involvement with others, including triangulation, and identification with parents.

Emotion-related Parenting Styles Self-test

This self-test (Hakim-Larson, Parker, Lee, Goodwin, & Voelker, 2006) is an 81-item true/false-format questionnaire consisting of four scales, each representing a different parenting style based on the meta-emotion theory. They are: the Emotion Coaching scale of 23 items (e.g., "When my child is sad, it's a time to problem solve"; "It's important to help the child find out what caused the child's anger"), the Laissez-faire scale of 10 items (e.g., "You should express the anger you feel"; "When my child is angry, I try to let her know that I love her no matter what"), the Dismissing scale of 25 items (e.g., "Childhood is a happy-go-lucky time, not a time for feeling sad or angry"; "I don't want to make a big deal out of my child's sadness"), and the Disapproving scale of 23 items (e.g., "When she gets sad, I warn her about developing a bad character"; "Kids get angry to get their own way").

Indigenous Parenting Style Scale

This scale was developed in Pakistan and consists of six factors: Controlling, Compassionate, Conventional, Supportive, Avoidant, and Aggressive Parenting (Batool & Mumtaz, 2015).

Intensive Parenting Attitudes Questionnaire

This questionnaire (Schiffrin et al., 2014) consists of 25 items that assess intensive parenting attitudes across five domains: essentialism, which emphasises that mothers make the best parents; fulfilment, the belief that parenting should be delightful and completely fulfilling; stimulation, or the idea that parents should continually engage their children in intellectually stimulating activities; challenging, the belief that parenting is very difficult; and child-centred, the belief that parenting should focus on the needs of the child more than the needs of the parents.

"One's Memories of Upbringing" Scale

This scale (Yangzong et al., 2016) is used to assess three dimensions of parenting style: rejection (seven items), emotional warmth (six items), and overprotection (10 items). Rejection is characterised by a critical and judgemental approach to parenting. Emotional warmth is shown through parenting attitudes of acceptance, support, and value, whereas overprotection is characterised by being fearful for a child's safety and having a high degree of control over them. The scale includes father and mother forms with 23 items each.

Parent–Parental Acceptance–Rejection Questionnaire

The Parent–Parental Acceptance–Rejection Questionnaire, to be completed by parents, has 24 items that measure parental acceptance and rejection of their children and adolescents. Its four subscales are: coldness/lack of affection (eight items), hostility/aggression (six items), indifference/neglect (six items), and undifferentiated rejection (four items) (Gomez & Suhaimi, 2015).

Parental Authority Questionnaire

This questionnaire was developed by J. R. Buri (Reitman et al., 2002) to reflect the three basic parenting styles from Baumrind's typology: authoritarian, permissive, and authoritative parenting. It is a 30-item test to assess parental authority or disciplinary practices from the child's point of view. It has been used in urban India (Raval, Ward, Raval, & Trivedi, 2013), Pakistan (Loona & Kamal, 2012), Arab societies (Dwairy et al., 2006), and Japan (Uji, Sakamoto, Adachi, & Kitamura, 2014).

Parental Authority Questionnaire—Revised

This questionnaire (Reitman et al., 2002) is a parental self-report version of the original, and intended for use with parents of children aged 3–8. It consists of 30 items, with three 10-item scales representing authoritative, authoritarian, and permissive parenting styles.

Parenting Style Self-Test—Revised

The original Parenting Style Self-Test was a true/false questionnaire to allow parents to assess their parenting style, whereas the Parenting Style Self-Test—Revised (Schwartz et al., 2006) is used to measure individuals' retrospective assessment of their father's and mother's parenting styles. The revised questionnaire consists of 162 questions: 81 each for assessing the parenting styles of both parents, covering the following four parenting styles: emotion-coaching parenting allows one's children to express emotions and to teach them how to deal with emotions; the disapproving parenting style punishes displays of emotions; the dismissing parenting style disregards, ignores, or trivialises displays of emotion; and the laissez-faire parenting style attends to emotions but not using emotional expressions to teach the child how to handle them.

The Parent–Child Interaction Questionnaire

This questionnaire (Lange, Evers, Jansen, & Dolan, 2002) is designed to assess the quality of the parenting relationship between the individual parents and any or all of their individual children. It focuses on attitudes and behavioural interactions between parent and child. There are two versions: a parent version (21 items) and a child version (25 items). There are two subscales: Conflict Resolution and Acceptance.

Parenting Style and Dimensions Questionnaire

This questionnaire (Roman et al., 2015) consists of 32 items assessing the perception of parents about their style of parenting: authoritarian, authoritative, and indulgence/permissive. Each dimension has four or five items.

Parental Self-efficacy Test

This test (Wittkowski, Garrett, Calam, & Weisberg, 2017) describes a parent's belief in their ability to perform the parenting role successfully. Higher levels of parental self-efficacy have consistently been shown to be correlated with a wide range of parenting and child outcomes.

Outcome questionnaires

Many outcome questionnaires are used in conjunction with parenting questionnaires to assess the outcomes for children of adopted parenting styles. Some are cited here, alphabetically, to give you an idea of the breadth of these measurements: Adolescent Perception of Parenting Measure and Academic Performance and Mastery Scales (Phillipson & McFarland, 2016); Alcohol and Drug Attitude Scale (Singh & Niwas, 2015); Child Behaviour Checklist (used in India, for example; Raval et al., 2013); Difficulties in Emotion Regulation Scale and Eating Attitudes Test (McEwen & Flouri, 2009); Disruptive Behaviour Disorder Rating scale (used in Pakistan; Loona & Kamal, 2012); General Health Questionnaire-12 and Brief Multidimensional Students' Life Satisfaction Scale

(Abubakar, Van de Vijver, Suryani, Handayani, & Pandia, 2015); Infant Behavior Questionnaire, Personality Inventory, and Work–Family Questionnaire (Woodworth, Belsky, & Crnic, 1996); Moral Values Internalisation Questionnaire (Karmakar, 2015); Peer Assessments of Social Behaviour (Chen et al., 1997); Psychological Control Scale–Youth Self Report and Interpersonal Reactivity Index (Yoo, Feng, & Day, 2013); Psychological State Scale and Multigenerational Interconnectedness Scale (Dwairy, Achoui, Abouserie, & Farah, 2006); Self-efficacy Scale (Leung & Shek, 2018); and the Self-esteem Scale (Lo Cascio, Guzzo, Pace, Pace, & Madonia, 2016).

Academic achievement of children

This is perhaps one significant outcome most parents of today are concerned with regarding the bringing up of their children. Many studies have examined this topic; a couple are mentioned herein.

A longitudinal study (Aunola & Nurmi, 2004) investigated mothers of 196 children (5–6 years) in Central Finland with reference to the effect of mothers' psychological control on their children's mathematical performance. Three conditions used were: during the children's transition from preschool to primary school, beyond the impact of maternal affection, and behavioural control. The results show that mothers' psychological control had a detrimental impact on the development of children's math skill only when mothers concurrently reported a high level of affection. There was no evidence that children's mathematical performance had any effect on their mothers' parenting styles.

Another study (Zakeri, Esfahani, & Razmjoee, 2013) examined 395 Iranian university students regarding the relationship between parenting styles and academic procrastination. The results show that warm, accepting parents, who use restrictions with logical thinking and encouragement about performing homework with their children, reduce their academic procrastination, thus increasing academic achievement. Conversely, parents who are sensitive to their children's developmental needs, but employ little emotional support and apply restrictions using severe discipline with poor verbal parent–child communication, decrease academic achievement in their children.

In summary, children whose mothers show psychological control and affection in their parenting are likely to demonstrate slow progress in their math performance during the transition from preschool to primary school.

Assessing your parenting style

We have now come to how to assess your parenting style. Table 8.1 below puts together a few pertinent parenting styles and practices for you to go through. Remember, *style* is a general strategy, and *practice* is a specific application. These are to give you more information in your search to know yourself better concerning parenting. Each style or practice includes a short list of items taken (but possibly modified) from the research literature and media. Add the ticks in each row in the right-hand column to give you the style and practice of parenting you have been adopting.

Note that the parenting style is identified first in the left column, then the related items (often statements) are placed in the column adjacent to it. In formal research studies, the parenting style is not named and the items are jumbled up for the user to tick. That way, participants will not have their parenting style in mind and will work on the questionnaire, which is fairer for the sake of research.

Here, to save the reader time and difficulty in reading the instructions of actual questionnaires, I have just compiled the relevant items or statements, so that you check the number of those that are appropriate to you, then add them up according to the style or practice. The more you have checked in each category, the more it is referring to your current parenting style or practice. To do this straightforwardly, think of your parenting style in the past week, month, or year, or in the period relevant to your child's age. Do not think too deeply, just whatever comes to mind. If an item does not apply to you, skip it.

It is likely that you would have used a style or a combination of them according to each child and situation. But you are likely to be quite consistent in your parenting practice. If, in the end, you use varied styles or practices, your opinions may not be in accordance with a stable parenting style. You may be doing what you consider is best at the moment for your child. In general, parents are quite consistent in their parenting, though they may not follow strongly a particular parenting style. Unless you are influenced by the literature or media

Table 8.1 Assessing your parenting style /practice

Father/Mother (circle one)			
		(√ Tick)	
Authoritarian Parenting	Parents should teach their children who is in charge in the family.		8 and above = High
	I do not allow my children to question the opinions and decisions that I make.		
	I often tell my children clearly what I want them to do and how I expect them to do it.		
	I let my children know what behaviour is expected, and if they don't follow those rules, they get punished.		
	I disallow most things my children want to do but only allow those that I approve of.		4 and below = Low
	Children have to be reminded and monitored of their activities and rules, and nagged if they forget.		
	It is for my children's good to have them do what I think is right, even if they don't agree.		*Note*: The higher the score, the closer to this style.
	When I ask my children to do something, I expect it to do to be done straightaway without questions or fuss.		
	Other parents should use more power and discipline to get their children to behave.		
	I get very upset and disappointed if my children try to disagree with me.		
	My children know what I expect of them and do what is asked simply out of respect for me and my authority.		
	Most problems in society could be solved if parents were stricter with their children.		
		12	

(Continued)

Table 8.1 (Cont.)

Father/Mother (circle one)		
		(√ Tick)
Authoritative Parenting	I have clear standards of behaviour for my children, but I am willing to change these standards to the needs of each child.	
	I manage activities and decision-making of my children by talking with them and using rewards and punishments.	8 and above = High
	My children know what I expect from them, but they feel free to talk with me when expectations are seemingly unfair.	
	Once family rules have been made, I discuss the reasons for the rules with my children.	4 and below = Low
	I always encourage discussion when my children feel family rules and restrictions are unfair or not quite their way.	
	I tell my children what they should do, but I explain why I want them to do it.	
	I listen to my children when making decisions, but I do not decide on something simply because they want it.	*Note*: The higher the score, the closer to this style.
	I expect my children to follow my directions, but I am always willing to listen to their concerns and discuss the directions with them.	
	I set firm guidelines for my children but I am understanding when they disagree with me.	
	If I make a decision that hurts my children, I am willing to admit that I've made a mistake.	
	I may appear quite controlling to my children, but they understand where I am coming from with reasons.	
	I often check on my children's schoolwork and progress, and they understand the reasons behind it.	____ 12

(*Continued*)

Table 8.1 (Cont.)

Father/Mother (circle one)		
		(√ Tick)
Eastern-style Parenting	Tradition and custom must be upheld in spite of the world modernising.	
	We discuss issues and problems as a family before making choices and decisions.	8 and above = High
	Everyone in the family or group is responsible to uphold the name of the family and our society.	
	Interdependence among us is valued over individual commitments.	
	Parental wishes and desired for their children come before the children's demands.	4 and below = Low
	Education is priority in life such that success in academic achievement is highly valued.	
	Appropriate punishment is meted out to discipline misbehaviours in children when they are growing up.	*Note*: The higher the score, the closer to this style.
	Children must respect their parents, elders, ancestry and religious worships.	
	Children are to be grateful to their parents for bringing them up.	
	Filial piety or its variation is upheld in the family.	
	It is normal for parents to control their children's behaviours, activities, and circle of friends. This is for their good.	
	Occasionally, children may decide on matters they prefer, but parents have to be convinced of them.	
		___ 12

(*Continued*)

Copyright material from Dr. Foo Koong Hean (2019), *Intercultural Parenting*, Taylor & Francis

Table 8.1 (Cont.)

Father/Mother (circle one)			
		(√ Tick)	
Filial Parenting	I believe children should be grateful to their parents for raising them.		
	I believe children should give up personal interests to fulfil parental expectations.		8 and above = High
	I consider my children's behaviour a reflection of how other people think of me and my family.		4 and below = Low
	I put my children's needs and safety come before mine.		Note: The higher the score, the closer to this style.
	When my children's academic performance is below my expectation, I become frustrated or angry.		
	I consider education a top priority in bringing up my children.		
	I am willing to do everything for my children's education and future, and make sacrifices when necessary for their best interests.		
	Filial piety means obedience and taking good care of one's parents or elderly family members. I value filial piety in my family.		
	I am willing to let my children live with me until they are ready to live independently.		
	Out of love, I believe parents should go the extra mile for their children.		
	I am always thinking of my children, and worry if they are not home or around me.		
	I am grateful if my children look after me or show concern when I am not well.		
		12	

(Continued)

Table 8.1 (Cont.)

Father/Mother (circle one)			
		(√ Tick)	
Indulgent Parenting	Children are free to make up their own minds, even if it is in disagreement with their parents.		8 and above = High
	I support my children even when they are not quite right.		
	I could make family decisions based mainly on what my children wanted.		4 and below = Low
	I am more of a friend to my children than a parent or caregiver.		*Note*: The higher the score, the closer to this style.
	I allow my children to do whatever they want mostly and make no attempt to curb their behaviour even if they disturbing or disrupting the activities of others.		
	I support my children's decisions without question or doubt most of the time.		
	I would give money to my children as long as they need it and ask for it.		
	I tend to give in to my children's demand mostly, however extreme they may seem to be.		
	I seldom set and enforce rules and standards on my children while they were growing up.		
	I would reward my children when I want them to do something necessary or right.		
	I give in to my children because they are my children.		
	Children should be given the best of life by parents whenever or whatever they could afford.		
		12	

(*Continued*)

Table 8.1 (Cont.)

Father/Mother (circle one)			
		(√ Tick)	
Negotiation Parenting	Parents decide what and how to do for their children when they are very young and not able to understand and make decisions for themselves.		8 and above = High
	Parents use business negotiation strategies, like logic and reasoning, to work with their children.		
	Families must not neglect their roots and culture.		4 and below = Low
	Knowledge from food, medical and neurological science are used to assist in bringing up children.		*Note*: The higher the score, the closer to this style.
	Smart parents nurture their children's thoughts, feelings, physiology, and actions so that they become wholesome successful personalities.		
	Smart parents harness children's strengths and build upon their weaknesses.		
	Smart parents understand themselves first and well before coaching their children.		
	Parents understand that they children have their own lives and paths, so they would let them go if they truly love them.		
	No matter how well parenting goes, children can still make mistakes in life; so parents are not to be blamed.		
	Parents and children are equal partners in the growing up and development process.		
	Parents know best when children are not able to understand the world they are in.	__12__	

(*Continued*)

Table 8.1 (Cont.)

Father/Mother (circle one)			
		(√ Tick)	
Neglecting Parenting	Parents need to consult with experts or authorities in order to raise children properly.		
	I do not give my children much support, whether emotionally or morally.		8 and above = High
	I often forget to give my children allowance even when they ask for it.		
	When my children were growing up, I made no effort to involve myself in their affairs.		4 and below = Low
	I am more often preoccupied with my problems and did not spend time with my children.		*Note*: The higher the score, the closer to this style.
	I am not concerned with my children social life and do not make attempts to find out.		
	I spend long periods of time away from home and makes little effort to contact my children.		
	I do not communicate much with my children and do not make the effort to do so.		
	I do not help my children much.		
	I am not concerned with my children's problems and actively avoid addressing them.		
	I live by my life mostly even in the presence of my family.		
	Children should grow up mostly on their own.		
	Parents have the right to be themselves in spite of having a family.	12	

(*Continued*)

Copyright material from Dr. Foo Koong Hean (2019), *Intercultural Parenting*, Taylor & Francis

Table 8.1 (Cont.)

Father/Mother (circle one)			
		(√ Tick)	
Permissive Parenting	In a proper home, children should have their way as often as parents do.		8 and above = High
	Children need to be free to make their own decisions about activities, even if this disagrees with what a parent might want to do.		
	My children do not need to obey rules simply because people in authority have told them to.		
	I usually don't set firm guidelines for my children's behaviour.		4 and below = Low
	Most of the time I do what my children want when making family decisions.		
	Most problems in society would be solved if parents would let their children choose their activities, make their own decisions, and follow their own desires when growing up.		*Note*: The higher the score, the closer to this style.
	I allow my children to decide most things for themselves without a lot of direction from me.		
	I do not see myself as responsible for telling my children what to do.		
	I allow my children to form their own opinions about family matters and let them make their own decisions about those matters.		
	I do not direct the behaviours, activities, and desires of my children.		
	Children are born free to be themselves.		
	There is no point having children if parents need to restrict their behaviour or control them in some way.		
		___ 12	

Copyright material from Dr. Foo Koong Hean (2019), *Intercultural Parenting*, Taylor & Francis

on parenting, you are likely adhering to how you have been brought up and/or how you desire to parent your child or children.

Do not judge yourself meanly if the parenting style turns out not to be your desired style or the better one recommended in the literature or here. Do not try to undo what you have done; just move on to the most suitable parenting style for you and your family.

Conclusion

There is little uniformity in measurements of parenting and outcomes.

Parenting styles are related to behaviour that occurs over a broad range of situations, thereby creating an atmosphere within which parent–child interactions take place. They are postulated to have similar influences across cultures. Parenting practices are situation-specific behaviours that may have different meanings in different cultures.

Critiques on parenting measurements are countless, as mentioned before. No one style dictates universal parenting, and no one measure is capable of checking the different parenting styles across the cultures. For example, Steinberg's group assesses warmth/involvement as a one-dimensional construct; low scores denote deficient warmth. There are no negative control components in this scale. A scale called Parental Warmth and Acceptance captures a bipolar construct, with a low score denoting deficient warmth, rejection, and hostility (Greenberger & Chen, 1996, cited in Stewart & Bond, 2002).

Parental supervisory and control practices are described differently in different scales. For example, the Child Rearing Practices Report (Chen, Dong, & Zhou, 1997) includes rejecting, and critical behaviours with firmness, whereas other scales just have firmness alone.

In summary, there is a consensus or there are similarities among investigators concerning warmth, regulation, and respect for the child's autonomy. However, at the practical level, grouping the constructs into dimensions and scales is highly variable. Warmth and dominating control are probably the only two dimensions of parenting style that may be universal (Stewart & Bond, 2002).

This is just a glimpse at the criticisms or dissatisfactions that researchers on parenting leverage on one another. It is meant not to discredit others, but to identify flaws or gaps in research for future directions and improvements.

So, as you have seen for yourself, parenting is a difficult concept or construct to define and measure. But given what we have achieved so far, we should be satisfied with what we have gone through, and move on to better things.

References

Abubakar, A., Van de Vijver, F. J. R., Suryani, A. O., Handayani, P., & Pandia, W. S. (2015). Perceptions of parenting styles and their associations with mental health and life satisfaction among urban Indonesian adolescents. *Journal of Child and Family Studies, 24*(9), 2680–2692. doi: 10.1007/s10826-014-0070-x.

Akhtar, P., Malik, J. A., & Begeer, S. (2017). The grandparents' influence: Parenting styles and social competence among children of joint families. *Journal of Child and Family Studies, 26*(2), 603–611. doi: 10.1007/s10826-016-0576-5.

Aunola, K., & Nurmi, J. (2004). Maternal affection moderates the impact of psychological control on a child's mathematical performance. *Developmental Psychology, 40*(6), 965–978. doi: 10.1037/0012-1649.40.6.965.

Batool, S. S., & Mumtaz, A. N. (2015). Development and validation of parenting style scale. *Pakistan Journal of Psychological Research, 30*(2), 225.

Chen, X., Dong, Q., & Zhou, H. (1997). Authoritative and authoritarian parenting practices and social and school performance in Chinese children. *International Journal of Behavioral Development, 21*(4), 855–873. doi: 10.1080/016502597384703.

Darling, N., & Steinberg, L. (1993). Parenting style as context: An integrative model. *Psychological Bulletin, 113*(3), 487–496.

Deci, E. L., & Ryan, R. M. (2008). Self-determination theory: A macrotheory of human motivation, development, and health. *Canadian Psychology, 49*(3), 182–185. doi: 10.1037/a0012801.

Dreher, D. E., Feldman, D. B., & Numan, R. (2014). Controlling Parents Survey: Measuring the influence of parental control on personal development in college students. *College Student Affairs Journal, 32*(1), 97–111.

Dwairy, M., Achoui, M., Abouserie, R., & Farah, A. (2006). Parenting styles, individuation, and mental health of Arab adolescents: A third cross-regional research study. *Journal of Cross-Cultural Psychology, 37*(3), 262–272. doi: 10.1177/0022022106286924.

Dwairy, M., Achoui, M., Abouserie, R., Farah, A., Sakhleh, A. A., Fayad, M., & Khan, H. K. (2006). Parenting styles in Arab societies: A first cross-regional research study. *Journal of Cross-Cultural Psychology, 37*(3), 230–247. doi: 10.1177/0022022106286922.

Esposito, A., Servera, M., Garcia-Banda, G., & Del Giudice, E. (2016). Factor analysis of the Italian version of the Alabama parenting questionnaire in a community sample. *Journal of Child and Family Studies, 25*(4), 1208–1217. doi: 10.1007/s10826-015-0291-7.

Favez, N., Frascarolo, F., & Tissot, H. (2017). The family alliance model: A way to study and characterize early family interactions. *Frontiers in Psychology, 8*, 1–11. doi: 10.3389/fpsyg.2017.01441.

Gomez, R., & Suhaimi, A. F. (2015). Malaysia parent ratings of the Parent–Parental Acceptance–Rejection Questionnaire: Invariance across ratings of Malay, Chinese, and Indian children. *Cross-Cultural Research, 49*(1), 90–105. doi: 10.1177/1069397114548647.

Hakim-Larson, J., Parker, A., Lee, C., Goodwin, J., & Voelker, S. (2006). Measuring parental meta-emotion: Psychometric properties of the emotion-related parenting styles self-test. *Early Education & Development, 17*(2), 229–251. doi: 10.1207/s15566935eed1702_2.

Karmakar, R. (2015). Does parenting style influence the internalization of moral values in children and adolescents? *Psychological Studies, 60*(4), 438–446. doi: 10.1007/s12646-015-0338-2.

Keller, H. (2013). Attachment and culture. *Journal of Cross-Cultural Psychology, 44*(2), 175–194. doi: 10.1177/0022022112472253.

Keller, H., Borke, J., Staufenbiel, T., Yovsi, R. D., Abels, M., Papaligoura, Z., ... Su, Y. (2009). Distal and proximal parenting as alternative parenting strategies during infants' early months of life: A cross-cultural study. *International Journal of Behavioral Development, 33*(5), 412–420. doi: 10.1177/0165025409338441.

Lange, A., Evers, A., Jansen, H., & Dolan, C. (2002). PACHIQ-R: The Parent–Child Interaction Questionnaire—Revised. *Family Process, 41*(4), 709–722. doi: 10.1111/j.1545-5300.2002.00709.x.

Leung, J. T. Y., & Shek, D. T. L. (2018). Validation of the perceived Chinese overparenting scale in emerging adults in Hong Kong. *Journal of Child and Family Studies, 27*(1), 103–117. doi: 10.1007/s10826-017-0880-8.

Lo Cascio, V., Guzzo, G., Pace, F., Pace, U., & Madonia, C. (2016). The relationship among paternal and maternal psychological control, self-esteem, and indecisiveness across adolescent genders. *Current Psychology, 35*(3), 467–477. doi: 10.1007/s12144-015-9315-0.

Loona, M. I., & Kamal, A. (2012). Role of perceived parenting styles and familial factors in prediction of teacher-report childhood behavior problems. *Journal of Behavioural Sciences, 22*(3), 49.

Maguin, E., Nochajski, T. H., De Wit, D. J., & Safyer, A. (2016). Examining the validity of the adapted Alabama Parenting Questionnaire – Parent Global Report Version. *Psychological Assessment, 28*(5), 613–625.

McEwen, C., & Flouri, E. (2009). Fathers' parenting, adverse life events, and adolescents' emotional and eating disorder symptoms: The role of emotion regulation. *European Child & Adolescent Psychiatry, 18*(4), 206–216. doi: 10.1007/s00787-008-0719-3.

Otto, W. J. (2016). What teachers should know about why these students perform so well: An examination of Korean-American achievement through student perspectives of East Asian parenting beliefs, styles and practices. *International Electronic Journal of Elementary Education, 9*(1), 167–181.

Phillipson, S., & McFarland, L. (2016). Australian parenting and adolescent boys' and girls' academic performance and mastery: The mediating effect of perceptions of parenting and sense of school membership. *Journal of Child and Family Studies, 25*(6), 2021–2033. doi: 10.1007/s10826-016-0364-2.

Raval, V. V., Ward, R. M., Raval, P. H., & Trivedi, S. S. (2013). Confirmatory and exploratory factor analyses of Parental Authority Questionnaire in urban India. *Journal of Child and Family Studies, 22*(5), 707–718. doi: 10.1007/s10826-012-9624-y.

Reitman, D., Rhode, P. C., Hupp, S. D. A., & Altobello, C. (2002). Development and validation of the Parental Authority Questionnaire – Revised. *Journal of Psychopathology and Behavioral Assessment, 24*(2), 119–127. doi: 10.1023/A:1015344909518.

Roman, N. V., Davids, E. L., Moyo, A., Schilder, L., Lacante, M., & Lens, W. (2015). Parenting styles and psychological needs influences on adolescent life goals and aspirations in a South African setting. *Journal of Psychology in Africa, 25*(4), 305–312. doi: 10.1080/14330237.2015.1078087.

Schiffrin, H. H., Liss, M., Geary, K., Miles-McLean, H., Tashner, T., Hagerman, C., & Rizzo, K. (2014). Mother, father, or parent? College students' intensive parenting attitudes differ by referent. *Journal of Child and Family Studies, 23*(6), 1073–1080. doi: 10.1007/s10826-013-9764-8.

Schwartz, J. P., Thigpen, S. E., & Montgomery, J. K. (2006). Examination of parenting styles of processing emotions and differentiation of self. *Family Journal, 14*(1), 41–48. doi: 10.1177/1066480705282050.

Seidl-de-Moura, M. L., Pessôa, L. F., Ramos, D. D. O., Mendes, D. M. L. F., Fioravanti-Bastos, A. C. M., & Dias, L. B. T. (2014). Beliefs of mothers, nannies, grandmothers and daycare providers concerning childcare. *Paidéia, 24*(59), 341–349. doi: 10.1590/1982-43272459201408.

Singh, M., & Niwas, R. (2015). Attitude of secondary school students towards alcohol and drugs in relation to their parenting. *Educational Quest – An International Journal of Education and Applied Social Sciences, 6*(3), 207–217. doi: 10.5958/2230-7311.2016.00008.8.

Stewart, S. M., & Bond, M. H. (2002). A critical look at parenting research from the mainstream: Problems uncovered while adapting Western research to non-Western cultures. *British Journal of Developmental Psychology, 20*(3), 379–392. doi: 10.1348/026151002320620389.

Uji, M., Sakamoto, A., Adachi, K., & Kitamura, T. (2014). The impact of authoritative, authoritarian, and permissive parenting styles on children's later mental health in Japan: Focusing on parent and child gender. *Journal of Child and Family Studies, 23*(2), 293–302. doi: 10.1007/s10826-013-9740-3.

Wittkowski, A., Garrett, C., Calam, R., & Weisberg, D. (2017). Self-report measures of parental self-efficacy: A systematic review of the current literature. *Journal of Child and Family Studies, 26*(11), 2960–2978. doi: 10.1007/s10826-017-0830-5.

Woodworth, S., Belsky, J., & Crnic, K. (1996). The determinants of fathering during the child's second and third years of life: A developmental analysis. *Journal of Marriage and Family, 58*(3), 679–692. doi: 10.2307/353728.

Yangzong, C., Lerkiatbundit, S., Luobu, O., Cui, C., Liabsuetrakul, T., Kangzhuo, B., ... Chongsuvivatwong, V. (2016). Validity and reliability of the Tibetan version of s-EMBU for measuring parenting styles. *Psychology Research and Behavior Management, 10*, 1–8. doi: 10.2147/PRBM.S111073.

Yoo, H., Feng, X., & Day, R. D. (2013). Adolescents' empathy and prosocial behavior in the family context: A longitudinal study. *Journal of Youth and Adolescence, 42*(12), 1858–1872. doi: 10.1007/s10964-012-9900-6.

Zakeri, H., Esfahani, B. N., & Razmjoee, M. (2013). Parenting styles and academic procrastination. *Procedia – Social and Behavioral Sciences, 84*, 57–60. doi: 10.1016/j.sbspro.2013.06.509.

Overview of parenting 9

Well, you have come so far, so what do you think of parenting now? To some of you, parenting is so complex, or it is so simple, yet regarding some of it you may say, "Wow, I have so much to learn." I hope this book has given you at least some idea of parenting in research and literature. To me, it is still supposedly a natural phenomenon but it is made complex and difficult by wanting to know more and do more for the children.

This final chapter summarises what has been discussed so far, with some tips on what to do if your parenting is not going smoothly and ideally. The reader will find a list of practical parenting behaviours introduced here to add flavour to your understanding of parenting. A conclusion closes the book.

Individualistic versus collectivistic cultures

We all come from one of two cultures, so to speak: individualistic or collectivistic.

For those of us from individualistic cultures, often from Western countries, the self is clearly an independent person. So it is more important to know more about the self than about others, as responsibility and decisions come from within. It is thus acceptable to say: "I am this and that. I want power and achievement, and self-glory, and *I* prefer people like me. I prefer to change the situation to suit myself than change myself to suit *my surroundings*. I'll compete for myself and attain my goals in life and my future. In the end, I'll leave autobiographical memories for others to appreciate and emulate. If I'm gone, the world is without the unique me, but you may copy me."

For those of us from collectivistic cultures, often from Eastern countries, the self is clearly an interdependent person. So, it is more important to know more about all of us than about the self, as responsibility and decisions come from without, often from a group. It is thus acceptable to say: "We are this and that. We want power and achievement, and group-glory, and prefer people like us. We prefer to change the situation to suit us than change us to suit our surroundings. We'll work together to attain our goals cooperatively and modestly for the group and our future. In the end, we'll leave a legacy of memories about ourselves for others to appreciate and emulate. If we're gone, we still have others to continue our lineage."

Such descriptions of individualistic and collectivistic people may seem extreme and polarised. Nevertheless, that is how we are brought up if the world is strictly divided into just these two groups. Fortunately, as we know, we have individuals within the collectivistic society, and collectivists within the individualistic society. Whether we conform or dissent, that is another story. Those who do will either be ostracised or tolerated, or be modified by the society. Consequently, we have a mixed world of individualists and collectivists, even within the family. We either observe this or not as people conform, rebel, or stay silent about their stand.

As the world spins and mixes, we have societies that are neither individualistic nor collectivistic but a mix of these. Some in these societies have claimed to be neutral to such a stand—they live for themselves and the group at large; distinctly, they may live for a conviction, like religion, or a cause unto themselves. Whatever stand a person or group takes, we would still observe such characteristics among them, though they may show up variedly according to the situation or self or group preference.

A better way to visualise parenting is from the angle of interpersonal relationships. In cultures where autonomy, personal achievement, and self-directedness are emphasised, parents will involve children in decision-making and provide explanations both for the rules they set and the consequences of one's behaviour. Authoritative parenting would be the most ideal style in such cultures; on the other hand, authoritarianism or strict parenting would be viewed negatively by children and contribute to adverse outcomes. Other cultural groups place more emphasis on group harmony, cohesion, and common goals. Respect for hierarchy and authority are considered paramount in maintaining the cohesiveness of the group. In such cultural groups, children would perceive strict parenting that is accompanied by warmth as acceptable. Studies among Asians illustrate that warm and strict parenting can coexist. Many countries with a strong tradition of relatedness and interdependency are becoming more modern and urbanised as their populations acquire more education. In such countries, a value pattern in which both economic independence and emotional interdependence are valued can emerge. This leads to parenting behaviour that encourages an autonomous-relational self. Parenting strategies aimed at encouraging an autonomous-related self may be especially salient for countries that are experiencing rapid social and economic changes (Abubakar, Van de Vijver, Suryani, Handayani, & Pandia, 2015).

Summary of outcomes of parenting for parents

As you can see from the chapters on parenting styles, there appear to be desirable styles according to cultures, and undesirable styles, again, according to cultures. Thus, it is a matter of practice and choice, which are governed by the situation one is in.

Let us say we start with Western parenting, as this book is in English, disregarding the historical beginnings of life and later developments. We then have, for this book, authoritarian, authoritative, indulgent, and permissive parenting styles, in which authoritative parenting becomes the desired style based on individualistic cultures and norms. This is supported by lots of research that authoritative parenting brings up better children and people of the future. Taking this as our reference, all other parenting styles are compared and evaluated, and thus verdicts regarding desirability or undesirability are rendered.

Eastern, collectivistic parenting styles are therefore seen as less desirable and do not bring up children and people of the future in the best way. Researchers on collectivistic parenting styles countered that, due largely to culture, collectivistic parenting styles are not less desirable;

they bring up children who are just as good if not better than those from authoritative parenting (Zhang, Wei, Ji, Chen, & Deater-Deckard, 2017). And other researchers, in search of an ideal or a better explanation, have come up with more parenting styles beyond those that are well established and measured (Bartholomeu, Montiel, Fiamenghi, & Machado, 2016). Hence, we have many more to learn from; for example, the positive styles like positive and supportive parenting, and my negotiation parenting, and the negative styles like harsh parenting and anxious, intrusive, and over-involved parenting.

Suppose we try to compare authoritative parenting and filial parenting (the information is extracted from Table 6.1 in Chapter 6). Point-to-point comparisons are made here.

Demandingness

Authoritative parents demand quite a bit from their children in conforming to standards, rules, schedules, and parental directions, but with logic and reasons. Children are free to voice their opinions if they find the rules/standards unfair or too controlling. Filial parents greatly demand these behaviours from their children, with logic and reasons but occasionally by virtue of parental decisions—for the good of the child, never mind whether he or she likes it.

Responsiveness

Authoritative parents respond greatly to their children's interests and needs based on short- and long-term goals. Children and parents work together on them for the future. Filial parents overly respond to their children's interests and needs, often based on parental wishes and goals as the children are growing up. Filial parents become overprotective and over-involved with their children.

Parent as source and role model

Authoritative parents are always a warm and accepting source for their children to turn to for support, whether physical or emotional. And these parents act as role models for their children to emulate. Again, children are free to voice their opinions with their parents as they develop. Authoritative parents would allow their children to develop individually. Filial parents are more than a source for their children; they provide even if their children did not ask for it. In return, filial parents expect their children to achieve success in school and life, and to care for them when they are old. Filial parents would develop collectively with their children.

Child's outcomes

Authoritative parents allow lots of self-control in their children so that they become self-reliant as soon as possible. Children are free to develop according to milestones set in medical science; otherwise, parents will intervene to assist the child's development. Filial parents do much of the controlling of their children, such that their children do not develop in the way they desire for themselves but more as the fulfilment of their parents' wishes and goals. Parental provisions turn their children into more self-centred people with an entitlement attitude.

Academically, both authoritative and filial parenting produce high achievers in school, but socially they are very different characters. Children of authoritative parents are socially competent, self-assertive, responsible, agentic, and explorative. Children of filial parents do less well in these areas as a result of having too much parental guidance and support; thus, the individual child needs to catch up on their social skills and individual rights.

According to studies (Sorkhabi, 2005; Foo, 2013), children of both these parenting styles are mentally quite healthy. Children of authoritative parents seem to fare better in most aspects of sanity of the individual as they are allowed to express themselves from day one. Children of filial parents are controlled so much in life that they do not express themselves much, so they may lack mental skills in handling awkward or difficult situations.

Extended family inclusion

Generally, authoritative parents rely much less on their extended families to assist them in parenting, such that grandparents are more like baby-sitters than involved in family affairs. Filial parents involve grandparents very much in caring and nurturing their children, such that the extended family is like one family. There is more sharing and helping in this aspect.

Overall, authoritative parenting demands lots from the parents in being role models and acting for their children, and demands lots of effort from them as well as abilities and resources. When their children are the difficult-to-manage type, these parents will need to seek help outside the home, or they will burn out. On the other hand, filial parents will burn themselves out sooner as they over-nurture their children, attending to almost every aspect of the child's life such that theirs are neglected. Parent–child dependence can be the result of filial parenting.

What you need to do as parents

As you can see from the discussion in the previous section, parenting is complex and parenting children is very dependent on one's choice and circumstances and what is said to be the better parenting style. If everything seems fine to you as parents, proceed as desired. If you want improvements, seek modification. If you desire an overhaul, seek change.

Whatever action you decide to take, there is always a way out. First, try your spouse or partner. If you have never talked with him or her about a parenting style or practice, do it now. It is better to cooperate than act alone, as the other may undo or cancel your actions. Working as a couple is much stronger than going it alone. No matter how smart you are, there will come a time when you cannot handle the matter in hand alone. It is like the way having a stranger talk to you can be easier than your family member. That is why we reveal all to a stranger called a doctor.

If this has been done and is not working, try talking to a close friend or relative. Do not sweep issues and problems under the carpet. Do not believe that keeping it secret means it will go away. Avoiding a problem is not solving it; we all know that cliché. Talk to him or her for a different opinion than yours. You will be surprised how helpful others' hints and tactics can be.

Alternatively, try social and printed media. There are lots of books and websites out there offering to help you with parenting. Go for the established ones, by which I mean those that have the backing of research, literature, and practical evidence. Subscribe to one for a short while to see the benefits. If it fails, try another.

If such self-help approaches are not working for you, try going to a professional: a family therapist or counsellor. Be prepared and ready to open up to get better. Be ready to try it out even if the proffered tactics do not sound right in the first place. Broaden your assumptions and beliefs.

Remember, it is for your children and *yourself* that some change is necessary. Parenting is a journey between a parent or set of parents and their child or children. Each child is different, even twins. Do not assume your son is like you, the father, for example, and your daughter is like your spouse or partner. Only about 50% of the child comes from you; even with that, the environment modifies his or her behaviour as he or she grows. You cannot control that. By keeping your child at home you deprive their brain of the chance to grow, develop, learn, expand, and trim itself into shape. By being let loose in their surroundings, your child will soon learn to be out of control or regulation.

I have provided below (see Table 9.1) a list of common parenting behaviours that will serve to give you, the parent, a better idea of what have you been doing or not (modified from McNeely & Barber, 2010). Note that the singular *child* and *parent* is used for simplicity. In reality both parents may be supporting the family of more than one child. Feel free to add your parenting behaviour to the table, with concrete explanations for it to help you improve.

Final word

If you are not ready for parenting, do not get into it, please. Because it means a lot to the life you are going to bring into this complex world. Notwithstanding the bliss of seeing the union of a sperm and egg grow and mature, the entire journey is arduous—yet memorable—if not well managed. Do not let a few minutes of fun end up in a lifelong agony of parenting and parenthood, and a regretful new life.

Table 9.1 Common parenting behaviours

Categories	Explanations	Remarks
Provide necessities	Parent provides items and services necessary for survival: food, shelter, clothes, and economic support.	This is a must for all responsible parents.
Take part in religious activities	Parent imparts religious belief at home to child or goes out to place of worship regularly with family. Family enjoys related religious activities together.	These indicate the importance of spirituality in the family.
Talk with me/ listen to me	Parent–child dialogue is kept open and free with adequate listening and talking.	This maintains relationships in the family.
No expression of hostility	Parent does not hit the child or yell at him or her.	Provided the child is easy to manage.
Expression of hostility	Parent threatens child with punishments or punishes him or her more than necessary.	Some appropriate punishment is fine; too much makes the child aggressive and vengeful.
Monitor/set limits	Parent observes, tracks, or regulates child's actions and behaviour, the peers he or she interacts with, events he or she attends, and his or her computer and school work.	This helps out in terms of guidance of the child's growth and development.
Show physical affection	Parent smiles, kisses, or hugs child. Child responds similarly.	This promotes bonding among members of the family.
Affection and encouragement	Parent encourages or emotionally supports child. Also shows love, gives attention, and treats him or her in a loving manner.	Human feelings often go with actions. When we encourage, some feelings go along with it. It is hard to hide real internal feelings. Real love is unconditional.
Give guidance/ advice	Parent teaches, advises, or appropriately guides child on the right path. Guidance does include a moral component.	Parents are role models.

(Continued)

Table 9.1 (Cont.)

Categories	Explanations	Remarks
Parent support for education	Parent provides emotional, instrumental, and financial support for education.	A must in today's world.
Do things with me	Parent performs activities or attends events with child.	This maintains the parent–child bond.
Give money	Parent gives child money or monetary gifts like allowances and bank/trust funds.	Money satisfies a major part of life.
Take care of me	Parent physically carries out a task that provides care for child.	A form of parental love.
Do not pressure me	Parent does not burden child with mental or physical stress and/or does not put him or her in a demanding situation.	Pressure produces stress and later mental health issues.
Do chores for me	Parent completes or assists with child's chores.	Role model or good guidance.
Protect me from harm	Parent defends or protects child from harm.	A natural parenting behaviour.
Buy/provide things I want	Parent gives child material items or gifts or spends money on them.	This does not include money spent on basic necessities or money given to the child directly.
Help me	Parent offers general help or assistance to child.	This does not include specific examples of help.
Demonstrate respect/trust me/ make me feel worthy	Parent shows or expresses respect, considers child's opinion, trusts child, or makes child feel worthy.	Respect is earned through reciprocity, not by demand.
Allow freedom	Parent grants child a heightened level of access, privileges, and/or freedom.	This builds and improves responsibility in a person.
Worry about me	Child reports parent as being concerned or worried about them.	Part of parental love; improves when child builds trust in parent.

(*Continued*)

Table 9.1 (Cont.)

Categories	Explanations	Remarks
Service for my well-being	Parent goes out of his or her way, denies own desires, and prioritises child to provide for child's needs.	Another form of parental love. Do not overdo this.
Encourage peer relationships	Parent supports and approves of child's development of friendships.	Socialisation is a must in life.
Discipline me	Parent corrects or disciplines child.	Only when necessary, with rules and reasoning.
Add responsibility	Parent gives child more responsibilities and duties.	Part of growing up and learning.
Celebrate with me	Parent organises gathering to commemorate an achievement or success. Child may do so for parent when he or she is ready to do so.	This keeps the family going forward with praises and rewards. A simple gathering serves just as well.
Visiting me/others	Parent visits child in his or her own home or vice versa. Also includes the family visiting relatives occasionally.	Maintains family bond and ties.
Over-reacting	Child reports parent gives him or her a long lecture, raises their voice, issues insults, says mean things, or calls them names, when he or she misbehaves.	Hurts parent–child relationship.
Over-involved with me	Parent is around child when he or she desires to be alone, "crashes" child's activities uninvited, takes on his or her issues to solve, or checks up on him or her.	Affects trust and faith in the child, unless it is genuinely for safety.
Talks too much	Parent nags child excessively over tasks that are done or not done, and threatens verbally to do things that he or she will not actually do.	Kills the power of words if action is not carried out.

(*Continued*)

Table 9.1 (Cont.)

Categories	Explanations	Remarks
Intrusive into my business	Parent does things for child even when he or she could manage them, like choosing classes, calling on a teacher, managing a timetable, laying out clothes, and intervening in problems.	Deprives the child of learning experiences and ability to be self-responsible and self-reliant.
Too soft with me	Parent does not take immediate or later action against a child who misbehaves or does wrong, does not following parental instructions or warnings, or ignores him or her.	This laxness in parenting spoils the child and reduces parenting control.

References

Abubakar, A., Van de Vijver, F. J. R., Suryani, A. O., Handayani, P., & Pandia, W. S. (2015). Perceptions of parenting styles and their associations with mental health and life satisfaction among urban Indonesian adolescents. *Journal of Child and Family Studies, 24*(9), 2680–2692. doi: 10.1007/s10826-014-0070-x.

Bartholomeu, D., Montiel, J. M., Fiamenghi, G. A., & Machado, A. A. (2016). Predictive power of parenting styles on children's social skills: A Brazilian sample. *SAGE Open, 6*(2). doi: 10.1177/2158244016638393.

Foo, K. H. (2013). Filial parenting is not working! In P. Mandal (Ed.), *Proceedings of the International Conference on Managing the Asian Century* (pp. 343–351). Singapore: Springer. doi: 10.1007/978-981-4560-61-0_39.

McNeely, C. A., & Barber B. K. (2010). How do parents make adolescents feel loved? Perspectives on supportive parenting from adolescents in 12 cultures. *Journal of Adolescent Research, 25*(4), 601–631. doi: 10.1177/0743558409357235.

Sorkhabi, N. (2005). Applicability of Baumrind's parent typology to collective cultures: Analysis of cultural explanations of parent socialization effects. *International Journal of Behavioral Development, 29*(6), 552–563. doi: 10.1177/01650250500172640.

Zhang, W., Wei, X., Ji, L., Chen, L., & Deater-Deckard K. (2017). Reconsidering parenting in Chinese culture: Subtypes, stability, and change of maternal parenting style during early adolescence. *Journal of Youth and Adolescence, 46*(5), 1117–1136. doi: 10.1007/s10964-017-0664-x.

Index

academic achievement of children 209–210
acceptance and rejection of children 148–152
achievement 67, 93, 101, 171, 204, 224; academic 25, 54, 80, 127, 198, 209; child 172, 204; cognitive 22; ethnic identity 167; individual 129, 133, 147, 159; personal 224; school 25, 54, 69, 75; science and math 75
adjustment 80, 159, 162, 180, 184, 203; academic and social 131; adolescent 74; emotional 111; health and emotional 111; health and psychological 129; maladjustment 74, 79; patterns 102; psychological 55, 74, 130; -related problems 102; socio-emotional 98, 162
adolescence 44, 73, 128, 132, 154; earlier/early 80, 107, 128; early to mid 132
adolescents 24–25, 44, 51, 53–54, 69, 74–76, 78–79, 101–102, 107, 108–111, 132, 134, 144, 158–159, 165, 167–168, 171–172, 184, 188, 203, 207; anxiety symptoms in 153–154; Chinese 80, 90, 96–97; early 56, 106; and internet 78; leisure time 78, 189; suicide 77; well-being 78

adulthood 9, 109, 131; early 74; emerging 58; Older 185; young 91
advocates 63, 92, 127
affluence 22, 91, 95
Africa 158
African American fathering 46
aggression 70, 74, 76, 90, 207; child/children's 18, 26, 53, 74, 97
Alabama Parenting Questionnaire 203
alcohol 76, 135, 148
anger 53, 59, 76, 130, 155
anxiety 53, 90, 98, 129–130, 166; in children 17, 153–154, 170; chronic 205; mothers 49
Argentine 159
Asian 79, 108, 112, 128–130, 147, 157–158, 167–168, 225
assertiveness 67, 78, 96, 132, 185; self- 67, 71
attachment 7, 16, 43, 52, 73, 138, 149, 183, 199; construct 2, 5; secure or insecure 26, 73; theory 16
attention deficit hyperactivity disorder 77
attitude 7, 16, 22, 46, 79, 110, 113, 156, 157, 167–168, 170; child 65; Confucian 112; entitlement 94, 227; let-fate/faith-decide-for-me 129; parenting 7, 17, 24–25, 52, 150, 152; punitive 171; self-compassionate 110

attitudinal bias 147
attributes 72, 148, 170, 203
attribution 72, 105, 148, 166; of punishment 72; of the self 167; theory 146–147
Australia 73–74, 132, 158, 183
authoritarian parenting style 65–66; *see also* parenting styles
authoritative parenting style 66; *see also* parenting styles
"authoritative parental behaviour" 67
autism 13, 92

Bahrain 109
Balkans, the 158
Baumrind, D. 64–73, 77, 79–80, 112, 171
Baumrind's parenting typology 64–68; evidence for 67–68
behaviour(s)/al 6–7, 23, 26, 40–42, 62, 79; adaptive 76; checklist 81; and Chinese parental 91; compliance 70–71; control 24, 27, 54, 56, 209; cooperative 67; culture-specific 79; dysfunction 69; ethics 113; in families 1, 62; family and parenting 93; modest 90; patterns 70; problem 67, 76; prosocial assertive 71; purposive 67; regulate/regulation 98, 100, 148; sexual 109, 148; situation-specific 79, 219; theories 41; well-adjusted 79; value-congruent 102
Belsky's process of parenting model 7
benevolent intention 129–131
binge eating 130
birth order of children 17–18
Block's Childrearing Practices Report 204
body stimulation 15, 134, 163, 199–200
Bowlby, J. 16
Brazil 132
breadwinner 30, 47; -caregiver model 59; fathers 106
Britain 95, 161
bullying *see* child behaviour

Cameroonian 8, 159
Canada 46, 76, 113
caregivers 7, 163, 180–181, 199–200; early 183; main 191; men as 45; mothers as 77; primary 42, 106; stress 21; younger 161
characteristics of fathers 53
child: communication 67; depression disorder 27; effortful control 154–156; first 17, 50, 100; forgiveness 97; -hood trauma 103; child behaviour 16–18, 26, 70–72, 76, 90–91, 97, 100, 105, 109, 128, 155, 158, 166, 171, 183–184, 199, 202, 226; adaptive 76; aggressive 74; anti-social 56; autonomous 168; bullying 75; callous/unemotional 136; checklist 81; compliant 154–156; cooperative 67; deceitful 136; disorders 21; disrespectful 157; disruptive 203; feeding difficulty 21–22; health risks 152; infant expressive 161; internalising and externalising 6, 28, 76; moral misbehaviour 202; passive reactions to 131; positive 19, 26; problems 18, 20–21, 54, 69, 76, 107, 129, 156; prosocial 132; purposive 67; responses 156, 200; risks 130; social and emotional 6, 67; violent 29; well-adjusted 79
Child Behaviour Checklist 81, 208
child outcomes 80, 180, 199, 227; measuring 202–210
childcare 28, 41, 46, 50, 56, 95, 98–99, 103, 106, 152, 161, 170, 179–181, 187–188, 193; by grandparents 184–186; in Hong Kong 190–191; by maids or domestic helpers 186–187; by nannies 182–184; in Peru 192–193; in Singapore 190; sharing 44; in South Africa 191–192; within family 43
childrearing 9, 21, 42, 44–45, 63, 72–73, 88, 103, 105, 113–114, 151, 153, 161, 167, 171, 191–192
children's literature 47
China 97–98, 127, 149–150, 158; grandparents in 187; Northern 162; urban 164
Chinese 8, 23, 80, 106, 111–112, 149–150, 153–155, 162–164, 171–172; American 127–128; *chiao shun* 90; Chinese Paternal/maternal Overparenting Scale 204; face of family 14; families

27; filial parenting 91–96; *guan* 90, 96; parents/parenting style 88–99, 171–172; *qin* 106; training 201; values 97
Chinese parenting style 89–91; evidence for 96–99
Chinese Paternal/maternal Overparenting Scale 204
Christianity 112
Chua, A. 126–127
cognitive dissonance 129
collectivistic 14, 27, 62–63, 73, 79, 126–127, 147, 171–172, 184, 187, 223–225; cultures 147, 171–172, 184; societies 14, 62; *see also* Eastern collectivistic parenting
Colombia 132, 149–150, 158
communication 6, 18–19, 40, 55, 74, 93, 101, 133, 136, 164, 168, 182, 185
emotional 6
means 93
parent–child 209
verbal and nonverbal 180
community: belief 135; engagement 111; family and 185, 192; Muslim 108; participation 44; religious 107; rural 110; school and 13; and society 182; urban 110
compliance 155–156; behavioural 70–71; with cultural norms 90; development of 134; dispositional 72; parenting practices and 155; with values 102
Confucian: attitude 112; Chinese families 127; ideas 102; teachings 92, 103; traditions 89; values 105
Controlling Parents Survey 204
co-parenting 16, 49, 185; grandmothers 188
co-sleeping 100, 106
culture: African 191; American 109; Argentine 159; Chinese 80, 106, 155; collectivistic 147–148, 150, 171, 184; Eastern 112, 127, 147; and family 138, 170; French 159; Hindu 160; individualistic 171–172; Israeli 169; Korean 106; Mongolian 162–163; Muslim 110; racial 88; and religion 19–20; -specific model 171; United States 159; Western 129, 133, 154–155, 199; *see also* individualistic versus collectivistic cultures
Czech Republic 76

delinquency 74, 76, 111, 156, 203; trajectories 75
demandingness 24, 70, 73, 81, 99, 134, 156, 226; dimension 75; parental 68; warmth and 64
depression 55–56, 74, 90, 98, 129–130, 162, 171–172; child's disorder 27
development: of autonomy 15; of a father's identity 45; of relatedness 15; sex role 40
developmental niche/microniche 8
developmental psychology 1–2
Differentiation-of-self Scale 205
domestic helper 13, 28–29, 93, 179; *see also* childcare, by maids or domestic helpers
drug use 76, 148

Eastern collectivistic parenting 88–122; application 114
Eastern countries 62, 73, 79 114, 224
Eastern versus Western parenting styles 171–176
education 17, 20, 24, 29, 55, 69, 74, 78, 93, 97, 99, 101, 103, 105–108, 114, 131, 137, 150, 154, 157–158, 181, 186, 192, 201, 225; *see also* literacy of parents
Egypt 109–110
emotional: dysregulation 97; intelligence 102
Emotion-related Parenting Styles Self-test 205
empathy 44, 94, 201
enhancing bias 166
environment 26, 33n1, 77, 81, 103, 179–181, 229; changing 102; cold family 156; competitive 91, 93; home 159, 180; metropolitan 93; protective family 150; safe 91; of Singapore 95; social 185, 201; virtual 201
error-related negativity 170
Europe 73, 158, 169; Western 189
European 76, 167, 189; American 90, 128 162–163, 166
extended family inclusion 227–228

Index

face-to-face contact 15, 132–133, 199–200
familism 8, 14, 16, 189
family 8–15; breakup 20–21; conflict 130, 167–168, 185; dysfunctional 109; Eastern 111; extended 101, 109, 190, 227–228; hierarchy 99; honour 108–109; Indian 100; Iranian 110; middle-class 29; relations 74; roles 76; rules 43; small 94; subsystems 14; *see also* work-family balance
Family Nurse Partnership 133
fathering 43–47; African American 46; versus mothering 39–59; self-efficacy and marital satisfaction 44
feeding practice 21–22, 100; unhealthy food consumption 100
feminist principles 46
fertility rates 22–23
filial parental love 92–93
filial parenting 91–96; *see also* Chinese parenting style
filial piety 89, 93–94, 96–98, 105, 112, 131, 162, 187; authoritarian 90, 96–97; reciprocal 89–90
Filipino 151
France 159

gang membership 155–156
Germany 8, 77, 158, 159, 161–164, 189
goals: common 111, 225; socialisation 8, 98, 108, 133–134, 162–164, 199
grandparents 13, 17, 22, 27–28, 46, 91, 93, 100, 179, 182, 227–228; in China 187–188; in South Africa 188–189; in Western Europe 189–190; *see also* childcare
Greece 75, 165, 189

harmony 90, 103, 112, 159, 161, 170, 172; group 105, 108, 111, 225
Hindu 99–100, 160; *Sanskar* 100–101; *swadharma* 100
homework 156–157, 167, 191, 209
Hong Kong 96, 127 191; *see also* childcare, in Hong Kong
human development 6
humility 97

ideal mother 48, 105, 181
ideologies 48; East Asian 202

immigrant 107, 131; Chinese 90; Indian 101, 168; Iranian 109; Jewish 168; Korean 106–107, 166–167; Mongolian 162; parenting 146; *see also* parenting, immigrant
immigration *see* immigrant
impulsiveness 78, 185
Incredible Years Toddler Course 132
independence 55, 80, 99, 109, 129, 161, 163, 168–169, 189, 204, 225; child's 128; lack of 95; model of 15
Indian 8, 26, 28, 73, 89, 98–102, 112–113, 147, 153, 158–162, 164–5, 207–8; American 157; Asian 167–168; families 100–101
Indian parenting style 99–101; evidence for 101–102
indigenous Chinese parenting 90
Indigenous Parenting Style Scale 206
individualistic 27, 62–63, 73, 81, 88, 111, 126, 147–148, 184, 187, 225; families 114; *see also* individualistic versus collectivistic cultures; Western individualistic parenting
individualistic versus collectivistic cultures 223–225
Indonesia 108, 110
indulgent parenting style *see* parenting styles
Intensive Parenting Attitudes Questionnaire 206
intercultural marriage 23
interdependence 15, 52, 80, 111–112, 128, 189, 225; familial 92
intergenerational dependence 99
internet 17–19, 78, 93, 97, 182; addiction 78; games 93; use of 23–24
Iran 77, 109–110, 209
Islam 79, 107–108, 160
Italy 132, 149–150, 165, 189

Japan 89, 102–104, 147, 207
Japanese parenting style 102–103; evidence for 103–104
Jewish 168–169
Jordan 109, 132, 149, 151

Keller, H. parenting model 8; *integrative model* 199
Kenya 132, 149, 151

Korea(n) 89, 104, 105–107, 112, 113, 129, 130, 131, 166–167; American families 106–107; *chek-im* 105; *Chemyon* 105; culture 106; *guan-sim* 105; *gyeum-son* 105; *Hyo* 105; immigrant 107; *jung-sung* 105; *Oryun* 105; *Samgang* 105
Korean parenting style 104–106; evidence for 106–107

life satisfaction 24, 42, 55, 74, 96–97, 130
literacy of parents 17, 20
love withdrawal 90, 107

Maccoby and Martin's additional parenting style 68–70; evidence for 69–70
Maccoby, E. 68
Malaysia 98, 108, 111
male child, preference for 27–28
marriage: age for 49, 50; arranged 168; career choice and 168; conflicted 52; having children soon after 170; mixed 23; and parenting 52; quality of 162; same-sex 42; strength of a 39; subsystem 14
Martin, J. 68
measurement 7, 16, 63–64, 70, 80–81, 198, 208, 219
mental health 8, 24, 54, 56, 104, 110–111, 131, 153
Mexico 8, 135
Middle East 73, 158, 169
mischievous 81
misconduct 69, 76, 108
mixed parenting group 63
mobile phone 18, 136; dependency 107
modernisation 91, 170
modesty 80, 107, 109
Morocco 109
mothering 15, 30, 39, 42, 48–50, 54–55, 74; intensive 48; *see also* fathering, versus mothering
mothers: Buddhist 50; Christian 49; Muslim 50
motivation: controlled 200; intrinsic 98, 103
Muslim 89, 107–110, 151, 168–170, 186; *gotong-royong* 108; *hormat* 108; *rukun* 108; *see also* mothers, Muslim
Muslim parenting style 107–110; evidence for 110–112

nanny 137, 182, 187, 193; nanny TV parenting 136–137; "nannying" 179; psychoanalytic aspect 183; *see also* childcare, by nannies
natural childhood 94–95
Netherlands, the 73–74, 149, 189
neuroscience 180–181
new parents 50–51
New Zealand 73, 107
North America 77, 158
Norway 134
nurturer 45, 100; male 106

obesity 21, 29, 130
object simulation 132
One's Memories of Upbringing Scale 206
operationalisation 7, 64, 201–202
outcomes 13, 16, 26, 39, 44, 47, 51–52, 69, 74–78, 80, 89–90, 92, 127, 129–130, 146, 163, 166, 168, 172, 180, 182–183, 198–203, 219; of fathering and mothering 53–59; of parenting 148–159; questionnaires 208; summary of 225–228
overconfidence 78, 185
overprotection 24, 73, 75, 103–104, 112, 128, 130, 153, 206, 226

Pakistan 111, 206–208
Parent as source and role model 226
Parent Authority Questionnaire 81, 114, 207; -Revised 207
parental: alienation syndrome 21; attitude, affection, and control 24–25, 54, 76, 106; avoidance behaviour 153; perceived behaviour 103; behaviours 4, 7–8, 16, 18, 68, 91, 93, 113, 133, 149, 157–159, 163, 185, 193, 202, 223, 225, 229; behaviour on brain development 132; beliefs 96; conflict 21, 97, 113; controlling behaviour 24, 27, 54, 56, 130; core behaviour 106, 209; critical behaviour 219; directive behaviour 128; gender-appropriate behaviour 43; goals 96; health-risk behaviour 148; interference 156; love 94, 112, 158–159; maternal behaviour 132; modelling behaviour 45; monitoring 104; negative behaviour 153; neglectful behaviour 64;

overview 223–233; positive behaviour 19, 24; roles 76, 108; separation 77
The Parent–Child Interaction Questionnaire 208
Parent–Parental Acceptance–Rejection Questionnaire 207
Parental Self-efficacy Test 208
parenting 5, 15–17, 107; cognitions 166–167; cultural differences/models of 15, 64; *Distal versus proximal* 133–134; distress 97; hostile 26; immigrant 166–168; inconsistency 25; influencing factors 17–32; maternal stress 157–158; mobile 136; neglectful 75; pattern 159; practices 16, 107; questionnaires/scales 203; strict 112; systems 15; training 98; virtues 106; younger versus older parents 170–171; *see also* parenting styles
Parenting Style and Dimensions Questionnaire 208
Parenting Style Self-Test—Revised 207–208
parenting styles: authoritarian parenting 27, 65, 76–78, 80, 98, 99, 102, 104, 109, 111, 131, 135, 149–150, 153–154, 157, 163–165, 170; authoritative parenting 22, 54–55, 66, 69, 70, 72, 74–78, 80, 96–98, 102, 104, 107, 110–111, 149–150, 154–156, 162–163, 165, 184; childhood 75; Eastern 88, 114; fifth 91; filial 91–96; and harmony 159; harsh 135–136; helicopter 126, 128–131; Indian 99–102; Japanese 102–104; Korean 104–107; and marital interactions 74; maternal 74; Muslim 107–112; nanny TV 136–137; negative 77, 107; negotiation 126, 137–138; Nordic model 134; over-involved 106, 112, 114, 131, 226; overprotective 102; paternal 74; perceived by children 164–166; perceived by parents 159–164; Permissive or indulgent parenting 21–22, 72, 76, 98, 104, 165, 184; positive 77, 126, 131–133; tiger 126–128; uninvolved or neglectful parenting 55, 68–69, 75–77, 111; Western 62–85

Parent–Parental Acceptance–Rejection Questionnaire 207
partner 45
perception 91, 106, 163, 172, 200; of adolescents 80, 172; of children's difficulty 97; of Eastern cultures 112; of parenting style 17, 25–26, 79, 96, 107, 134, 159, 164–165; of parenting/parents 22, 25–26, 158, 208; of reciprocity 182; of a shared identity 186
perfectionism 77
permissive or indulgent parenting style 64–65; *see also* parenting styles
personal competence 76
personality 6, 41, 53, 95, 103–104, 179, 181, 183, 201; child's 199; of parents and children 26–27; religious 111; traits 7, 17
Philippines, the 98, 132, 149, 151, 190
Portugal 76
provider 45
punishment 24, 63, 71–73, 88, 90, 98, 112–113, 146, 164–165, 168–169, 200, 204; corporal 46, 106, 134–135, 162–163, 203; disciplinary strategies 97; parenting styles 72, 90; physical 109, 135

qualitative method 202
quantitative method 202

reciprocity 14, 73, 89, 111, 182, 189
regulation: external 98, 101; identified 98, 101; integrated 101; introjected 98, 101
rejection 20, 53, 71, 81, 148–154, 203, 206, 219
religious 19–20, 23, 100, 110, 112–113, 169; classes/studies 75, 108; personality 111; worldview 111; *see also* community
responsiveness 68, 73, 226
restrictiveness 71, 81, 96
role modelling 45, 226–227
role: of members of a family 42–43; of significant others 179–195
Russia 74, 98, 169

Saudi Arabia 109
school achievement 54, 69, 75
self: -actualisation 109; -control 24, 44, 67, 70, 97, 137, 154, 202, 227; -effacement 105, 166; -efficacy 44, 98, 129–130, 162, 200; -esteem 24, 42, 44, 48, 54–55, 70, 74, 76, 96, 98, 102, 104, 127, 130, 147, 162, 200; -regulation 68, 103, 114, 154, 163; -sacrificing 94
sexual: abuse 104; activities 192; behaviour 109; orientation 13, 48, 59n1; preference 39
shaming 24, 90–91, 107, 127–128, 167
significant others 15, 17, 28–29, 59, 94, 179, 193; opinions of 59
Singapore 91, 92–96, 98–99, 126-7, 183; *see also* childcare, in Singapore
Slovenia 76
social/socio-economic status 29, 53–54, 99, 160, 162, 165, 185
social: media 25, 146; phobia 153–154; skills 54, 78, 132, 150, 185, 227; support 7, 42, 53, 74, 97, 171
South Africa 77, 147, 158; *see also* childcare, in South Africa; grandparents, in South Africa
South America 73, 158
Spain 76, 78, 133, 189
stay-at-home: dads 46–47; mums 49–50, 105
stigma 106
substance use 76
success 6, 107, 127, 147; academic 29, 93, 129, 131, 227; career 95; children's 20, 40, 91, 101; of the family 168; parenting 105, 128, 136, 166, 172, 208; reproductive 23
suicide 77, 103
supportive: parents/parenting 20, 42, 71, 114, 127–128, 131–132, 151, 157–158, 188, 226; social arrangements 46
Sweden 76–77, 132, 134, 137, 149, 152, 165, 189

Taiwan 154–155
teachings: Confucian 92, 103, 112; filial 89; Islamic 107; religious 113
Thailand 132, 149, 152

theories/models: attribution 147–148; behaviouristic 41; biological 40; Carol M. Worthman's composite bioecocultural model 8; cognitive-developmental 6; Darling and Steinberg's contextual model 199; evolutionary 6; family alliance 14, 201–202; family systems 52; Integrative Parenting 64; Keller's integrative 199; psychodynamic 6; psychological 40; *self-determination* 200–201; social cognition 6, 58; sociological 41; socio-psychological 6; Wendi Otto's East Asian 201
tobacco 76
tradition: Arab 109; Arab Muslim Israeli 169; Cameroon 160; Colombia 150; Confucian 89; Indian 99, 160; Iranian 110; Jordan 151; Korean 105–106, 131; Mexican 135; Muslim 50, 107; South Africa 188–189, 191–192; Sweden 152; Thailand 152
training 80, 171; Chinese 90, 201
travel 55

uninvolved or neglectful parenting style 68–69; *see also* parenting styles
United Kingdom 76, 133, 154–155
United States 24, 46, 64, 74–75, 78–80, 96, 98–99, 109, 129–130, 132, 135–136, 147–149, 152, 154–156, 158, 164–168, 180–181, 187

victimisation 75

warmth 20, 24, 52, 64, 66, 68, 73, 76–77, 79–80, 112, 127, 129, 134, 148–153, 161–162, 165, 171–172, 180, 184, 225
well-being 27, 43, 51–52, 54, 77–78, 104, 107, 110, 127, 129, 131, 157, 167, 180, 183, 189, 200–201
Western countries 62, 73, 169, 223
Western individualistic parenting 64
Western parenting styles 63–64, 69, 73, 79, 80–81, 91, 111, 198; application of 73–80; comparing 146; versus Eastern 171–172; four 64, 69, 89
withdrawal 24, 71, 78, 90, 107, 185
work–family balance 30
Worthman, C. M. *see* theories/models

For Product Safety Concerns and Information please contact our EU representative GPSR@taylorandfrancis.com
Taylor & Francis Verlag GmbH, Kaufingerstraße 24, 80331 München, Germany

www.ingramcontent.com/pod-product-compliance
Lightning Source LLC
Chambersburg PA
CBHW070600300426
44113CB00010B/1341